The Road to Dungannon

The Road to Dungannon
Journeys in Literary Ireland

MICHAEL PATRICK PEARSON

McFarland & Company, Inc., Publishers
Jefferson, North Carolina

All photographs courtesy John Lawrence

ISBN (print) 978-1-4766-9159-6
ISBN (ebook) 978-1-4766-5041-8

LIBRARY OF CONGRESS AND BRITISH LIBRARY
CATALOGUING DATA ARE AVAILABLE

Library of Congress Control Number 2023030198

© 2023 Michael Patrick Pearson. All rights reserved

No part of this book may be reproduced or transmitted in any form or by any means, electronic or mechanical, including photocopying or recording, or by any information storage and retrieval system, without permission in writing from the publisher.

Front cover photograph by John Lawrence

Printed in the United States of America

*McFarland & Company, Inc., Publishers
Box 611, Jefferson, North Carolina 28640
www.mcfarlandpub.com*

For Jo-Ellen, from the beginning and forever, the love of my life,
so Irish—a Kiernan and a Kennedy by birth—
that she can wear her heritage with insouciance
while I toil digging in the bog of the past
to discover a remnant of mine.
And for our sons—Shane, Ian, and Owen—
an bothar maith—the good road is open to you.

Contents

Prologue: Where the Ladders Start	1
1. The Rocky Road to Dublin and Beyond	11
2. Memory and Imagination	27
3. Joyce and Modern Ireland	44
4. Yeats, Sligo, and the West	71
5. J.M. Synge and the Aran Islands	86
6. Frank O'Connor and Cork	98
7. Edna O'Brien—A Country Girl in the West	117
8. Seamus Heaney and Northern Ireland	127
9. Writers of the New Ireland	144
Epilogue: Hunter and the Hunted—Ireland Today	184
Acknowledgments	188
Appendix: A Starting Point—Books, Music, and Film	189
Index	197

"I must lie down where all the ladders start/
in the foul rag and bone shop of the heart."
—William Butler Yeats,
"The Circus Animals Desertion"

"The bogholes might be Atlantic seepage.
The wet centre is bottomless."
—Seamus Heaney, "Bogland"

"...a writer who goes back to his native place
is rather in the position of Heine's monkey chewing his tail.
Objectively he is eating, subjectively he is being eaten."
—Frank O'Connor, *Irish Miles*

Prologue: Where the Ladders Start

"You can read too much or too little. They're both bad."
—Edna O'Brien in an interview
with Andrew O'Hagan, December 15, 2020

We never said much about my grandfather, my mother's father, from Ireland. She claimed she didn't know much about him, but even as a child I sensed something shuttered in her when it came to speaking about Alfred Hunter. When I got old enough for her to tell me that Alfred had abandoned her as an infant in the cradle, leaving her with her mother, Jenny Finlan O'Pray, and her three much older half-brothers whose surname was Fluhr, I suspected that she knew more than she was willing or able to say aloud. That part of her past had turned for her to stone that she could not quarry into language.

I was a curious kid (a nature I surely inherited from her) and learned what I could about her father—that he emigrated from Northern Ireland, staying around the Bronx and their apartment at 574 East 156 Street just long enough to leave her with a name, and then disappeared as precipitously as he had appeared on Ellis Island a few years before. My mother was open-hearted and candid, but I never pressed her too hard on the story of my grandfather because a pained expression would cloud her attentive, smiling blue-grey eyes and she'd pat my arm and sigh.

"What do you care about all that, Michael?" she'd ask rhetorically, as if the skeleton of that dead world and that decayed history was best left buried in the bog.

She'd brush a strand of dark brown hair away from her forehead and gaze out our grimy kitchen window in the Bronx, a faraway look shadowing into her eyes, as if she were being admonished by her ancestors in a Druidical whisper, *Say nothing, say nothing.*

I didn't read Seamus Heaney's "Whatever You Say, Say Nothing" until after she died, but I immediately thought of her when I traveled through the shivering lines of the poem. In part, the "Irish thing" that Heaney referred to seemed aligned to my mother's rejecting of that part of her past, refusing to recall any details that Jenny O'Pray had given her, and I saw the innocent topography of her face and her devout Catholicism in Heaney's words—"The times are out of joint/But I incline as much to rosary beads."

"Each of us has a cross to bear," she'd say and leave it at that.

When I reached adulthood, I came to recognize her restraint as, perhaps, an Irish way of dealing with personal history. In a manner, her silence had a kinship with what might have been my grandfather's "Northern reticence, the tight gag of place." For a woman who was otherwise always an open book for me, my mother kept the story of my grandfather tightly shut. As a young man, I wanted to know more, but finally I determined it was her story, and I let it go in pursuit of my own life, my own narrative. I married, raised three sons, eventually traveled with my wife (a Kennedy and a Kiernan by maternal and paternal heritage but an American to the core) to Ireland, and left it to the bog to hide or preserve what it would of the past and my grandfather's story.

Then Alfred Hunter became my history and my story, my inheritance. Two months after 9-11, my mother died, and it was suddenly too late to ask her any questions about my grandfather. I had never encountered anyone with more curiosity or passion for life than my mother. It may be too simple to say that—for a woman, born on November 23, 1911, who had found a way to see each moment with clarity and hopefulness through two world wars, the Korean Conflict and the Vietnam War, through the Depression, and the ordinary burdens that any individual must endure—the image of the Twin Towers in her beloved New York City took the life out of her but that seemed the case to me. It was as if she decided in the two-hour span that it took the Twin Towers to collapse on that Tuesday morning that the world as she wanted to know it had ended.

Shortly after 9-11, a fortnight before her 90th birthday, her eyes went unfocused, as if she were gone already. Before that she had been active, vivacious, eyeing the world like a young girl eager to discover what each day would offer, always asking questions and prepared for new adventures. Then she stopped being interested. It all happened so quickly, as quickly as the towers' collapsing. One day she was healthy and happy, and then she lost her enthusiasm for living. In a matter of weeks, she faded from us. I never got to ask her again about Alfred Hunter—or anything else—the mystery of Ireland, the possible reasons for his escape act or for hers. Of course, I understood that her desire to disappear made sense—she was 90 and the world had shifted on her in a manner that must have felt seismic. She left me to figure out Alfred Hunter on my own. And with her gone, he seemed a riddle that I was obliged to solve in order to know her and myself properly.

I wasn't sure exactly where to uncover the story of my long-lost grandfather. There were no uncles or aunts left from my mother's family. My older sister knew less than I did. There was no household Bible, no stash of letters in an attic, no oral histories—just a resounding silence and blank pages. I knew that I might find out more than I bargained for, that I might discover a thief, a coward, a murderer or, worse perhaps, a banality.

Whoever he was, I guessed that Alfred Hunter was shaped by Ireland, and I reasoned that the best way for a professor of literature to discover that country, and perhaps my ancestor and myself, was in its books. The spirit of adventure and the inclination to travel have been, for as long as I can remember, two of the principal driving forces in my life. As a kid growing up in the Bronx, I had dreamed day and night of being elsewhere, of discovering a world beyond the silence and obedience of Catholic school, away from the rattle of the subway train that ran under the sidewalk beneath my bedroom window and far from the tight perimeter of squat apartment buildings, toward the open road and the endless sky. Our apartment was claustrophobic, and my father drowned his chronic unhappiness in drink and cigarette smoke, often making that 500-square-foot home feel like a prison cell. Early on, books saved me, not metaphorically but truly, allowing me to find a way out of that space and into a world as big as my imagination could reach. For much of my childhood, I disappeared into the white heat of stories. Without them, I might never have found my way out of the fog and ruin that for me was often the Bronx of those years. I fell in love with books the way I fell in love with basketball and football and girls. My first adventures were in books, and then books led me into the worlds they described.

From the time I read some children's versions of Homer's *The Odyssey* and Cervantes's *Don Quixote* in elementary school and then on to Twain's *Roughing It* and *Adventures of Huckleberry Finn* as a teenager, I had gone AWOL from that confining apartment and from the sour looks and strictures of Brother Boniface and Sister David in primary school. I loved those three protagonists—Odysseus, Don Quixote, and Huck Finn—because all of them seemed to me more heroes of the imagination than the physical world. They suggested to me that living by my wits and dreams, that making up the stories that would lead me through the days and weeks and years ahead, was feasible. Books shielded me from my father's despair and some teachers' sadism. I hadn't yet read Ellison's most famous novel, but I was the invisible boy, nonetheless. I was there at St. Philip Neri Elementary School and in the cramped living room on 198 Street in the Bronx, but I was gone, even though no one knew it but me. From childhood to adulthood, from St. Philip Neri Elementary and Mt. St. Michael High School to Fordham University, I was steeped in the rites of the Catholic Church—Baptism, First Holy Communion, Confirmation, and Confession—but the idea of pilgrimage was of my own variety, leading me not toward Rome but to secular landscapes like the big sky country of the American West or to dear, old, dirty Dublin. I had little interest in saints. Instead of wondering about St. Anthony of Padua or St. Teresa of Avila, I was fascinated by Lawrence Ferlinghetti and Jack Kerouac and Ken Kesey.

Eventually, around eighteen or nineteen years of age, I drifted away from Saturday afternoon Confession and Sunday Mass, but the attraction of pilgrimage never lost its luster for me. The idea of the search, the spiritual quest, followed me as much as I sought it. My dissertation topic for my Ph.D. at Penn State focused on the philosophical essays and the novels of the Catholic writer Walker Percy, who defined his first novel, *The Moviegoer*, as "the pilgrim's search outside himself rather than the guru's search within." Percy found his voice, as the biographer Paul Elie says in *The Life You Save May Be Your Own*, by "telling the story of someone else.... In order to find himself, he had to lose himself; he had to look outside himself, going on a pilgrimage."

At twenty-four years old, I went against the academic grain to write my dissertation on Walker Percy, in opposition to the advice and consensual wisdom of the conservative English faculty at Penn State (a group of men who believed a writer's value increased substantially after he had the good sense to die). Percy's second novel, *The Last Gentleman*, had sent shock waves of recognition through me when I read it as an MA student at the University of San Francisco in 1972. One Sunday afternoon, I was in Live Oak Park in Berkeley, near where I lived at the time, just finishing up a ragtag pick-up basketball game, when Greg Waller called me over to the shaded bench where he sat. He reached down for a beaded bag below the bench, his dark ponytail swinging against the baby carriage where his son, Moby, slept, innocent of what his school life was going to be in a few years when the teachers read the roll looking for Mobius, and he said call me Moby. If Moby's schools were anything like what mine had been, he was in for years of subtle and explicit torture.

Greg lifted a water-stained, well-used paperback out of his bag and said, "I think you'll get this. Not everybody would, but I'm pretty sure you will."

Crucifix on the Aran Islands.

The book he handed me, *The Last Gentleman*, had no cover and a faded library stamp in the corner that announced the price of the used book—*5 cents*. "It's pretty far out," he said. "Mind watching Moby while I get in the next game?"

He didn't give me a chance to ask why he'd thought I would appreciate the novel, given I was as fallen as any Catholic could be and had never been to any Southern state in America and, at that time, had no plans to do so. I'd seen *Easy Rider* a few years before in the Loew's Paradise Theater in the Bronx, and that had scared me off any trips below the Mason-Dixon line.

The first line of the novel—"One fine day in early summer a young man lay thinking in Central Park"—caught me like the beginning of a fairy tale for adults. I flipped the pages back and found two epigraphs. The first, from Kierkegaard, said something I didn't understand but that felt true and worth thinking a lot about—"If a man cannot forget, he will never amount to much." What was I to forget in the course of remembering? The second epigraph was attributed to a writer I had never heard of—Romano Guardini—and it made the hairs on the back of my neck stand up—"We know that the modern world is coming to an end.... Loneliness in faith will be terrible. Love will disappear from the face of the public world, but the more precious will be that love which flows from one lonely person to another ... the world to come will be filled with animosity and danger, but it will be a world open and clean."

I was just married and dizzily in love with my beautiful wife and the adventure we shared in San Francisco, a city that took my breath away, a geography for me of first and enduring passion. Everything seemed new about that time and place—our love, the strong breeze, gentle rains, the sensual hills and voluptuous Victorian houses, the gauzy, shifting curtain of fog, every piece of the world slightly out of reach, breaking my heart with the knowledge, even at twenty-two years old, that time inevitably transforms experience into memory.

The Last Gentleman sat in a box for our year in the Bay Area, the intimation of pilgrimage in its opening line coming to me like a mantra in my sleep and daydreams, along with the question of what I was to forget and remember and how I was to protect my good fortune as Charles Mansons lurked in the world and the Vietnam War raged on, and Jimi Hendrix, Janis Joplin, and Jim Morrison, not much older than I, burnt out like shooting stars.

When I finished my MA, Jo-Ellen and I returned to the Bronx because I had a job teaching English in a junior high school and because, most likely, we could think of nowhere else to go but back where we started. The Bronx had not changed and didn't seem to acknowledge the change in the two of us. It wasn't long before the junior high school where I taught felt to me like a

Image of Jimi Hendrix, St. Andrews Church, Dublin.

prophecy of Guardini's world, "filled with animosity and danger." And it wasn't long before I felt compelled to open the box that housed the water-stained copy of *The Last Gentleman*. I read the novel more than once in the Teachers' Room of JHS 113, talk crackling around me like a foreign tongue. At times, when I caught my image in the glass bookcase in the room, I was startled to recognize my features and not those of the protagonist of the book, Will Barrett. He seemed to be an unstated challenge to me—*will you bear it* he seemed to ask. I had little in common with Williston Bibb Barrett, of course, other than he reminded me of Huck Finn, Odysseus, and Don Quixote, and they were as much a part of my DNA as any actual ancestor. On paper, my resume didn't match Will Barrett's at all. I wasn't wealthy. I hadn't gone to Princeton, and I wasn't the scion of a noble family. And I surely wasn't a Mississippi boy. But I imagined that I was Will Barrett looking for a sign. Very much like him, I had no idea what sign I was seeking or what was missing in my life. But I knew there was a question that needed answering—or asking—maybe not a mystery to be solved but one to be entered into, as Gabriel Marcel had phrased it.

Something about Walker Percy's voice seemed to be speaking for me and through me, not merely to me. I admired Percy, the convert—a doctor who left medicine for writing, a Protestant skeptic who became a devout Catholic, a scientist who took on the raiments of the philosopher, a pilgrim who dug for meaning amidst the ruins of the modern world, a man who chose literature as a way of making sense of the world. In a way, *The Last Gentleman* and Walker Percy guided me out of the Bronx, toward a Ph.D. and in the direction of a new world. After I finished my degree at Penn State and started a career as a professor of literature and creative writing, I read all of Percy's novels, finding myself aligned to many of his watchers, waiters, and listeners.

In my first decades as a professor, I re-read the books I had to teach—Hawthorne, Melville, Twain, Cather, Faulkner, Steinbeck, Fitzgerald, Hurston, Wright, and others—and I immersed myself in writers who I suspected might offer me the mysterious sign I sought. I gravitated toward authors who grappled with questions of memory and identity and meaning. I drifted from one writer to another—*The Magus* by John Fowles or *One Hundred Years of Solitude* by García Márquez or *Edwin Mullhouse* by Steven Millhauser. There was no chronology or alphabetical order in my pilgrimage in books—Anne Tyler's *The Accidental Tourist*, Nabokov's *Pale Fire*, Amado's *Dona Flor*, Joseph Heller, Graham Greene, Robert Penn Warren, Toni Morrison, Richard Ford, Flannery O'Connor, Kurt Vonnegut, Cormac McCarthy, Tim O'Brien, Orhan Pamuk, Thomas Pynchon, Annie Dillard, Virginia Woolf,

Camus, the Brontë sisters, Tolstoy, Lawrence, Sartre, Dickens, all of Joseph Mitchell and John McPhee. The books I read led me to deepen my own search by writing my own books.

First in 1991, I wrote *Imagined Places: Journeys into Literary America*, tracing the relationship between six writers and the landscapes that nurtured them or that they made famous—Frost and Vermont, Faulkner and Mississippi, O'Connor and Georgia, Steinbeck and California, Twain and Missouri, and Hemingway in Key West. I went to those places to understand the literature, drawn by what Robert Coles had described as "the call of stories" to see the imagined places, to go where the stories started, to let my explorations shine a light for me on the books I admired. Other narratives of literary adventure followed. I felt a bit like Percy's Will Barrett in *The Last Gentleman*, looking for a sign through his telescope. But for me the instruments of the search were the books that had called to me over the years. Shortly after finishing *Imagined Places*, I wrote *A Place That's Known*, a collection of essays about literature and travel. Other books, fiction and nonfiction, followed. In 2008, in a sort of teasing homage to Twain, I wrote a narrative about traveling around the world twice (in 2002 and 2006) aboard ship—*Innocents Abroad Too*—connecting journeys to Japan, China, Vietnam, India, Kenya, South Africa, Burma, Brazil, Cuba, Egypt, and Spain to the writers from those lands who had made me dream since childhood of those countries. Most recently, in 2015, I wrote *Reading Life*, reversing the course of *Imagined Places* by focusing on works of literature that were formative for me. I wanted to understand place through that literature, to discover the meaning of my own life

Gate, County Armagh, Northern Ireland.

in the literary works that defined me. Without exactly intending to, I found myself immersed in a story that amounted to an autobiography in which I tracked my life in books. One track in that book of a dozen chapters—*Reading Life*—took me to Ireland with the words of Yeats, Joyce, Frank O'Connor, and Edna O'Brien beckoning me to find out if their stories of Ireland would lead me to understand what my grandfather's story might have to do with my own.

    Not long ago, when I glanced back at the books I had written over the past three decades, I saw a connective tissue I had not been aware of—the same sense of displacement and homelessness that Walker Percy's characters grappled with in each of his novels. It was Odysseus's desire to return to where his story began, Telemachus's longing to know his father. That search for home, for the father I knew too well at times and never enough, for the grandfather I knew not at all, was at the heart of everything I had written. In *Irish Classics*, Declan Kiberd persuasively remarked, "A concern with absent or inadequate fathers is to be found in the classic works of Irish modernism from Joyce's *Ulysses* to Synge's *Playboy of the Western World*...." And Alfred Hunter, I suspected, might be discovered in the literature of Ireland, where my heart had been leading me all along. Those seven books I had written led to this one. The search for home started in Ireland, and it would start in stories and in the books of that country.

Chapter 1

The Rocky Road to Dublin and Beyond

> "I wanted real adventures to happen to myself. But real adventures, I reflected, do not happen to people who remain at home: they must be sought abroad."
> —James Joyce, "The Encounter"

The first time I went to Ireland, in 1993, the country was in an economic decline, and my wife and I were robbed on a train and trapped in a snowstorm for two days. Other than a weekend in Toronto when Jo-Ellen and I were teenagers in 1969 and I was pondering my options for avoiding being drafted and sent to fight a war in Vietnam that I didn't feel was righteous, and a day trip to Tijuana the following year when the draft lottery freed me from such decisions on our carefree journey across America, we had never been outside the United States. In 1993, we left our three sons in Virginia Beach in the care of my mother and sister and headed to London for a week and then took a train to Holyhead to catch the ferry to Dun Laoghaire, where we had a reservation for a car rental so that we could drive around the island, from Dublin to Cork and on to Galway and the west.

On the train from London to Holyhead, Jo-Ellen napped, and I went up to the restaurant car to get something to eat. I was a Bronx boy, after all, and arrogant in my sense of my own worldliness and on this well-appointed train through rural England, what could happen? I should have remembered reading right before we landed in Ireland that the unemployment rate had reached 22 percent. When I got back to our seats, Jo-Ellen still lay in a beautiful and innocent sleep, and I saw that in the rack above her head, the leather jacket my sister had given me just before we departed was gone and with it my wallet and credit card and traveler's checks. If it hadn't been for a kindly, soft-spoken Englishwoman who bore a striking resemblance to Dame May Whitty in Alfred

Hitchcock's *The Lady Vanishes* and who convinced us to take a loan of twenty pounds, we would not have had enough cash to buy the required tax and insurance for the car rental we had arranged in advance for Dun Laoghaire. On our way from Dun Laoghaire to Dublin, it started to drizzle, then rain, then pour from the sky in a Biblical fashion that would have made even Noah and his family take notice.

We were told by a man with an untrustworthy grin that we would find an American Express teller machine on Upper O'Connell Street. But, as the crowds took on a surreal aspect in the lengthening and darkening shadows of the late Dublin night, I started to consider that we had become characters in a story imagined by Joyce. I felt like Leopold Bloom in Hades, isolated and lost. A few months before, I had been lost in a passage in Ulysses that began "Now who is that lankylooking galoot over there in the mackintosh? Now who is he I'd like to know? Now I'd give a trifle to know who he is. Always someone turns up you never dreamt of. A fellow could live on his lonesome all his life." I never did figure out all the lonesome mysteries contained in Ulysses, and I feared that I'd be just as lost on those dark, foreign streets of Bloom's city that night.

If God were a shout in the streets, then the god shouting on the grey, rain-slicked streets leading into Dublin that night was none other than Bacchus. The rain blew at me sideways, and our situation seemed as hallucinatory as the Circe episode of *Ulysses*. People drove with what seemed mad abandon to me, groups of revelers yelled, lights flashed, horns honked, drunken screams of *feck you and feck her* filled the air like an off-key litany, umbrellas turned inside out and flew like birds from outstretched hands into the black sky. I considered for a moment that Freud had been right when he said that the Irish were the only race that could not profit from psychoanalysis. Under different circumstances, I think I would have loved that first chaotic experience of the city, its shouts and drunken laughter, its swelling crowds and shifting lights, and I might have agreed with Susan and Thomas Cahill—"Dublin should first be visited by night. In early morning, when the air is heavy with white smog from thousands of chimney pots and the sky is overcast, Dubliners are silent, white-faced people, who greet the day begrudgingly and often belatedly. Toward evening the rhythm of the city quickens, the noise level rises, and faces flush."

My first view of Dublin that night was not Joyce's center of paralysis but a pulsating, throbbing city that felt dizzying and unstable. On many later visits, I would fall breathlessly in love with that rough and handsome city, but on that first night I wanted to be anywhere but dear old dirty Dublin. The gears on the transmission whined and grinded

Chapter 1. The Rocky Road to Dublin and Beyond

angrily as I tried to downshift from 4th to 3rd with my left hand as the car bucked and slid through the downpour. Then, somewhere near the Abbey Theater, the car sputtered and stopped abruptly. I got out and pushed it through the slanting rain to the side of the road, managed through prayer rather than mechanical know-how to get it started again, and discovered shortly that for me pushing a car through the midnight rain in Dublin was an easier task than driving on country lanes in the pitch darkness.

Once I replaced our traveler's checks, we escaped in our rental car to a farmhouse in Prosperous, in County Kildare, about twenty miles to the west of Dublin. At that time, the farming community seemed aptly named, a rich landscape of rolling hills and manor houses. In contrast to Dublin, it was peaceful. A few years later, after the roar of the Celtic Tiger had turned into a feeble whine, Prosperous was anything but. In 1993, though, it looked like a place on the rise. From our farmhouse room, Jo-Ellen and I could hear birds twittering nearby and the intermittent barking of dogs in the distance. At breakfast, the woman of the house, Kathleen Phelan, complained in lilting Irish tones about her five grown children and the hard times that she already saw coming to Prosperous. Kathleen's husband had been forced into an early retirement, and she decided the only way to survive was for her to transform her home into a B&B.

"But, ah, your trouble," she said, after Jo-Ellen told her about my stolen jacket, and our lost credit cards, "you're on holiday and shouldn't have that happen. You shouldn't have to watch your bags every second. If you had to do that sort of thing, you might as well stay home, lock the door, and watch *Far and Away*. But you've made it here, and it's a bad wind that doesn't bring good to somebody, eh? And it brought you here to have a lovely breakfast with me."

Statue of Jim Larkin on O'Connell Street.

Lovely was Kathleen's favorite word. And if we chose tea over coffee, that was *lovely*. And a walk after breakfast, that too would be *lovely*. But even if her go-to word was *lovely*, her world showed some cracks beneath the surface of the l's and y's. Her house had once been a substantial country estate but now it was frayed around the edges. She looked to me like the landed gentry in decline, an example of what a man on the ferry from Holyhead to Dun Laoghaire had said to me, "Ireland may be the only third world country in Europe, an economic as well as a geographical afterthought."

The Ireland of the early 1990s was not the Ireland of the early twenty-first century, when the Irish GPD grew by over 200 percent and the diaspora halted and young Irishmen and women came home. Kathleen Phelan's country was reminiscent of the Ireland of the recent and far past, the island of poverty and emigration.

"We take pride in our education," she said, brushing away a stray auburn lock that had drifted toward her brown eyes and speaking with quiet pride about her children's accomplishments. "We just don't have many opportunities to use it here. So, our children head to England or Canada or America. Ours is a land of elsewhere." Referring to the long history of diaspora in Ireland, she said, "We've always lost our young people. We've had American wakes for centuries. And in a way we still have them. Things are rarely logical in this country. When people complain about car accidents or littering, the government passes a law to fine litterers or lower the speed limit. Then they don't enforce the laws. That way everybody's happy. That's Ireland, for you. Keep everybody happy, even though sadness is as much a part of the national character as music and literature are."

On the road, as we headed toward Youghal, where John Huston opened his 1954 film adaptation of *Moby Dick*, Jo-Ellen gazed out the window at the Irish Sea, and I mulled over Kathleen's insights about her homeland. She offered so much down-to-earth wisdom during a breakfast that stretched to the edges of the dining room table—baked beans, eggs, grilled tomatoes, mushrooms, fried potatoes, scones, and tea. Ireland, for her, was a multi-layered soil, art, music, myth, and religion all sifting into one another. It was a land invaded and oppressed, where people had struggled for centuries to recapture their land and language and sovereignty. For her, it was a country of silences and leave-takings, a place of heartbreaking hardship and breathtaking beauty, music and laughter springing from tragedy and fatalism.

We stopped in Moby Dick's Pub in Youghal, Kevin "Paddy" Lineham's place, and proud he was that John Huston had used his pub as the location for Peter Coffin's Spouter Inn. There were six men at the bar

Chapter 1. The Rocky Road to Dublin and Beyond

and two young boys sitting in one of the booths when we walked in. A television was on, showing Gregory Peck, a supernatural white streak painted across his cheek, speaking in the Shakespearean intonations of Ahab. A few men in the bar resembled, to one degree or another, Richard Basehart and his tight-lipped handsomeness in his portrayal of Ishmael. It was Ireland in the 1990s, and no one came close to looking like Queequeg. No one paid any attention to the film, which played like a visual Muzak as the men sipped their pints and talked to one another. Not even six-year-old Gerald or five-year-old Kevin gave the film any notice.

"I saw it before about ten times," Kevin said to me.

"I've seen eleven," interjected his younger brother.

Youghal was Huston's stand-in for Melville's New Bedford, Massachusetts, the whaling village from which the Pequod sailed toward its tragic destiny with the fabled white whale. Youghal may have looked more like a nineteenth-century New England coastal town than most places in Massachusetts, but it was actually a walled seaport known for the Collegiate Church of St. Mary, which residents claimed to be the oldest church in Ireland. More than one of the townspeople claimed that the church harkened back to the fifth century and the monastic order founded by Declan of Ardmore. Some spoke of Declan and Sir Walter Raleigh, who made a brief sojourn as Lord Mayor of Youghal, as if they were neighbors who recently died. As Paddy Lineman said to me in his pub over the din of customer chatter and Ahab's soliloquies, "Your man Raleigh brought the potato to Ireland. I love my potatoes, don't get me wrong, but I'm not sure if his introducing the Irish to them makes him a hero or a villain." And Paddy's ambivalence made perfect sense to me. I was married to an Irish girl who loved potatoes in every shape and form—baked, fried, mashed, what have you—but the Irish dependence on the potatoes as their staple food may have been the curse that exacerbated the famine of the mid–nineteenth century. Then the country of six million people ate potatoes for breakfast, lunch, and dinner, an average some say of fifteen pounds per day for each person. When the potato crop failed year after year beginning in 1845, the country was destroyed.

In 1993, Youghal was a town of moss-covered stone walls and crumbling turrets. In the graveyard of St. Mary's, tombstones leaned against one another in the lush grass like old friends huddling against the elements. During the brief afternoon sunshine that slid between bouts of rain, the streets were crowded with rosy-cheeked people intent on going from one shop to another. But at night those same people seem willing to stay still, sitting for hours in the pub conversing. That evening

Jo-Ellen and I sat with many of them in the gregarious smoke and the blurred murmur of pint-soaked talk in a pub called the Nook. One old gentleman hobbled in, and the bartender raised his voice over the crowd noise.

"How's the farm, John?" he asked.

"Rotten," John replied. "I'm just here in town to fill a prescription ... a pint of dark, if you don't mind."

It wasn't until more than an hour later, when John and I were in the midst of our own conversation, and he had bought both Jo-Ellen and I pints in sympathy for our troubles with "those English thugs" who took my jacket, that I realized that this was an example of the citizens of two countries separated by a common language. The barman had not been asking John about his farm at all. John was not a farmer but an accountant. He had been asking John about his *form*, that is, his health. When I explained my misunderstanding to John and the barman, I became a sort of curiosity for them and that made them want to buy Jo-Ellen and me more drinks. Men gathered around and toasted our innocence and tried to explain the complicated mysteries of the Irish character to us.

"I was in America once," one explained, "and saw a funeral. The people acted like business as usual. No one stopped what they were doing. I knew I wasn't in Ireland."

"In England," another one chimed in, "if you ask two questions, they call a solicitor. In Ireland if you ask two questions, they give you three answers."

"My whole family has strayed from Catholicism," another said. "I remember when I was a boy, one of my classmates had done some mitching, you know, doing the dodge from school, and the Christian Brothers, damn them, caught him, tied his hands behind his back, and whipped him with a bamboo stick, the poor lad. That did me for Catholicism."

"They're as bad as the IRA," the man next to him said, shaking his head from side to side. "They should be stuck in the darkest hell, both the Church and the IRA. Maybe send them off to live together in the northern part of England."

The bartender didn't seem to care for the political tone of the conversation and spoke up.

"One on me lads," he said. And then he continued in a wonderful non sequitur, "I was riding on a train to Limerick years ago, sitting next to a man who never spoke a word until we were nearly there when he said one thing: 'Jaysis, I hate work!' Then he fell silent again. He never spoke another word for the rest of the trip, but I've always remembered that beautifully articulated philosophy that ranks in my mind with the wisdom of Aristotle."

Chapter 1. The Rocky Road to Dublin and Beyond 17

That started the men's conversation in another direction.

"You know why they invented liquor, don't you? Two very good reasons. First, so that the Irish couldn't take over the world. Second, so that every ugly woman would have a ride home at the end of the night."

"I asked my friend Murphy if he talks to his wife while he's making love," a man who had just strode into the circle said, nodding his Donegal cap to Jo-Ellen in a courtly gesture before continuing, "Certainly, Murphy told me, if there's a phone handy."

The jokes and stories kept coming, and even seemed to make a modicum of sense in a decade when Guinness and smoke-filled pubs and political incorrectness all held sway, and the anecdotes were lyrical and poetic, crude and inappropriate, pertinent and meandering, and sometimes all of those things at the same time. With each additional pint of Guinness, the conversation made more sense. The atmosphere in the Nook didn't feel to me very different from the one I remembered from Darby O'Gills in the Bronx, the local for my friends and our fathers. The resemblance seemed even closer when the music started up in the next room—"Wait Til the Midnight Hour," "Jumpin' Jack Flash," "Knockin' on Heaven's Door"—came thundering through like a call from the 1970s, the music connecting me to them, Ireland of the 1990s to America of the 1970s, maybe even connecting my grandfather's experience to mine. The room next to the bar was packed with young men and women, listening to music that linked us. Now I was with their parents, peering into the smoke, looking for some clue in their eyes to who my grandfather might have been. But I realized it was into the eyes of the teenagers I should have been gazing because they were the age Alfred Hunter had been when he determined to leave Ireland and find a new life in America.

So, Jo-Ellen and I drifted into the young people's section of the pub. When the musicians left the stage in the wee hours of the morning, a raven-haired young woman named Rosemary took up her guitar at our table and sang Cat Stevens's "Father and Son." She never said why she picked that song to sing in the hushed room. Her voice was sweet and soft, and I imagined she chose the song for me, that "same, same old story" of fathers and sons, that she sang it, an incantation, to bring Alfred Hunter out of the shadows of the past.

It was the middle of March in 1993, and our flight home from Shannon Airport was canceled because of a monster snowstorm—not in Ireland but on the East Coast of the United States. With a taunting irony, for five days in a row the gods had given us an uncommon sunshine in Western Ireland and left us to worry about our three sons waiting for us at home with family members that had to eventually return to their own

Temple Bar, Dublin.

houses in different states. We got back—three days later than expected and on an Aeroflot jet that appeared to be held together by shoelaces and glue. After we returned home and hugged our kids, we searched our bags for the name and address of the woman who had lent us the twenty pounds, but it was nowhere to be found. One more piece of evidence, we thought, that would prove to the English that the Irish were untrustworthy.

It was ten years later that I opened a zippered compartment of my old suitcase and found a copy of *Joyce's Dublin: A Walking Guide to Ulysses* by Jack McCarthy. The book had been given to me by the writer John McPhee. I was happy to find the missing book but even happier to discover what was inside it. Folded into the book was a scrap of paper with the Englishwoman's name and address. A decade late I was able to send her money back to her along with a gift and, hopefully, improve Irish-English relations and redeem the Kennedy-Kiernan-Hunter name.

Over the next two and a half decades I traveled back to Ireland a half dozen times, and on many of those trips I followed in the tracks of Leopold Bloom, trying to find a way through Joyce's compassionate and generous Alfred Hunter to my cryptic ancestor of the same name. Nearly twenty years later, in 2012, I was in Dublin again, leading students around the city, as I was led, unbeknownst to them, by the ghost

Chapter 1. The Rocky Road to Dublin and Beyond

of my grandfather. We were there for Bloomsday, what many of my undergraduates thought would be something akin to the Running of the Bulls in Pamplona, of course without the scarfed Spaniards and minus the charging bulls. They had all read *The Sun Also Rises* the past semester, and they saw Jake Barnes and Leopold Bloom as one and the same, I think. I wasn't sure exactly what to expect, and perhaps my hopes were aligned to theirs—a Bacchanalian re-enactment of the novel, a Mardi Gras for bookish nerds who wanted to step from the pages of a novel into the life it described. Whatever Bloomsday turned out to be, I reasoned, who couldn't love a country that gave itself over with fervor to focus on a work of literature, especially one by a man who spent the last forty years of his life in exile reflecting on the claustrophobic character of his birthplace? What a country and what a people! They demonized him when he was a living writer and then canonized him when he went silent.

Bloomsday turned out to be less of an orgiastic event than I had anticipated; if anything, it was muted—and maybe a few Spaniards and bulls would have added to the excitement. A half dozen costumed men and women ambled along Grafton Street but Mardi Gras it wasn't. There were a few readings of Molly Bloom's soliloquy in pubs around the city and a couple of re-enactments of scenes from *Ulysses* in locations that ran from Dublin to Dalkey. It all seemed virtuous rather than venereal, and Joyce would surely have declared it too tame for his taste. I might not have noticed that it was all happening in the streets around me if I hadn't checked my calendar and noted that it was June 16.

So, a few days later I decided to take a more dangerous approach to Joyce—"See Dublin and Joyce's *Dubliners* by Bike"—a Joycean bike ride that none of the students opted to participate in because riding a bicycle in Dublin seemed to them—fair enough, probably—a death wish. And in not joining the bike ride, they may have shown more sense than their professor. The ride was led by a convivial Sean Farrell, a middle-aged man who had been riding bicycles around the capital of Ireland for a quarter of a century. Sean showed no fear as he wiggled between cars and pedestrians, as if he believed wholeheartedly in the good will of the thousands of car and bus drivers who swerved around us on every street. Or, perhaps, I thought, he had decided our yellow high-vis jackets emblazoned with the silhouette of James Joyce would ward off demons and distracted drivers. Or maybe it was just Irish fatalism: if it was our time to die, so be it. In any case, there were seventeen people besides Sean who picked up their bicycles on Fade Street that morning and angled into the heart-thrumming traffic. We made a path through the humming streets and the stories of *Dubliners* as we snaked around buses and cars. I would rather have followed Leopold Bloom in his perambulations through *Ulysses* and squinted into the hazy light for a glimpse of Alfred Hunter, but for most cyclists *Ulysses* would have likely seemed more dangerous than a line of buses on Nassau Street.

The penniless Joyce had been a *flaneur malgre lui* in Dublin and its environs, and on our bicycles we had something close to a walker's perspective. Slowly, eighteen bicycles pulsing up one street and then down another, we came to the Canal Bridge that stood between innocence and experience in "The Encounter," and then we stopped on Hardwicke Street, once a stately block of Georgian homes that were made into boarding rooms in Joyce's day and provided the setting for "The Boarding House" of his story. The fate of that street had slipped even further since Joyce's depiction of it in the early twentieth century. Two of our cycling group left us there, as if the sad fate of the street was too much for them to bear. One was an older man. The other, his companion, was a middle-aged woman in a green chiffon dress and black high heels. It seemed to me a strange outfit for a bike ride, but it was only a few days after Bloomsday, and it might have been her nod to Joyce's Molly. Who was I to tell the citizens of Ireland how to dress on Bloomsday or a few days after? Her green chiffon dress blowing in the breeze, the woman waved enthusiastically as she sped off. Her dress flew up behind her like the green flag of a modern united Ireland. Down the way from the downtrodden townhouses was the church that Mrs. Mooney in "The Boarding House" dreamt of seeing her daughter marry the trapped Mr. Doran. To the left of the church, two idle construction cranes dominated the post-boom landscape. To the right of the church, the faded façade of The Children's Hospital framed the grey horizon. Hanging from the side of the church, like a reminder of Mrs. Mooney's covetousness, fluttered a 20 by 40-foot banner advertising office space for let from Arthur Ryan Property Consultants. Underneath the banner, a dark-skinned Roma woman with a baby strapped to her breast, was bent into the wind as if she had been invented by Joyce to highlight the inertia of the city.

One hundred years after Joyce published *Dubliners*, Kevin Barry, one of the most highly acclaimed contemporary Irish writers, came out with a twenty-first-century portrait of the city in *Dark Lies the Island*, and his estimate of its residents—that so many were "soul sick"—suggested that neither the Celtic Tiger, the unmooring of the Catholic Church, nor entry into the European Union had changed the country in many of its fundamentals. When we reached North Richmond Street, the locale for "Araby," Sean waved his arm and shouted over the noise of the traffic, "You can ride the bikes, all right. Don't worry that it's a one-way street now. Mr. Joyce would love that, eh?"

Chapter 1. The Rocky Road to Dublin and Beyond

We parked our bikes near 13 North Richmond Street, where Joyce lived for some years of his nomadic adolescence. A freckle-face boy screamed "Ma" at a second-floor window, and he could have been one of the boys in Joyce's story, or he could have been one of my street companions on Bainbridge Avenue in the Bronx. North Richmond Street, like the streets of my Bronx childhood, was a gritty brick neighborhood that had either forgotten its past or remembered it too well. Half-torn garbage bags rose in small mounds on the curb, pigeons feasted on debris in the middle of the blind street, the Gaelic Football Stadium hovered in the distance, and the remaining cyclists roamed about like visitors from an alien planet—or like characters who had stepped out the pages of a book on to the pavement of the city. A man in a first-floor flat cater-cornered from Joyce's old residence opened the faded lace curtains and peered out warily. Cardboard boxes propped open the window, and paint peeled from its sides like melting wax. The man stared out at us with pinched lips and narrowed eyes.

All this seemed at the heart of Joyce's *Dubliners*, similar to where I grew up in the New York City, and, I suspected, it had a kinship with the environment in the North from which Alfred Hunter had made his first escape. I realized at that moment, like Alfred Hunter in his second escape, that I too had run from the Bronx. I had left my city and my borough behind, but, unlike my grandfather, I had taken my love with me.

The bike tour ended at Finn's Hotel, where Joyce met Nora Barnacle for their first date. We stood in a circle gazing at the hotel as if we would not be surprised to see Joyce come limping out, swinging his cane. Alice Coughlin, the tour host, bid us farewell with a joke about how easy it was to get Americans to believe "any cock and bull story one could make up about Ireland's most famous writer." I was thinking about other things, my past and my lost grandfather most probably and barely heard her teasing remarks. One of the Dublin cyclists, a young woman named Sinead, came over to me and apologized.

"Don't worry a bit," I said without realizing I was probably confirming Alice's characterization of obtuse Americans, "I was barely listening."

"Well," Sinead said, "we were insulted for you then." She smiled so brightly I felt my heart expand for the past and the present, and I fell in love with Ireland and its mysterious reality all over again and thought Alfred Hunter, whether he had any redeeming qualities personally, had brought me home. He had given me Dorothy Hunter Pearson, the most important person in my youth, and he had given me Ireland, a country I loved even if I didn't always know why. For those two blessings, I could forgive almost anything.

The next year I arrived in Dublin in early summer when an unusual sunny spell had taken over the city. My class had just read *Skippy Dies*, and Paul Murray had come to the seminar at Trinity to talk about his novel. From the sleepy-eyed question-and-answer period with him, I guessed that most of the students had not finished the 700-page book. I felt sorry for them. It's a wonderful narrative, and the majority of them had missed their opportunity to go behind the screen and ask the wizard how he did it.

I was disappointed for them—and with them—and I took off to St. Stephen's Green to consider the state of education in America. As I sat on a bench in the precarious sunshine, my thoughts circled back to *Skippy Dies*, a tale of the new suburban Ireland, a place as shallow and modern as any enclave outside of New York or Boston, a novel about a group of youngsters who struggle with the same issues their American counterparts in the Facebook and Twitter and mall-grazing brave new world, face. And, perhaps, the lassitude I saw in some of them was no different than what existed in the college cohort of my own time, a laziness that my memory now romanticized out of existence. I gave up the thought with a sigh and pulled James Plunkett's *Strumpet City* from my backpack. His 1969 tale of the Great Lockout of 1913 had been chosen as the One Dublin One Book choice, following in the wake of Flann O'Brien's *At Swim-Two-Birds*, the first city pick in 2006. The classics that followed O'Brien's comic masterpiece—*Dracula, Gulliver's Travels, The Picture of Dorian Gray,* and *Dubliners* led up to the committee choosing Plunkett's historical novel of the city in the early twentieth century. The book had the compelling feel of a nineteenth century epic to it, a Dickensian brand of sympathetic realism that made me wonder if the past of the city were ever truly the past.

Toward the end of the afternoon, two middle-aged women strolled over to the bench where I was reading. The one, slim and bedecked in an orange sundress and oversized brown sunglasses that could have put her comfortably on Madison Avenue in Manhattan, surprised me with what seemed to be a stage Irish accent and the syntax and the idiom to match.

"I have a desperate pain in me back, Mary," she said. "Why don't we sit ourselves down?"

For some reason, when I first looked at her, I'd forgotten I was in present-day Ireland and the *me* and the *desperate* brought me out of the novel and back to St. Stephen's Green. Two teenagers wearing New York Yankees t-shirts jostled one another as they passed by, and one bellowed, "For fuck's sake, Aiden, I told you I'm not going with her tonight. So, stop asking me, will ya?"

Chapter 1. The Rocky Road to Dublin and Beyond

"Down be a gawn now," his companion responded. "Just see her once, won't ya?"

Gertie, the woman in the sundress, glanced quickly in the direction of the disappearing Yankee shirts and turned again to Mary.

"Let's sit down and rest our bones for a while, all right," she said, pointing to the section of my bench that was unoccupied. "For heaven's sake, I can't step another foot now. I'm about destroyed."

From the moment they sat down with a shuddering sigh and turned toward me with a nod, I could see that Gertie was gregarious, even a bit flirtatious, while Mary was shy, barely raising her eyes when she muttered a quiet sentence or two—"I was a teacher for years like Gertie, but I taught the little ones."

It didn't take Gertie long to peer over my shoulder to see what I was reading.

"Ah, that's a fine book, it is," she said with an approving squint of her eyes. She then held her head at an angle as if she were about to sneeze. "Everyone in Dublin is reading it now. We're one city one book, you know. We're a literary town, we are. When I was a snip of a girl, I fell in love with Fitz in that story. Now I think I'd love Mr. Yearling."

I'd read enough of the novel to know that she was alluding to two of the most compassionate male figures in the book. And she kept the posture of an imminent sneeze for the next half hour as she talked about Irish history and literature—everything from *Ulysses* and *Finnegans Wake* to the films *Michael Collins* and *The Wind That Shakes the Barley* and plays like *The Cripple of Inishmaan* and *The Playboy of the Western World*.

"Ah, such a twisted history we have," Gertie said.

"History is a nightmare from which the Irish are trying to awaken, I suppose," I said in response.

Both women could have rolled their eyes at my pretentiousness, but both smiled broadly, and Gertie let her fingertips drop to my forearm and linger there.

"That Joyce," Mary said, glancing at her friend and then letting her eyes drop to the ground, "you can't escape him here."

She pushed her chin deeper into her chest and shifted her eyes quickly in my direction and then away.

"Excuse my French," Gertie said, "but even in a city of statues, you can't miss Joyce. The prick with a stick is what we call his highness."

The sky began to cloud over, and the temperature dropped discernibly. Gertie fluttered her eyelids, smiled coquettishly at the word *prick* and whispered the phrase one more time, giggled and glanced down at my hands. We talked for a bit about her upbringing in Sligo, and I told her what little I knew of my long-lost grandfather.

"He was a playboy of the western world, I bet," she said. And then asked, "So, are you here in Dublin on your own?" A pause. "Or with your wife."

"With my wife," I told her. "She's back at Trinity, getting a break from me."

Gertie didn't respond, but, surprisingly, Mary looked up and spoke forcefully.

"Young men may loot, perjure, and shoot and even have carnal knowledge," she intoned like a schoolgirl reciting a poem she was asked to memorize for class. "But, however depraved, their souls will be saved if they DON'T go to Trinity College."

Reciting that couplet seemed to take all the wind from her sails, and she looked down at her shoes, collapsing back into her slouching posture. Then the weather and the conversation stalled together. A well-nourished, shirtless young man, tattooed from wrist to shoulder, chest and back, waddled past us, bringing with him, it seemed, a clap of thunder and in seconds a hard rain.

"Ireland has her madness and her weather still," Gertie said, the retired English teacher showing her past once more. Then she grabbed Mary's elbow and produced her exit line as they dashed off under the umbrella she had just raised. "Enjoy your stay in the city. Nice weather for ducks! I hope you find the dosser you're looking for."

The rainy weather followed us to Mary's home ground in Sligo. On our way to Yeats country, we passed through the village of Cong, what still looked like a movie set for the fight in *The Quiet Man*. We negotiated the winding roads as if we were really pondering the discrepancy between the Romantic Ireland and the Real one, for me the possible intersection between my imagined Alfred Hunter and the actual one hidden from view. The question of the relationship between Romantic, mythic Ireland and the historical, political reality was the same negotiation that Yeats engaged in with his poetry from the outset until his death. Before sunset we stood alongside the poet's simple gravestone in the unadorned Drumcliffe Churchyard in the long shadow of Ben Bulben. The famous lines etched in his tomb—"Cast a cold eye/on life, on death/Horseman, pass by"—seemed frozen in the falling light. For my students and my colleague on the trip, John McManus, the mountain held a more compelling view, more than the poet's stony epitaph.

The mountain was both awe-inspiring and daunting. From our perspective, the north face seemed a sheer limestone cliff. Of the eleven students on our bus, only four decided to hike with my colleague, John, the bus driver, John Gavin, and I to the top of Ben Bulben. It wasn't easy to find an appropriate spot to start the climb amidst the bramble

Swans, St. Stephen's Green, Dublin.

and rocks. John Gavin stopped the bus on a narrow country lane to inquire from a passing farmer where we might find the right path up the mountain.

"How are you getting on?" Gavin asked the countryman driving the tractor. "We're trying to find a way up the mountainside."

After a considerable amount of hemming and hawing, the farmer made it clear that there was no easy way to do that as far as he knew, but he suggested that we try going down the road for a while until we came to a place where the lane curved and allowed a path through some brush.

"No worries," Gavin told the farmer. "Enjoy your day."

Turning to us in the back of the bus, Gavin explained, "We may be the only conversation he's had all week. We're his bit of craic for a while, I think. But if we don't head up the mountain now, we'll never make it to the top and back by nightfall. Let's go. This will be deadly, sure."

So, he parked on the side of the road, and we headed to the top. It was nearly nine p.m. by the time we reached the wind-blown crest, and Gavin raised his hand in triumph, even though the words he shouted through the blasts of wind sounded less-than-heroic, "I'm about destroyed with hunger. Let's get back to Sligo and have a pint."

About an hour later in the bar of the Glasshouse Hotel, as we gazed at the Garavogue River, what the locals call Sligeach, we had our pint, and a few more for good luck. The next morning Gavin dropped us off in Rossaveel to catch the ferry to Inishmaan. On the day we stepped on the island, there were fewer than two hundred people living there, and besides our group there were only a half dozen people on the ferry. The few people waiting on the dock had the same chiseled, faraway look that I saw in the characters in Robert Flaherty's 1934 documentary, *Man of Aran*. The landscape of the island had a lunar feel to it, that is, if the moon had been carefully segmented by hundreds of intricately made stone walls. The boreens were unmarked and, given that everyone on the island knew his neighbor and there was only one bar (a modest local tavern) and one—occasionally opened—restaurant (Inis Meain, the kind of upscale restaurant and hotel one might expect to find on Martha's Vineyard or Catalina, with prices to match), there didn't seem much need for signs. One of the few places marked on the island was Synge's Chair, a curving throne of stones built on the edge of a high cliff, where on many occasions the writer sat contemplating the landscape and the people he brought to comic and dramatic life in his nonfiction and plays.

My students and I spent much of the morning in the thatch-covered cottage that Synge lived in each summer from 1898 to 1902, collecting stories from islanders and working on plays like *Riders to the Sea* and *The Playboy of the Western World*. The man who showed us the place, Kieron, from the Mac Donnchadha clan that had owned the cottage for years, had grown up there, sharing the three tiny rooms of the place with his ten siblings. Kieron stood leaning into the shadows of the smoke-wrapped entryway. His grey hair was damp and tousled from the wind and rain. His weathered skin had the same dark hue as the limestone found near the cliffs. His hooded eyes registered a remarkable blend of innocence and foxlike awareness. Without offering any eye contact, he told us bits and pieces of his island story. He had been away from Inishmaan only once or twice and never beyond Galway.

"I have a bit of land over there," he said, pointing toward the southern part of the island. The *over there* was stretched to a mournful cadence it was hard to imagine the phrase being capable of reaching. "I have some sheep and cows and vegetables, all right."

Between terse statements, Kieron held the silences like a man not used to speaking. He seemed to cherish the silences, as if the crowd of us made him uneasy, as if English were a language he had learned as a child and not used again until now, straining his best to remember how to string words together into one sentence, then another. The students asked him more questions than I suspect he had been asked in quite some time and, finally, he stepped out of the entrance to the cottage, shook the smoke and ash from his clothing as if they were snowflakes. Then he angled his gaze toward the shoulder of one of the male students, asking in a diffident whisper as he looked at the far horizon, "What kind of cows do you have at your house?"

Chapter 2

Memory and Imagination

> "He disappeared in the dead of winter.... What instruments we have agree/The day of his death was a dark cold day."
> —W.H. Auden, "In Memory of W.B. Yeats"

Alfred Hunter was a shade under six feet tall and had a sly, funny manner. He hardly ever allowed his controlled features to break into a wide grin, but his grey-blue eyes always stayed awash in the sort of half-light that implied something comic had just happened. The scar on his left cheek, probably from an accident on the family farm in Northern Ireland, looked like the waning crescent of the moon when he arched his eyes to question an utterance he thought irrational. His parents were successful farmers, somber and practical people. They loved Alfred but thought him a quare lot because as a boy he read Dickens by the hour and they thought him too dreamy to make his way in the hard world. They probably would have been beside themselves if they knew he saw himself as a character of the David Copperfield variety, a man who would soon be the hero of his own life. Even when he left home for a new world, he likely took that boy with him, cradled in his heart. Alfred may have had a kinship with both James Joyce and me in his fascination with the wily Odysseus, more attracted to the dreamer than to the more standard Greek heroes like Achilles or Hector. Ultimately, though, he may have been more like Tennyson's narrow-hearted Ulysses, "always roaming with a hungry heart," a man who could not "rest from travel," a man for whom knowledge was more important than loyalty and love. At least this is the way my grandfather came to me in my daydreams.

Then there are the modest facts about the Alfred Hunter I found in online documents. He left Ireland, the youngest of four siblings, an older brother and two sisters. His father, William Hunter, remarried and had nine more children, leaving Alfred and his brother disenfranchised, without any real inheritance on the farm in Dungannon.

In America, alone and lonely, Alfred met Jennie O'Pray, ten years his senior, a sweet-tempered woman with three sons, and with her he fathered a daughter on November 23, 1911, a baby girl—Dorothy Hunter. By this time, he was twenty-five years old and had left Dickens behind for good, or left that story for his grandson's dreams. Without entrusting anyone with a note, he skipped town, leaving Jennie and Dorothy and the three male stepchildren whom he determined not to know at 574 East 156th Street in the Bronx.

Alfred didn't make it easy for me to track him after he arrived at Ellis Island. I thought of Stephen Dedalus, most likely echoing Joyce's own sentiment, telling his headmaster Mr. Deasy in *Ulysses* that history is a nightmare from which he's trying to shake himself awake. I felt I had the opposite problem: trying to dream my way back in time. At first, it seemed all Alfred Hunter left behind was my mother and his name. It took me a few months to figure out that he had been an electrician on the *SS Mongolia* and that by 1920 he had found himself a new wife—Eleanor—rented a house in Irvington, New Jersey, for $84 a month, and started another family. Eventually, he had three children—two boys and a girl—Warren, Sabina and Stanley. The 1930 census lists Eleanor as the head of household—so Alfred may have been out to sea. Or perhaps he had done a second disappearing act already because by the 1940 census, he had vanished and his youngest son, Stanley, was in a boys' home.

The search for Alfred Hunter initially had the contours of a dark melodrama but it eventually took on the outlines of a slapstick comedy, what seemed to me something like an eighteenth-century novel by Henry Fielding. What started as a somber melodrama—a Dickensian tale of abandoned babies, deserted wives, scarred anti-heroes, seafaring escapades, and a discovered demesne, manor house, and affluent relatives—deteriorated into some blend of French farce, complete with mistaken identities, dinners with strangers, a busted birthright, and a brand-new mystery.

It started this way: my memory of a conversation my mother had with me when I was in grade school. Our seventh-grade class divided itself along a simple boundary—either you were of Irish or Italian descent. Pearson, my father's anglicized German surname, didn't readily fit into the group from Villa Avenue or the one from Bedford Park Boulevard. I felt a kinship with the Irish lads, but my name didn't seamlessly fit into the stew of O'Learys and Mahoneys and Fitzpatricks.

"My father was from Northern Ireland," my mother said when I told her about my school identity crisis. "I didn't know him and really don't want to talk about him. But you can take his name—Alfred Hunter—to school with you. It may sound English, but he was Irish enough, surely.

Chapter 2. Memory and Imagination

Empty bench, Rosses Point, Sligo.

It's about time he did some good in this family. Take the Hunter name. It's yours."

Many years later, I went to Ireland a number of times, imagining that I followed in Joyce's footsteps, going out into the world in order to turn experience into story. I had fallen in love with the landscape, the music, the people, the history, and literature of the country. I didn't have much evidence to solve the mystery of my grandfather—just the date of my mother's birth and the fact that Alfred Hunter had come from somewhere in Northern Ireland and landed like a Viking raider in New York City. Basic biology told me that his arrival had to have been some time before the spring of the year she was born. I searched the Ellis Island immigration records and found only one likely candidate—Alfred Hunter, born in Killyman, Dungannon, County Tyrone, on May 28, 1886. He had arrived on Ellis Island in 1908. His father was William Hunter and his mother's maiden name was Elizabeth Jane Orr. They had lived in Dungannon for a few generations, the family most likely emigrating in the eighteenth century from Scotland or the English highlands. Eliza Jane died when Alfred was nine years old, in 1895, and Alfred's father remarried and began having his next set of heirs—ten of them. In a fog of shifting primogeniture, Alfred and his siblings born of Eliza

Jane saw the farm and their inheritance slipping away from them. Two went to Canada, one to Australia, and Alfred, in his 21st year, shipped out from Londonderry on the *SS Columbia* to New York City. Most likely he had the money for a second-class passage, which meant a little more space and four meals a day rather than the three given in steerage. At the end of the two-week journey, he landed on Ellis Island with $28 in his shoe and a note in his pocket listing the address for his Uncle James McComb in Hudson, New Jersey. He arrived in New York Harbor three days after his twenty-second birthday, on May 31, 1908. The ship's manifest describes him as 5' 10" tall, with fair skin, blue eyes, and brown hair. His profession is listed as a farmer, and he'd come to America with only the money in his pocket and the sponsorship of his uncle in New Jersey.

I had no trouble finding Alfred's birth certificate in Dungannon. Nor did I have any difficulty locating my distant cousin, Raymond Hunter, who still owned the farm with his wife, Jill, and lived there six months of each year. The other half of the year Raymond, a dairy company executive with an honors degree from Oxford and a doctorate in Agricultural Economics from Queen's University Belfast, lived in the United States in a rented American McMansion in Celebration, Florida, southwest of Orlando and near enough to Disneyworld to hear children scream out Mickey's name on a quiet night. With Irish good humor and English practicality, in the shadow of Goofy and Cruella de Vil, Raymond served as a consultant to companies around the world. The Hunter farm in Drumkee, Dungannon, County Tyrone, consisted of a few hundred acres with a view of miles and miles of bocage that might remind one of Southern England, a quilted landscape of brilliant pastures painted green by the constant rains, a pastoral setting with groves of trees and winding country lanes bisecting an emerald geometry. On a clear day, the Sperrin Mountains rose in the far distance to compete with a view of the low hanging clouds.

In 2017, my wife and I took the train from Dublin to Portadown Station in Northern Ireland. Raymond Hunter—tall, white haired, bespectacled, and bearing a Goofy sort of handsomeness—picked us up and drove us to the farm. The homestead was made up of two ample houses, a complex of pig sheds and cow barns, acres of rolling pastures sprinkled with complacent cows, and a million-dollar windmill that powered the entire operation. Raymond looked British, like a sensible butler in Downton Abbey, but his accent was Irish through and through. He gave Jo-Ellen and me each a pair of Wellingtons from the dozen he had waiting in the foyer. Then, like a real estate agent showing us part of a condo we would never be able to purchase, he took us to the empty pig barn,

Chapter 2. Memory and Imagination 31

clean enough to be a pre-school. After that, he introduced Jo-Ellen to a quartet of cows while I took what felt like a family photo—cows and cousin and my brightly smiling wife.

Then we returned the boots to the foyer, retrieved our shoes, and met Raymond's 97-year-old mother, Ruby. An hour later, Raymond and Jill took us to lunch and on a tour of Dungannon Town, the Castle Caulfield, the Hill of the O'Neill House (after all, we were within spitting distance of the O'Neill Dynasty and my wife's stepfather had been an O'Neill), and on to the cemetery, where my ostensible great-grandfather, William, was buried next to his second wife, Margaret Jane.

By the time we left Dungannon that night, I felt as if I had done the reverse immigrant trick. The typical Irish emigration story amounted to a tale of hardship and hunger, escaping poverty and prejudice for a brighter future in Australia or Canada or the United States. The usual storyline tracked an Irish immigrant from shack to sturdy suburban homestead—or better. Even Frank McCourt's about face in *Angela's Ashes* recounted the funny and tragic trajectory of his family from an impoverishment in Brooklyn to a worse one in Limerick. And he ultimately followed the worn path with his protagonist running from Ireland to the new world. As McCourt said in his memoir, his was a "miserable childhood: the happy childhood is hardly worth your while. Worse than the ordinary miserable childhood is the miserable Irish childhood, and worse yet is the miserable Irish Catholic childhood." So, McCourt had the memoirist's trifecta—childhood misery, Catholicism, and damp Ireland. On the other hand, I may have had my share of misery in my childhood, as well as a strong dose of Catholicism, but I was lower middle class and never knew hunger or squalor. However, I didn't know the majesty of the Hunter farm, and I imagined it must have been a sad slide for Alfred to leave those bucolic rolling acres for an apartment in the Bronx and an escape to, of all places, New Jersey. When I compared the one-bedroom apartment I grew up in, spending twenty-one years in those crammed spaces before I got married and left for San Francisco, I envied the pigs on Raymond's estate. My maternal heritage amounted to a loss of status, not a slow climb up in a new country.

Raymond and I kept in touch over the next few years as he tried to help me search for Alfred Hunter's death certificate. I did everything I could, outside of hiring Sam Spade, to find out where Alfred went after he slipped moorings from his second family. Without his death certificate, I could not complete the paperwork for an Irish passport. But weeks turned into months and then years, nothing. Alfred had covered his tracks well. He had vanished into thin air. He was like an IRA operative on the run.

My relationship with my new Hunter relatives deepened, visits, calls, and emails, every few months, Raymond's brogue crackling over the phone line. The last time he called, in the spring of 2022, he was visiting his daughter in New York City, and I could hear the thunder and sirens competing in the background.

"It's bucketing down here right now," he said. "But we head out on our drive to Florida tomorrow, sun or hail. How about lunch?"

So, with Jill, he stopped at our home in Cape Charles on the Chesapeake Bay, had lunch with us and examined the paper evidence of our familial relationship that I had gathered and laid before him on the dining room table.

"Wait a minute," he said, the beginnings of a smile creasing his eyes. He squinted. "Wait a minute." He paused and ran his index finger up and down one of the pages. Then, his eyes widening, he stared at my mother's baptismal certificate, which recorded her name as Dorothy Hunter, born in the Bronx, and listed Jennie O'Pray as her mother and Alfred Hunter as her father. The date of her baptism was January 14, 1912, a month and a half after her birth. Her birth certificate for November 23, 1911, had her mother's name as Jeanie Hunter and her father's as Alfred Hunter and their residence as 574 East 156st in the Bronx. Jeanie's age was listed as 34 and her number of previous children was three. Alfred was listed as 35 and born in Ireland. Other than some alterations in the spelling of names, and the fact that my mother was Dorothy Hunter on her baptismal record and Helen Fluhr Hunter on her city birth certificate, discrepancies that could be easily explained by whimsical record keeping and name changing in the early twentieth century, I wasn't sure what was making Raymond's brow wrinkle. But when he came to my grandparents' certificate of marriage and Alfred Hunter's birth certificate from Northern Ireland, his eyes narrowed even more dramatically.

"Hmmm, we may have eaten lunch with you on false pretenses," he said, his eyes shining in a playful smile. "Look at this."

He placed Alfred's birth certificate alongside my grandparents' record of marriage, and I saw the two undeniable discrepancies that he saw. I had glossed over them as if they were another example of early twentieth-century bureaucratic whimsy.

"Our genetic bond may be broken," Raymond said, leaning his head back and laughing. "Your scapegrace may not be mine. But, not to worry, it looks like we surely both have reprobates in our genealogy and they're each named Alfred Hunter."

His Alfred Hunter had been born in 1886, which would have made him 22 years old when he married my 30-something-year-old maternal grandmother. For a long time, I had imagined my grandmother as an

Chapter 2. Memory and Imagination

older woman and a widow with three sons who had fallen in love with the dashing young Irishman, Alfred Hunter. The age discrepancy I imagined away, but the marriage record I now had listed Alfred's birthplace as County Armagh in 1876, not the County Tyrone ten years later when the Alfred Hunter of Raymond Hunter's clan had been born. On the marriage certificate lying on the table in front of me, it said that Alfred's parents were James Hunter and Hannah Williams, both of County Armagh in Ireland. So, as Raymond drove back toward Disney World, I watched my heritage evaporate, the Alfred Hunter of Tyrone fade, along with William and Margaret Jane's graves, the whole gentleman's farm up in smoke. I was left with a new Irish grandfather, a heritage no longer associated with manor houses and the Protestant Ascendancy and more likely connected to the typical story of Irish emigration—poor, hardscrabble, and desperately seeking a new life and fresh identity in America. I was left with a different Alfred Hunter, probably one more fitting of the circumstances of my own growing up in a cramped one-bedroom apartment in the Bronx. A tongue-in-cheek email came from Raymond a few weeks later. "Dear Michael," it said:

> Are you removing our genetic bond and telling me that I might no longer have a black sheep in my family? What happens if you fail to find any upright citizens in your lineage? How are you going to incorporate this latest twist into your book?

So, there we stood, Raymond and I, he in Florida and me in Virginia, like characters in a Woody Allen story, stepping from the pages of our own fiction into a world in which the fiction seemed as reliable as the facts. He ended his email by saying that he had enlisted his sister-in-law, who lived in London, to "dig up any dirt on this disreputable person using the Alfred Hunter name without our permission." Then he thanked Jo-Ellen and me for our hospitality and detailed his visit to Virginia Beach and Ocracoke Island in North Carolina on his way back to Florida. His next email a few weeks later was chock full of detective work and a certificate from The Births and Deaths Registration (Northern Ireland) for my new, if not improved, maternal grandfather.

"Jill's sister, Joan, has been hard at work confirming that indeed there was a James Hunter who married a Hannah in 1871 in Co. Armagh," he wrote. "She also found an 1872 birth certificate for their son Frederick George Hunter and another for Edmund Hunter, born on April 4, 1876. This Edmund most surely is your Alfred, who must have altered his first name to connect him to the Great Saxon king in order to impress the Americans he encountered or to make himself harder to find by the Irishmen and women he left behind."

Raymond's sister-in-law dug deeper still, going back to my great-great grandfather, Moses, a farmer in the mid–1800s in Drumkee, in the same townland as Raymond's clan. Based upon the will that Joan discovered, Moses was William Hunter's brother, and our family connection, although frail, still existed. The birth records that Joan sent showed that Moses had a son born in the 1840s, in the tragic midst of the Irish Famine, and those facts "would tie into the likely birth of the Armagh James Hunter who married Hannah Williams in the 1870's." So, I traded one mystery for another, one sad-eyed Odysseus for a different one of the same name. One rich ancestor for a poor one. My last email to Raymond alluded to a herd of black sheep or at least the two tinted sheep that linked us together in a shared heritage, starting a friendship that I sensed would survive on sly humor and the sort of negative capability that seemed to me patently Irish.

* * *

My newly discovered Alfred Hunter, born in County Armagh on April 4, 1876, under the given name Edwin Gray Hunter, most likely was orphaned when he was a young child. His father, my great-grandfather, James Hunter, a publican, and his mother, my great-grandmother, Hannah Williams, had both been widowed, and this was their second marriage. That would place the births of my great-grandparents at some time during or near the Great Famine, *An Gorta Mor*, of the mid–nineteenth century in Ireland. Most certainly, the stories of Black 47 would have been part of their growing up, even part of their experience and memory, and surely they would have passed along that history, like survivors of an inexplicable natural disaster, to their son Edwin. He may have changed his name from Edwin Grey Hunter

Poster in the James Joyce Centre, Dublin.

Chapter 2. Memory and Imagination

to Alfred Hunter when he decided to leave Ireland to make a new life in the United States, or it may have been changed for him by adoptive parents or the social welfare system he certainly found himself in when his parents died less than a decade after he was born.

Alfred's parents would have made him aware of the Great Hunger, their holocaust. They would have described the blackened earth, the sickening smell, the deathly silence, the packs of feral dogs digging up the shallow graves of the famine dead, the emaciated women in rags carrying dead infants, the men walking twenty miles to distant towns for food because they were too proud to let their neighbors see them begging. Ireland during the Great Famine was a one-way road out for many. In the historian John Kelly's assessment in *The Graves Are Walking*, the majority of Irish citizens were desperate to leave. There was "the overpowering desire to get out ... husbands deserted wives, parents, children, brothers, sisters...." For millions looking to escape the horrors of poverty and famine, the motto was "anywhere but here." For many Irish, the English in general were genocidal monsters, and Sir Charles Edward Trevelyan, the Assistant Secretary for the Treasury in the mid–nineteenth century who administered the callous and inadequate response to the Irish famine, became the poster boy for the monumental indifference of the British government. Trevelyan's pitiless economic theory that argued the righteousness of a philosophy of natural causes dismissed the mass starvation in Ireland as a consequence of Divine Providence. He determined that the only cure for the famine was private enterprise and free trade. Feeding the poor, he believed, would only exacerbate the Irish tendency toward sloth and dependence.

In a letter to an underling, Trevelyan made clear his heartless opinion of the Irish culture in general. "The great evil with which we have to contend," he lectured, "is not the physical evil of the famine, but the moral evil of the selfish, perverse, and turbulent character of the people." He seemed convinced that his charge from the Almighty was to rehabilitate the morals of the feral Irish, not to feed the victims of crop failure, and for the most part the punitive Poor Laws and the workhouses with their austere conditions and prison-like atmosphere did just that. Trevelyan was convinced that God had sent a plague to teach the Irish a lesson, and he was not going to interfere with God's designs. His philosophy was parroted by many English politicians and writers. James Wilson of *The Economist* serves as an example: "It's no man's business to provide for another." John Kelly described the workhouses that rose from this economic and social philosophy: "The task of the Irish (and English) workhouse was to rehabilitate the afflicted by further afflicting them—by making poverty so unendurable, its victims would embrace the virtues of the saved: industry, self-reliance, and personal discipline." Trevelyan's gospel of self-help might seem to some a foreshadowing of a modern-day Republican Party platform in America. Compassion and self-awareness were not linchpins of the British government policy and its response to Irish suffering and death in the mid–nineteenth century, even when one of their own newspapers, the *Illustrated London News*, castigated their countrymen for irresponsibility: "We have not done our duty by Ireland.... There is only one book that the English believe in—the ledger."

In 1845, the typical summer rains in Ireland were heavier than usual, and the sodden fields began to show signs of the disaster to come. Potatoes turned black and oozed a putrid slimy substance. It was years before Victorian pundits shifted the blame from the savage Irish who stood in the harsh light of God's judgment to the actual culprit—a fungus called Phytophthora infestans, a phrase that combined Greek and Latin and essentially meant *decaying plant that infests*. The terrible odor that came with the diseased tubers occurred because the potato was being eaten and decaying from the inside out. The wet Irish climate fostered spore reproduction, and winds spread the sickness from plant to plant. The disease started in Europe, but it didn't take it long to conquer all of Ireland. Soon after it arrived in Ireland, it made its way to Armagh and most certainly dramatically affected the lives of the Hunter clan. They would have viewed farmers weeping in their destroyed pastures like mourners at a state funeral, and they would have observed dazed men and women sprinkling holy water over their potatoes and muttering prayers as they examined their crops.

According to John Kelly, in County Longford, where my wife's paternal ancestors, the Kiernans, farmed the land, "people walked ten miles to purchase meal." Often men and women went these distances out of pride, not wanting to advertise their poverty to their neighbors. By the worst year of the famine, 1847, hundreds of thousands were dying or fleeing the country. The fields had rotted, the stench was universal, and the sight of starving men, women, and children on the roadsides and in villages was commonplace. Some armed themselves and robbed and killed to feed their families, but for the most part a horrible silence permeated the countryside and fatalism became embedded in the culture. Many mothers and fathers begged not for food but for coffins to bury their loved ones. If they were evicted from their cottages, families waited by footpaths to die, bones protruding, faces hollow, eyelids enflamed, their lips foaming green from eating nettles and grass, their bodies cannibalizing themselves. Often hunger edema set in, their bodies swelling grotesquely in what seemed like some insulting masquerade

Chapter 2. Memory and Imagination

of overeating. By the end of the famine more than a million of them had starved to death. And another million fled the country, many of them dying of Typhus and other fevers on coffin ships headed to America and Canada. Between 1845 and 1850, more than one-third of the population was dead or gone. In 1846, Armagh organized a day of solemn prayer, and it might be fair to assume that Alfred's parents were there asking for God's mercy for the living and the dead.

There were British politicians, tutored in a Victorian religiosity and laissez-faire economic policy, who believed that the potato blight was sent by a God who intended many Irish to die, not to emigrate. Clearly, more than one third of the citizens of Ireland during the famine years did not subscribe to that idea. Most of those who could leave, left. Others couldn't leave. Many others died. Alfred Hunter, because as an orphan he had not many options or because of his sense of the history of tragedy in his homeland, was among the millions who left and found his way to America in the nineteenth and twentieth centuries.

By the time Alfred Hunter stepped onto American soil and walked the streets of New York City in 1907 or 1908, the ads that proclaimed NINA and the Irish Need Not Apply signs posted in shop windows were less common, but they were still there and surely a fresh part of the communal memory and general attitude in New York City and elsewhere in the United States. But the Irish had populated the slums before Alfred arrived and, although they had infiltrated city hall, the police and fire departments, and the construction trade by the early twentieth century, the Paddy Wagon was still part of the vernacular, and the Irish had a growing reputation for drinking and waywardness. So, Edmund Hunter changed himself into Alfred Hunter and fled Ireland to confirm his new identity. He met Jennie O'Pray and stayed long enough in the Bronx to see my mother born, and then he left again for parts unknown. He may have been a Protestant and Jennie O'Pray was as Catholic as they come. In those times, that could have been considered a mixed marriage. He might not have wanted the trouble, and leaving may just have become an inevitable part of his cultural DNA.

It's likely that my newly discovered Alfred Hunter ran from Armagh and the familiar nightmare of Irish history and his own poverty that reminded him of the stories of the Great Famine. I read everything about the island's past in case I needed to know it in order to know him. The evidence shows that as early as 8000 BC, hunters and food gatherers found their way across a land bridge that existed between England and Ireland. Ireland then was, of course, sparsely populated and showed no sign of artistic activity. Nor did it leave any mark of agricultural occupation. Ireland's first livestock breeders and crop growers were probably Neolithic people from Britain or the European continent who began arriving around 4000 BC. They built homes and stone boundary walls like the ones I had often seen in the West of Ireland and the Aran Islands. They also constructed megalithic monuments like Newgrange, passage tombs, cairns and dolmens, used for burials and rituals. It was during the Bronze Age that Ireland's first metal workers exploited the land's rich metal deposits to produce copper and bronze axes, spearheads, shields, cauldrons, and craftsmen's tools and later neck, arm, and waist ornaments. Around 600 BC iron replaced bronze and the first Celtic peoples probably came from central Europe to the island. Then in 55 BC the Romans invaded England but generally stayed clear of Ireland, what they called *Hibernia*, "the land of winter." Refugees and trade increased and so, perhaps, did the cashels, the ring forts that were built to protect the people in a time of invasion.

The true written period of Irish history came in the fifth century with St. Patrick and the advance of Christianity. Christian monks—literate in both Irish and Latin—helped shape in a narrow scope a literate society. The monasteries rose up, becoming not just centers of piety but of learning and the production of art. Ireland began to take on the name "the island of the saints." Monks copied manuscripts—many of them, like the *Book of Kells*, which was created around 800 BC—magnificently illuminated works of art and literature. By the eighth-century Ireland had established its hierarchical society—kings, clerics, and poets regarded as sacred in the society. Law tracts were heavily influenced by the scriptures, and poets were understood to have semi-mystical powers. Kings and chieftains believed that the fili, the poet-seers, had the skill to curse their enemies and bless their friends with prosperity. That may have been where the Irish came to accept the sanctification of the lie. And in a country that was to be overrun by foreign armies, learning how to lie artfully to officials was the foundation of survival. The Irish reputation for deceit, guile, craft, and wordplay may have been part of the necessary mechanism they had to deal with invaders.

For the Irish, literature and politics were always at a bloody crossroads. Over the centuries, their country had been colonized and their native language had been banned. Modern writers like Synge, Yeats, and Joyce re-created and re-imagined Irish culture and life—and attempted to revitalize their language, making English in an Irish idiom. Most great Irish writers found their books banned in their own country, and for many of them—like James Joyce, George Bernard Shaw, Samuel Beckett, or Edna O'Brien—the outsider's perspective became the fundamental way of looking at their homeland.

Irish writers and the Irish people had to find a way to deal with

Chapter 2. Memory and Imagination

invaders from the very beginnings of their history. In 795 AD, Vikings began to attack the coast of Ireland. The Vikings established ports in Dublin, Waterford, Wexford, Cork, and Limerick. It was the Vikings who named the point where the Liffey and the then-visible Poddle River met as "Dubh Linn," *black pool*. For three centuries, the people of Ireland lay in fear of Viking invasions. A ninth-century quatrain found in the vellum margins of an ancient monastic manuscript suggests the relief that inclement weather might bring to residents of the island: "Bitter is the wind tonight,/It tosses the ocean's white hair:/Tonight I fear not the fierce warriors of Norway/Coursing the Irish sea." Frank O'Connor, one of the writers who translated the poem, remarked, "In London during the Second World War, we waited for a moonlit night to sleep safe in our beds. In Ireland of the ninth century, they waited for a storm."

In 1014, the consolidated forces of King Brian Boru defeated the Vikings at the Battle of Clontarf. But the sense of peace and safety was short-lived. Chieftains angled for power for the next century, and in 1171, Henry II of England received a papal license to invade Ireland and "aid in the process of Church reform." Technically, Henry was a Catholic but barely so—something like most twenty-first-century Catholics in Ireland and when he established the English lordship over the country, it began the process of bifurcation that led to the rift between Catholic and Protestants that still exists in many respects today. The conquest of Ireland took centuries, the British monarchs soon discovering that it wasn't easy to transform Ireland into a little England. But that didn't deter Henry II or future kings from greedily eyeing the rich land they could bestow on favorites. However, the British government didn't like it when English settlers assimilated too well, and in 1366 the Statutes of Kilkenny were born—a set of laws designed to prevent the English from becoming too Irish. The statutes forbade intermarriage, dressing like the Irish, or even adopting Irish children. So, the course of colonization ran over the centuries. The country was transformed—the woods were cleared, making for arable land, trade soared, and the native Irish were made into second-class citizens. Swift's "A Modest Proposal," written in 1729, gives a pointed picture of the twisted relationship he saw between the landlords and the born and bred Irish. His metaphor for the relationship between the British landlords and the Irish centered upon a cannibalizing of Irish infants, an immodest proposal that he implicitly argued was already a reality.

* * *

Over the decades and centuries, though, the inability of the English colonizers to uproot the most powerful Irish chiefs and kings and later the failure to eradicate the Irish heritage, language, and culture made for a violent stalemate. Colonization created a landlord society, a divided people that led, ultimately, to a divided island. From the beginning, many in the British government and citizenry saw themselves as a conquering people chosen by God to civilize the barbaric Irish. In the fourteenth century, Famine and the Black Death devastated the Irish economy, and the island lost its status as a revenue maker for the British crown and instead became a drain on its resources. Landlord absenteeism and feuding among the nobles increased. By the Middle Ages, the area from Dundalk to Dublin became *the Pale*, the four obedient shires, and the rest of Ireland was *beyond the Pale*, in the estimation of the British government a wild place outside civilization and law. By the sixteenth century, Henry VIII and the Protestant Reformation had their effect on Ireland, as did Oliver Cromwell in his savage campaign in the mid–seventeenth century, a brutal anti–Catholic, anti–Irish, pro-landlord assault on the country. Cromwell's cruel response to the Irish rebellion was a 40-week reign of terror between August 1649 to May 1650, and he remains in the Irish consciousness nearly four centuries later as a war criminal who epitomizes British barbarity. After Cromwell strangled any remnants of an Irish uprising, more plantation lands were granted to English families (4,000 to 12,000 acres) to "build substantial residences, foster agrarian innovation, and exploit natural resources." More landlords became absentees, and more rebellions sparked throughout the land. The tensions never really ceased, and when King James, the last Roman Catholic monarch in England, came to the throne in 1685, Irish Protestants feared a loss of their dominion. But in 1690, at the Battle of the Boyne in Drogheda, the forces of King James and the Catholics were soundly defeated by the troops of William of Orange, and that battle is still a symbol for Protestants in Northern Ireland of their ascendancy over the Catholic majority.

During the late seventeenth and early eighteenth centuries more draconian laws sought to curtail and neuter any Catholic power in the country. The Penal Laws officially disenfranchised Catholics, excluded them from the legal profession, prohibited them leasing land long term, holding firearms, or serving in the military. Catholics were not allowed to educate themselves outside of Ireland, inherit Protestant land, or hold a seat in Parliament. One of the stipulations stated that "no person of the popish religion shall publicly or in private houses teach school, or instruct youth in learning within this realm."

As the colonial stranglehold tightened, history headed toward the rebellions, civil wars, and terrorism that tore Ireland apart in the twentieth century. The first significant and unsuccessful rebellion against

Chapter 2. Memory and Imagination 41

the British came in 1798 with the legendary Wolfe Tone and his struggle to end British rule. The rebellion failed, Tone was captured, and rather than allow his captors to hang him, he slit his own throat. After the debacle of the 1798 rebellion, many of the restrictive anti–Catholic Penal Laws were rescinded. In the same year that Tone died, Daniel O'Connell, who came to be known in his country as The Liberator, was called to the Irish Bar. Soon after, he was elected to Parliament, and as the first Irish Catholic MP, he launched a campaign to repeal the Act of Union and make Ireland a sovereign republic. He was immensely popular, a golden-tongued orator who took on a mythic status in his country, even though he failed to get the Act of Union repealed.

In the nineteenth century, Catholic clergy rose in numbers, and the political power of the Catholic Church grew exponentially. The Church became the power behind schools, orphanages, hospitals, and asylums, wielding a nearly unchecked authority until the scandals of the late twentieth and early twenty-first centuries. The Great Famine of 1845–1850, the potato blight, devastated the country, and emigration became a way of life, for many the only chance at survival. The instinct to leave became for many—Alfred Hunter among them—the only way forward. Loss and tragedy gave rise to another political hero—Charles Stewart Parnell—and another wave of Irish nationalism. Like O'Connell, Parnell fought for home rule, but sexual scandal with his long-time mistress, Kitty O'Shea, a married woman, brought Parnell's political career to an abrupt end. He was abandoned by conservatives and the Catholic Church, and he died at 45 years old with his dream of a free Ireland unfulfilled.

Irish nationalistic fervor held strong in the wake of Parnell's abandonment and death. Organizations like the Gaelic Athletic Association (which fostered traditional Irish sports such as hurling) and the Gaelic League (which promoted the Irish language) grew strong. Sinn Fein ("We Ourselves") rose up as a political entity that would eventually morph into the warlike Irish Republican Army. Ireland stayed neutral in World War I, even though more than a quarter of a million Irish men served in the British Army, but many people in the country felt that they had their own revolution to fight. In 1916, the Easter Uprising lasted less than a week, but left shock waves that altered the course of modern Irish history. If the British had not made martyrs of the rebels by executing more than a dozen of them—including Patrick Pearse, Thomas MacDonagh, Joseph Plunkett, John MacBride, and James Connolly—after their surrender at the GPO, the Easter Rising might have gone down in history as a dismal military, political, and social failure. Instead, the actions of the British government made the rebels mythic heroes to the people, and even Yeats, in all his ambivalence, memorialized them in "Easter, 1916" for the transformation they created, the "terrible beauty" they left in their wake.

The Rising of 1916 led to the founding of the Irish Free State, but that took a civil war between the supporters of the treaty, led by Michael Collins, and those who sought a dissolution of the union between Britain and Ireland, led by Eamon de Valera. Collins was ambushed and assassinated in West Cork by Republican forces. From 1922, the founding of the Irish Free State, the island was divided into twenty-six counties in the Republic and six in Northern Ireland. Three of the four provinces—Leinster, Munster, and Connaught—were in the Republic, and the majority of Ulster became part of Northern Ireland, Armagh, my grandfather's home ground among them. The Troubles—violent bombings and brutal murders that lasted from the 1960s until the Good Friday Agreement of April 10, 1998—became another bloody footnote to the history of the Irish struggle against the British Empire for peace and sovereignty.

Bloom's door, 7 Eccles Street.

Much of Irish literature in the twentieth century examined this blood-stained intersection in Ireland's story—mass murders in Derry and Belfast, IRA bombings throughout the land, Unionist Ulster Volunteer Force slaughters of innocents and guilty alike, hunger strikes, more martyrdoms, and more firmly entrenched feuds and hatreds. Writers like Yeats, O'Connor, Brendan Behan and others depicted the paralyzing effects of the long-held animosities and grappled with ways to repossess their language and culture, their history and myths. As Frank O'Connor once said, "Irish literature in the first part of the nineteenth century was a tale of two cities—Dublin and London." That didn't change much in the twentieth century.

Auden's line from "In Memory of W.B. Yeats"—"poetry makes nothing happen"—has much truth to it, but so does Oliver St. John Gogarty's statement from the floor of the Irish Senate—that without literature, Yeats and he and his colleagues would not have been representatives of an independent Ireland. What Gogarty may have been alluding to was the deeply rooted heritage in Ireland between state and poet, the power of Irish bards and Irish chieftains connected from the earliest times, words being a weapon as potent as dynamite. The Abbey Theater; the poetry of Yeats, Heaney, and others; the drama of J.M. Synge and Martin McDonagh; the fiction of Joyce and the satire of Flann O'Brien were all as revolutionary as any Easter Rising, as subversive as a car bomb, and a way of attempting to repossess their country. In their work was the narrative of Ireland's struggle, a tale of two countries connected and separated on one island, a portrayal of betrayal and emigration, and in between the lines of all of their stories lurked for me the ghost of Alfred Hunter, son of Armagh, emigrant, escape artist, mystery, grandfather.

Chapter 3

Joyce and Modern Ireland

> "Ireland," says Bloom. "I was born here. Ireland."
> —James Joyce, *Ulysses*

The first time I read James Joyce's *Dubliners* I was a junior in Mount St. Michael High School and was supposed to be concentrating on the poetry of John Keats for my Tuesday morning English class. I slumped there in the back of the room, my face hidden behind the forest of crew cuts and sports coats in front of me and braced on the desk a weighty hardcover anthology of English literature opened to "Ode on a Grecian Urn." Propped on my lap, half hidden in the shadow of the desk, sat a battered paperback copy of Joyce's short stories. As the lay English teacher, Ichabod Crane's twin, closed his eyes, waved his skinny arms, and intoned Keats's words about the still unravished bride of quietness, the mad pursuit, and beauty being truth and truth beauty, I lost myself in "Araby." I was convinced that Joyce's Dublin was just a metaphor for my life, and that the un-named narrator of the story was me, his longing for Magnan's sister was my current unrequited love and his inability to escape the confines of Dublin my entrapment in the Bronx. Joyce's Dublin with its dreary streets and priest-ridden corridors felt precisely like my home ground. The day before, leaning against the warmth of the radiator in my apartment on a rainy Monday afternoon, I had read the first two stories in the collection, "The Sisters" and "An Encounter." In the background, the subterranean D Train rattled our bedroom window, and the sound of my father opening beer cans in the kitchen punctuated the silence between trains.

Both "The Sisters" and "An Encounter" held me in thrall for different reasons. I had glanced at the table of contents of *Dubliners* and knew that the last, long story was "The Dead." I suspected that "The Sisters," with its emphasis on the death of Father James Flynn, began a circle that closed with that final narrative. The word *paralysis* appeared three times in "The Sisters." Father Flynn reminded me of many of the

Double rainbow over Joyce Martello Tower.

religious brothers and priests I saw each day in the Bronx, disappointed men, paralyzed, I imagined, by the prohibited pleasures and required sacrifices of their everyday existence. There was something secret and unknowable about them. "The Sisters" ended with Father Flynn's strange behavior, "sitting up by himself in the dark in his confession box, wideawake and laughing-like softly to himself" and the final line, "there was something gone wrong with him...." What was that unspecified sin that Father Flynn was guilty of, that Old Cotter alluded to at the dinner table? "The Sisters" seemed to me a story constructed, as my life up to then was built, on what didn't happen, on what was left unspoken, except, that is, for the Catholic platitudes I had heard thousands of times in school and church—*he had a beautiful death, God be merciful, he's gone to his eternal reward*. The silhouette of the Catholic Church fell upon the narrator's life in Joyce's story, just as that shadow fell over mine. "The Sisters" seemed to me then a question without an answer, a tale without even a clear question, as if it were demanding that I frame the inquiry myself. "An Encounter" had even darker tones. At first glance, the story appeared to be about an innocent escape from school, the narrator and his pal Mahony mitching so that they could play cowboys and Indians on the outskirts of town. For the narrator, the dime novel adventures he and his friends read, like the comic books I devoured as a child, "opened the doors of escape." Like the narrator, "I wanted real adventures to happen to myself. But real adventures, I reflected, do not happen to people who remain at home." The narrator gets more than he bargained for in his day of playing hooky. Sometimes, I had learned myself even at that age, the walls of the prison are safer than the wider world. The narrator discovers this: he meets a shabbily dressed old man, with yellow teeth and an unsettling interest in his adolescent love life. The dialogue turns even more disturbing as the old man excitedly talks about chastising boys—"...they ought to be whipped and well whipped ... a good sound whipping ... a nice warm whipping.... He described to me how he would whip such a boy as if he were unfolding some elaborate mystery. He would love that, he said, better than anything in this world." The narrator runs from the sordid old man toward his friend Mahony—"How my heart beat as he came running across the field to me! He ran as if to bring me aid. And I was penitent for in my heart I had always despised him a little." The callowness he may have scorned in his friend he now prizes as he shudders in the face of an understanding he would rather not acknowledge. It reminded me of an encounter I had had in a Manhattan apartment building the year before as I worked as a Saturday delivery boy for a pharmacy on 77th Street and Lexington Avenue. I looked much younger than my 15 years, and the maintenance man in a luxury building who propositioned me probably took me for 12. I had no Mahony to run toward, but I used my friend Frank Fitzpatrick, who had gotten me the job, as my fictional co-worker waiting for me down the block so that I could make my escape.

    A similar loss of innocence paints the surface of "Araby." Everything about Dublin in the story seemed perfectly familiar to me. The tension between blindness and sight in the first paragraph felt like a portrait of my own struggle to see anything with clarity in the confused fog of sexual urges and religious admonitions I stumbled through each day. Like the un-named narrator, I lived in a world of street-level sensation and spiritual high ideal. The narrator could have been describing my friends and me—each day bolting from our apartments—"The cold air stung us and we played till our bodies glowed." The way the speaker sees Mangan's sister—"her figure defined by the light from the half-opened door"—was the way I saw every girl I fell in love with at first sight, from a shadow, in a shadow. The narrator carries the grail of his "confused adoration" as he walks the "flaring streets, jostled by drunken men and bargaining women, amid the curses of labourers, the shrill litanies of shop boys...." And when I finished the story, as my class turned to "On First Looking into Chapman's Homer," I thought I understood the disappointment the protagonist of "Araby" justifiably felt in failing to bring home a gift for Magnan's sister. Based upon my sixteen years of experience, I was convinced that, finally, all romance might be doomed to failure.

Not until I re-read the story in college did I calculate the narrator's blindness as he gazed up into the darkness of the hall, his eyes burning with anguish and anger. Then, as a cunning nineteen-year-old looking back at my raw younger self, I estimated the immaturity of the narrator of "Araby" and what clues Joyce had given me that I had been too dull to comprehend when I first read it in high school. I learned even later

Ha'penny Bridge, Dublin.

that the story was based—as so many of the tales in *Dubliners* were—on Joyce's actual experiences. A bazaar called "Araby" came to Dublin in 1894 when Joyce was twelve or so, about the age of his lovelorn narrator. The Dublin fair, similar to the smaller county fairs in Ireland at the time, might have had more than a trace of Irish nationalism in its entertainments with the balladeers, something Joyce alluded to in "Araby" in the street singers crooning a *come-all-you* about the Fenian leader O'Donovan Rossa. I discovered that Joyce had written two essays about the Irish poet and nineteenth-century Orientalist James Clarence Mangan some years before *Dubliners* was published. Deep inside the story I had initially thought simply about a teenager's shattered ideals and lost love or adolescent blindness were much more sophisticated and complicated ideas about Romantic figures, nationalist constructs, a writer's hidden self-portrait, and a young narrator who, as the critic Heyward Ehrlich said in a 1998 article in *The James Joyce Quarterly,* played "the Manganian hero one more time, alternatively inventing, effacing, and enlarging himself, now in the Araby of his own memory.... 'Araby' seems another fictional biography of Mangan, the Irish Orientalist, or perhaps an early fictional autobiography of Joyce in the process of reinventing himself." The layers of revelation—about fictional characters, about Ireland, about Joyce himself—might serve me, I thought much later, as a training ground for the excavation that would be required for me to get a clearer view of my grandfather and the piece of his past that was part of me.

I read one more brief tale from *Dubliners* on the number 16 bus home from high school that day. "Eveline" came at me like a plaintive warning, a portent of what my own story might become if I wasn't careful—or rather if I was too careful to take a chance. Eveline Hill longs to escape the narrow confines of her life in Dublin. Her mother has died, leaving the nineteen-year-old Eveline to care for two younger siblings and face the drunken belligerence of her father. But a young man named Frank, on a visit back to Dublin after supposedly making a success in Buenos Aires, will rescue her, of that she is convinced. He wants to take her back to Argentina and marry her. As I gazed out the grimy bus window at the clogged streets and crowded stoops and slumped shoulders of workers returning to their apartments after a long day, I dreamt of the fair winds that I imagined floated through the happy avenues of Buenos Aires. Eveline's choice seemed simple to me then—"Escape! She must escape! Frank would save her." The last page of the story brings us to her departure. Eveline prays to God "to direct her, to show her what was her duty." The boat whistle announces its departure, she moves her lips in silent prayer, and Frank seizes her hand. But a "bell clanged upon her heart" and she clutches the iron railing, refusing to go. "She set her white face to him, passive, like a helpless animal."

When I re-read the story in college and once more after graduate school, I wasn't so sure about the clarity or simplicity of Eveline's choices. Was Frank "kind, manly, openhearted," as he seemed to Eveline? Did he have a home waiting for her, as she assumed? When he sang about "the lass that loves a sailor," she was always confused, and I wondered if the adverb "pleasantly" made her confusion less problematic or more so. I began to consider that her father's view of Frank as a "bounder" might have some validity in the text. I began to acknowledge that no question Joyce ever posed came with a straightforward answer. Joyce had written "Eveline" right around the time he met Nora Barnacle in Dublin in June 1904. Eveline's ambivalence about emigration could have been Joyce's hesitation concerning leaving Ireland, his uncertainty about his choice to link his fortunes with Nora on the continent. Marriage itself is an emigration and exile, of sorts. It wasn't a coincidence that it took Joyce more than a quarter of a century to officially marry Nora.

"Eveline" started me thinking about the historical dangers of emigration to the Irish of the nineteenth and early twentieth centuries. The risks to women like Eveline and Nora emigrating would have been significant, but even a young man like my grandfather, Alfred Hunter, must have felt such jeopardy like a gathering storm. I tried to imagine for Eveline Hill or Alfred Hunter the courage required to leave family and friends and homeland, the will necessary to relinquish the known and face the perils as well as the possibilities that a new world would present.

Statue of Oscar Wilde, observed by statue of naked woman.

Years later, when I read Joyce's 1906 letter to his publisher Grant Richards, I remembered myself on that bus in the Bronx reading the story—"My intention," Joyce wrote to Richards, "was to write a chapter of the moral history of my country and I chose Dublin for the scene because that city seemed to me the centre of paralysis." He went on to say, "I have tried to present it to the indifferent public under four of its aspects: childhood, adolescence, maturity, and public life." Ireland was always a nightmare and a dream for Joyce. The river Liffey was always filthy and beautiful. Dublin was forever dear and dirty. The country, the river, the people held their own opposition in his mind, as the Bronx and my grandfather, Alfred Hunter, did in mine.

Joyce wrote "Eveline" and some of the early stories in *Dubliners* for George Russell's magazine *The Irish Homestead* under the pseudonym of his alter-ego Stephen Dedalus, and he wrote them just a few months before he sailed away with Nora Barnacle from the same North Wall docks that paralyzed Eveline. Was he playing out his wishes or his fears? Was distance the only way he could face the locus of his imagination? A few years before his death he was asked by a friend why for decades he had not returned to Ireland. His response: "Have I ever left it?"

Some years after abandoning Ireland, Joyce found himself in Rome, oppressed by the heat, the pressures of a growing family, and his failures as a writer. He started to resemble Eveline, nostalgic for home, longing for "rashers and eggs in the morning, the English variety of sunshine, a beefsteak with boiled potatoes and onions, a pier at night or a beach and cigarettes." Distance and time, in that moment, softened his view of his native land. "Sometimes thinking of Ireland," he said, "it seems to me that I have been unnecessarily harsh. I have reproduced (in *Dubliners* at least) none of its ingenious insularity and its hospitality." Many critics feel that the last and the greatest of his stories in *Dubliners*—"The Dead"—written at least one year after any others in the collection—came from this complicated attachment Joyce felt to Dublin and Ireland in general. Toward the end of his career, he said that if the Dublin of his time were to be destroyed, it could be recreated from his works. And most readers would agree that he ended up both mapping the city with a cartographer's precision and imagining it with the genius of a prophet.

Around the time he began to write "The Dead," when Joyce was living in Rome (a city he disliked because it reminded him of "a man who lives by exhibiting to travelers his grandmother's corpse") and working unhappily as a bank clerk, he wrote to his brother Stanislaus, "I have a new story for *Dubliners* in my head. It deals with Mr. Hunter...." When I read those sentences, many decades after that bus ride back from Mt. St. Michael and far into my career as a professor of literature and creative writing, I thought, "Ah, Mr. Hunter, certainly...." The Mr. Hunter Joyce alludes to in the letter to his brother became, of course, Leopold Bloom in *Ulysses*. Joyce's Alfred Hunter was not my grandfather, as much as I would have shouted with glee if he had been, but when I read in Richard Ellmann's biography of the writer's encounter with my grandfather's namesake, the whole incident felt like more to me than a coincidence or interesting Joycean footnote: "Joyce was said to have been dusted off and taken home by a man named Alfred H. Hunter, in what *Ulysses* would call 'orthodox Samaritan fashion.' Hunter was rumored to be Jewish and to have an unfaithful wife, two disparate points that became important later to Joyce. With Hunter, Joyce was only distantly acquainted, having (according to Stanislaus Joyce) met him only once or twice. This very lack of acquaintance was memorable, since Joyce regarded himself as hemmed in by indifference or hostility and was surprised that someone unfamiliar, of temperament and background opposite to his own, should have unselfishly befriended him. Here might be one of those 'epiphanies'—sudden, unlooked-for turns in experience—which could prove the more momentous for being modest." I thought, *Joyce can have his epiphany and I can have mine.* Maybe clues to my grandfather's

Chapter 3. Joyce and Modern Ireland 51

life could be found in the comic heroism and compassion of Leopold Bloom. I imagined that Bloom's kindness, Alfred Hunter's benevolence, might have been some part of my grandfather's nature. Like Bloom, my grandfather was a nobody, but like Joyce's character, he was important, a mystery worth pondering. Could he have abandoned my mother and disappeared forever for some reason that would allow me to forgive him? Was there something about her own father that my mother never knew or failed to imagine?

When I read Richard Ellmann's analysis of Bloom's rescuing the drunken Stephen Dedalus, I inserted my Alfred Hunter into the scene: "The kindness of Bloom in *Ulysses* on June 16, 1904, begins with animals and ends with human beings. So, he feeds his cat in the morning, then some sea gulls, and in the *Circe* episode a dog. He remembers his dead son and dead father, he is also concerned about his living daughter, and he never forgets his wife for a moment. He helps a blind man cross the street. He contributes very generously—beyond his means—to the fund for the children of his friend who has just died; and, when he begins to see Stephen as a sort of son, he follows him, tries to stop his drinking, prevents him from being robbed, risks arrest to defend him from the police, feeds him too, and takes him home...." Joyce's Bloom, based in part upon his picture of Alfred Hunter, is a portrait of a wandering Jew. A wanderer, I envisioned, like the Alfred Hunter who started a family in New York City and wandered away to parts unknown. I decided he could have been a Ulysses who failed to find his way home. And I found myself agreeing with Joyce that the Ulysses story was the most human one in all of world literature. Joyce had recreated Alfred Hunter as Leopold Bloom, a comic hero who ends up back in Ithaca with Penelope. My Alfred Hunter never found his way back. But he might have tried.

I think I was afraid in high school to read the rest of the stories in *Dubliners*, fearful that the other tales would show me more of my future or past than I could face then, that I had too much in common with Eveline and the anonymous narrators of "Araby" and "An Encounter." Gradually, after graduate school and during my scholarly and creative life, I came back to them and to all of Joyce, even eventually to *Finnegans Wake*, although I understood less of that novel than I did of quantum mechanics. It's a novel, I fear, that must be studied in a graduate class with an intelligent guide and other sympathetic and baffled readers, not read on a screened-in porch over a humid Virginia summer. *Finnegans Wake* may have confounded me, but it didn't stop me from circling back to Joyce's writings that made more sense to me. *Finnegans Wake* offered a puzzling but wonderful music, a polyglot language of puns and parentheses that, like the dreamscape Joyce intended, always stayed just a millimeter or two out of reach. Its first line, beginning in mid-sentence—"riverrun, past Eve and Adam's, from swerve of shore to bend of bay, brings us by a commodious vicus of recirculation back to Howth Castle and Environs"—twists back like "Finn, again" to the last line—"a way a lone a last a loved a long the." Joyce said he wanted to end *Finnegans Wake* with the least forceful word he could find and said, "I found the word which is most slippery, the least accented, the weakest word in English, a word which is not even a word, which is scarcely sounded between the teeth, a breath, a nothing, the article *the*."

When I returned to *Dubliners* after being lost in the dream of *Finnegans Wake*, it was "The Dead" that opened my heart to his other works and led me to Leopold Bloom and back directly to Alfred Hunter. "The Dead" is inextricably linked to the first two stories in *Dubliners*, to "Sisters" and "Araby," but it serves as a coda for all fourteen stories that precede it. Richard Ellmann, the most respected of Joyce biographers, calls "The Dead" a linchpin in the writer's work, "his first song of exile." In it, Joyce expressed his undeniable and everlasting attachment to Dublin and Ireland. As with everything Joyce wrote, "The Dead" has an autobiographical root. Ellmann makes this clear in his discussion of the story: "Joyce's habit of ferreting out details had made him conduct minute interrogations of Nora even before their departure from Dublin. He was disconcerted by the fact that young men before him had interested her. He did not much like to know that her heart was still moved, even in pity by the recollection of the boy who had loved her. The notion of being in some sense in rivalry with a dead man buried in the little cemetery at Rahoon was one that came easily, and gallingly, to a man of Joyce's jealous disposition." Joyce seemed mesmerized by the word *betrayal*, and the jealousy that many of his characters feel has a source close to the writer's own anxieties.

Like so many of the characters in the other stories in *Dubliners*, Gabriel Conroy longs for escape. He yearns for the exotic as much as the young narrator of "Araby" does. At his aunts' party, Gabriel is irritated by Miss Ivor's suggestion that he should go to the West of Ireland and get to know his own land, and hear his own language. "Irish is not my language," he tells her testily. Irish nationalism means little to him. He'd rather go cycling on the European continent than discover his wife's home ground in the West of Ireland. Around the time Joyce was writing "The Dead" in Rome and then later finishing it in Trieste, riots broke out in response to John Millington Synge's production of *The Playboy of the Western World* at the Abbey Theater in Dublin in early 1907. Synge had taken Yeats's suggestion and found stories in the West of Ireland and in the folk tales of the Aran Islands. Ostensibly, the riots exploded when the word "shift" was uttered in the play to describe a woman's undergarment. Of course, the source of the riots ran much deeper than the crowd's desire to defend Irish womanhood. Joyce had received and rejected the same advice that Synge had followed, and his depiction of the conflict with Irish nationalism that gets expressed in Gabriel is as autobiographical as the jealousy over the dead lover.

In the course of "The Dead," Gabriel shows himself to be a prideful snob about his country, its history, and its people. It's as if Joyce were shining a light on his own prejudices, trying to make a subtle correction of his often-eviscerating portrait of Ireland, trying to fill in what he admitted to his brother Stanislaus he had left out of the picture: "I have not reproduced its [Ireland's] ingenuity and its hospitality, the latter 'virtue' so far as I can see does not exist elsewhere in Europe."

In Gabriel's thoughts, even his aunts are "only two ignorant old women." He smirks at the "three syllables Lily [the servant girl] had given his surname." He is a self-centered Romantic, as adolescent in his own way as the narrator of "Araby," but without youth as his defense. He sees his own wife, Gretta, with the same cataracted eye as the narrator of "Araby" sees Mangan's sister. Toward the conclusion of the story, as the party is ending, Gabriel stands at the foot of the staircase straining his ear to hear Bartell D'Arcy sing *The Lass of Aughrim*. "He was in the dark part of the hall gazing up the staircase. A woman was standing near the top of the first flight in the shadow also. He could not see her face but he could see the terracotta and salmon pink panels of her skirt which the shadow made appear black and white. It was his wife.... He asked himself what is a woman standing on the stairs in the shadow, listening to distant music, a symbol of." He sees her no more clearly than the narrator of "Araby" sees Mangan's sister in the half-light. No more clearly, perhaps, than Joyce saw Nora Barnacle.

What the scene and his wife evoke in Gabriel amount to "a keen pang of lust." As they stand at the hotel door, Gabriel "felt that they had escaped from their lives and duties, escaped from home and friends and run away together with wild and radiant hearts to a new adventure." Trembling with desire, his heart thumping in his chest, Gabriel watches Gretta for a sign of ardor, but he sees her hazily through the fog of his longing. When he realizes that she has been thinking not of him but of her long-lost teenage lover Michael Furey (as Nora once told Joyce she remembered the tubercular Michael Bodkin, who had left his bed to sing to her in rainy weather), Gabriel, similar to the narrator of "Araby"—"A shameful consciousness of his own person assailed him. He saw himself as a ludicrous figure, acting as a pennyboy for his aunts, a nervous well-meaning sentimentalist, orating to vulgarians and idealizing his own clownish lusts, the pitiable fatuous fellow he had caught a glimpse of in the mirror. Instinctively he turned his back more to the light lest she might see the shame that burned upon his forehead." This could be the teenage narrator of "Araby" grown but little changed as he gazes up into the darkness, seeing himself as a creature driven and derided by vanity, his eyes burning with anguish and anger.

The story ends after Gretta has sobbed herself to sleep, with Gabriel acknowledging his ordinariness. But that might be a genuine epiphany for him and for the reader. Gabriel gazes at his sleeping wife without resentment. Generous tears fill his eyes. He feels pity for her, for his aunts, for all the dead and for all the living who will die. With the snow "general all over Ireland," Gabriel, shedding perhaps his animus for Miss Ivors and her nationalism, imagines a journey westward toward memory and history. He envisions the snow "falling on every part of the dark central plain ... softly falling into the dark mutinous Shannon waves ... falling, too, upon every part of the lonely churchyard on the hill where Michael Furey lay buried ... falling faintly ... and faintly falling, like the descent of their last end upon all the living and the dead." Death and memory are general, like the snow all over Ireland, and Gabriel's moment of recognition, the humbling of his pride and the shedding of his self-absorption, may arrive with his appreciation of a common humanity and shared fate, of the relationship between the living and the dead.

I didn't want to admit it to myself, but when it came to Alfred Hunter, I was as purblind as any character in *Dubliners*, as the narrator of "Araby" or Gabriel in "The Dead." Gradually, over the years, as my teaching and writing career turned in a gyre of its own making, spinning from literary criticism to journalism to creative writing and then, ultimately, into some amalgamation of all three forms, I began to focus on the writings and biography of James Joyce, on Irish literature and history, on travel to every corner of the island, as if I were drawn to all of it by the specter of Alfred Hunter.

In my imagination, I kept conflating James Joyce and Stephen Dedalus and Leopold Bloom and Alfred Hunter, as if understanding one would help me understand the other. Joyce's life was well recorded in his literary works. All I had of Alfred Hunter was what resided in my imagination, along with a few spare documents in my desk drawer. But just as Joyce *was* Stephen Dedalus and Leopold Bloom, I imagined myself as both of those characters and Alfred Hunter, as well. They were all part of me. Joyce's exile was mine too. Stephen Dedalus's search for a father was mine, as well. His Dublin was my Bronx. In *Ulysses*, Joyce described in noble mock-heroic terms the ordinary man, the uncommon common

Chapter 3. Joyce and Modern Ireland

Dublin at night.

man. I suspected my ancestor Alfred Hunter was that too, a man leaving no mark I could discover in the world except my mother. That mark, though, was extraordinary. Alfred Hunter, my lost ancestor, never got to know how he had changed the world by bringing Dorothy Hunter, filled with a sense of curiosity and grace and unyielding love, into it. Initially, Alfred left me no trail but the writings and the life of the author of *Dubliners*, *A Portrait of the Artist as a Young Man*, *Ulysses* and *Finnegans Wake*. And that was the path I followed to see if the story of Joyce's life led me any closer to Alfred Hunter and my own life.

* * *

From an early age, Joyce carried the weight of the nine syllables of his full name—James Augustine Aloysius Joyce—with a sense of his own grand importance and predestined genius. He was born on February 2, 1882, into a Victorian Age that his writing surely helped to dismantle. At his confirmation ceremony at Clongowes School, he chose Aloysius as his saint's name, as Edna O'Brien explains, "in imitation of Pascal, [a saint who] would not allow his mother to embrace him because he feared contact with women." Joyce never seemed averse to contact with women, but his contact with his mother was complicated and became the subject of much of the story of his alter-ego, Stephen Dedalus.

Joyce's familial story, akin to William Faulkner's, was a tale of decaying privilege and standing. John Joyce, James's father, came from a middle-class family in Cork. His university education opened up a sinecure for him as a tax collector in Dublin, and his wit and singing talent (he thought himself to be the best tenor in Ireland), his unconquerable confidence and skill as a raconteur, along with his rakish good looks and his inherited property in Cork, made him the kind of eligible bachelor that blinded the good sense of Mary "May" Jane Murray, ten years his junior and light years his superior in terms of responsibility and compassion. He first saw her singing in a church choir, and he determined at that moment that she would be his. And even though John's mother thought May "beneath" him, he married her in 1880.

It wasn't long before John Joyce, as Richard Ellmann suggests, a talented, reckless reprobate, started to fill their home in Rathgar, an upscale Dublin suburb, with children and debts. And it didn't take much time for his true character, as Edna O'Brien describes it, to surface—"a great raconteur and one whose wit masked a desperate savagery." His surname may have derived from the Latin meaning *joy*, but for his family he had little of that emotion to share with them. Before her death at age forty-four, the deeply religious May, like many Irish women of the time, "a cracked vessel for childbearing," gave birth to sixteen children, ten of whom lived to fill the crowded homes James Joyce resided in during his unsettled and unsettling growing up in and around the city of Dublin. Very quickly, John Joyce demonstrated far more flair for drinking and telling stories than he did for hard work or fatherhood. John may have fantasized about a stable family life and gentility, but he was constitutionally unsuited, from all accounts, to the work necessary to achieve either. He did recognize, however, that his oldest son, whom the family called "Sunny Jim," a nickname wonderfully unsuited, except when he was in his cups, to the man James Joyce would become, was a prodigy, and he sent him at six years of age to Clongowes College to be educated by the Jesuits.

But other than his insight into his oldest son's brilliance, John proved himself to be consistently irresponsible and self-centered, traits that, except for his sacred commitment to writing, James would inherit with a vengeance. John was an ill-tempered Irish Rip Van Winkle, a dissolute dreamer, inclined to alcoholism and glibness, by turns fearsome and jovial, with a stunted conscience and little concern for the hopes and welfare of those around him. At one point, hoping to be supported by his brilliant son James, whom everyone in the family felt was destined for artistic greatness, and in the hopes, perhaps, of sneaking back into the semi-gentility he had let slip from his grasp, he urged his son to apply for a position at the Guinness Factory. In drunken rages, John bullied and beat his wife and children. Over the years, he mortgaged and lost all of his inherited properties, and over the course of the lives of James and his nine siblings, John moved them from one temporary residence to another around Dublin, more than a dozen habitats whose only consistency was their steady downward spiral. James called these dwelling places "haunted inkpots."

On his quest to stay one day ahead of the eviction process and a few yards ahead of the landlords, John worked one con game after another to avoid paying his rightful bills. One of Joyce's biographers, Gordon Bowker, describes the nomadic life the elder Joyce forced his family to endure, "flitting from one address to another, often pursued by angry landlords waving unpaid bills. As John found more and more solace in drink, and his rake's progress continued, the Joyce's goods and possessions diminished." Most of John Joyce's children feared or despised him but perhaps because he saw himself in his father, James held an affection for him until his dying day. In Edna O'Brien's words, "no wrong done by his father wrankled him because they were both 'sinners.'" It's easier to understand his brother Stanislaus's hatred for his father or his sisters' fear and alienation from him than to comprehend James's intermittent sympathy over the years. For instance, when May Joyce was dying of cancer, as she lay there retching and screaming in agony, John marched into her bedroom with a few drunken companions and shouted, "I'm finished. I can't do any more. If you can't get well, die. Die and be damned to you!" Stanislaus was, understandably, never able to forgive his father for such a breach of decency and compassion, but James found a way to retain an affection for his self-absorbed, irresponsible, cunning, and calculating father. He saw himself in his father's eyes.

As all of the biographers point out, despite his fractured family life, James was a brilliant student, and, in Ellmann's words, by the age of twelve he cultivated an indifference to the chaos and instability of his home life and "was learning to pick his way among the family ruins as nimbly as an archeologist." Among the positive lessons James did learn from John Joyce was to have a high opinion of himself and to take Dublin into his marrow and memory. James literally followed in his father's footsteps, becoming an Irish flaneur, taking what Ellmann describes as "preposterously long walks" around the city. When he wasn't walking, he was reading voraciously. Once he liked a writer, he read everything by that author. But, as Edna O'Brien says, Joyce's discovery of Henrik Ibsen was "as definitive as Saint Paul's conversion on the way to Damascus." She goes on to say, "Ibsen he placed above Shakespeare as a dramatist. Ibsen he revered because of his contempt for falsity and hypocrisy."

Carrying Ibsen's banner throughout his university years, Joyce became the most famous, although not the only important writer, to attend UC Dublin. His friends and acquaintances recognized his brilliance and feared it because Joyce was not a man to forget a slight, real or imagined. "Forgiveness," Edna O'Brien says, "was anathema to him."

In the line before and after him at UC Dublin were Gerard Manley Hopkins, Flann O'Brien, Liam O'Flaherty, John McGahern, Mary Lavin, Colm Toibin, Emma Donoghue and Roddy Doyle. Joyce may have been the only one of the lot, though, who upon graduation believed himself to be the Dante of Dublin. His mind, he felt, was more interesting than the country itself, and he explored the story of that mind in relation to Ireland for the next four decades. Before he even graduated from UC Dublin, he wrote his first play—*A Brilliant Career*—a prophetic title. He inscribed the play "To My own Soul I dedicate the first true work of my life." It would be the only work he would dedicate to anyone. His younger brother's view of him as "proud, willful, and selfish" appears close to the mark.

While at university, Joyce avoided the crowded and unhappy life amidst his family and spent much of his time at the National Library reading or at what became his home away from home at the Sheehy's house, classmates who had an urbane and stable environment that seemed a world away from John Joyce's drunken belligerence. Besides the predictable and jovial nature of the Sheehy household, the linguistically precocious Joyce was amused by what Gordon Bowker termed the epicene nature of their surname. The boy was surely father of the man who would write *Ulysses* and *Finnegans Wake*.

After reading an article Joyce wrote, the Irish novelist George Moore told friends that the young writer was "preposterously clever." So, when the twenty-one-year-old Joyce knocked unannounced on the Dublin door of critic and poet George Russell, he was something of a known quantity. Russell too recognized him as a young genius, albeit proud as Lucifer, and he wrote to Yeats about him. Upon his first meeting with Yeats near the National Library in Dublin, Joyce asked him how old he was and remarked that he had met him too late to teach the poet anything. Yeats's first impression was that "such a colossal self-conceit with such a Lilliputian literary genius I never saw combined in one person." That assessment very quickly underwent a radical change. Yeats, like Lady Gregory and others, recognized Joyce's natural talent, and they both did what they could to nurture his career. In 1902, in a grand gesture flinging off the shackles of his country, Joyce left to study medicine in Paris. He soon returned from his failed experiment in France to be at his mother's deathbed, refusing her last request to kneel and pray at her bedside, his refusal like Lucifer's *non serviam*, one he later transformed into Stephen Dedalus's rejection of his mother in *Ulysses*.

Ultimately, all the stories Joyce wrote were the story of his life. If what Bernard Malamud said in *Dubin's Lives* is valid—"all biography is fiction"—then the reverse holds up as well—*all fiction is biography.*

Chapter 3. Joyce and Modern Ireland 59

Everyone Joyce knew, every place he lived, every story he heard became a part of his fiction. For a brief time, he lived in a Martello tower in Sandycove, just south of Dublin City Center, in what was conceived by his medical student friend Oliver St. John Gogarty as a budding writers' colony. Agreeing to do housekeeping to pay for his bed and board, Joyce lived there in the hopes of working on his first novel. The experiment lasted less than one week but was immortalized in the opening pages of *Ulysses*. He made a quick exit when one of the Martello tower residents, Samuel Trench, woke up in the middle of the night screaming that a black panther was attacking him and fired off a few pistol shots into the walls too close for comfort to Joyce's head. That night was a near as Joyce ever came or wanted to come to battle.

On June 10, 1904, the twenty-two-year-old Joyce encountered a twenty-year-old Galway girl, Nora Barnacle, walking along Grafton Street. They made a date to meet the next evening in front of 1 Merrion Square, Oscar Wilde's childhood home. Nora worked as a chambermaid at Finn's Hotel, near Trinity College, and the job held her from keeping the appointment. A plaintive letter from Joyce set another meeting for June 16, and that date Joyce memorialized as the single day that the plot of *Ulysses* takes place, the Bloomsday that would be celebrated on June 16 in countries around the world more than a century later. Joyce's relationship with Nora—always passionate and volatile—intensified quickly. In less than four months, they decided to run off together to the European continent. The woman he had met for the first time on June 10, 1904, would become his lifelong companion and, a quarter of a century later, his legal wife.

When Joyce left Dublin with Nora in October 1904, bouncing from Paris to Rome to Trieste to Zurich and back to Trieste, he found work as an English language teacher in Berlitz schools, employment that barely sustained the two of them. A few years later, by the time they had their two children—Giorgio (named after his dead brother George) and Lucia (named for light but destined to be cast into the darkness of mental illness)—they could not have survived without the stability and financial assistance of his brother Stanislaus. James had learned the fundamental narcissist's lesson from John Joyce and followed in his father's scrounging footsteps, more in the pattern of the stereotyped Welch-man than Irishman, it seemed. Joyce appeared always ready to have friends, family, or patrons pay his room and board and family expenses. His pleading letters to family and friends swung from arrogance to self-pity and back again. He seemed to believe he lived—and deserved for his blessed virtuosity and for the books he was fated to write—a charmed life.

No matter how many bad decisions he made, how many times he

begged friends and acquaintances for loans, no matter how many jobs he lost or discarded, he landed on his feet and stayed true to his art. Oliver St. Gogarty, three years older than Joyce, was the son of a Dublin doctor and in medical school when Joyce became his close companion. Some of Joyce's friends, like Gogarty, for example, may simply have been terrified that he planned to demonize them in his fiction, and loans became a way of appeasing the man with the power of words. Joyce was like the ancient Irish *fili*, the poet feared even by kings for the curses they could level in satirical verse. Joyce's relationship with the sharp-witted Gogarty, a self-styled Oscar Wilde who called Joyce the Bard, ranged from intellectual jostling to outright venom, and Gogarty had probably been wise to dread Joyce's pen because he was portrayed by the writer as the scabrous and cynical Buck Mulligan, stately and plump, dressed in a yellow gown and carrying a razor and shaving bowl, in the opening lines of *Ulysses*, intoning about the snot-green, scrotumtightening sea as he walked around the Martello tower.

It may have been Joyce who started the joke circulating in Dublin that as a poet, Gogarty made a good doctor, and as a doctor, he made a good poet. Ultimately, though, Joyce's imagination was a sympathetic one, and as he did for most of his characters from actual life that he wove into his fiction, Joyce gave fair play to Gogarty, making him in *Ulysses* a Falstaff to Stephen Dedalus's self-conscious Prince Hal. Even Joyce's father, John, who was reasonably bludgeoned in his son Stanislaus's memoirs, was handled sympathetically at times in James's work—be it "The Dead" or *Ulysses*. As James Joyce admitted to a friend after *Ulysses* was published, "The humour of *Ulysses* is his [John Joyce's]: its people are his friends. The book is his spittin' image." The other Joyce children came, for good reason, to hate their father, but if James saw his flaws with a gimlet eye, he held an affection for him anyway. As a writer, Joyce was able to see his characters whole. Colm Toibin in *Mad, Bad, Dangerous to Know: The Fathers of Wilde, Yeats and Joyce* offers a cogent explanation of the writer's well of empathy: "John Stanislaus Joyce's son [James] forgot nothing. And nothing was resolved from his staying away from Dublin. His father remained raw and present. Because Joyce found the space between what he knew about [his father] and what he felt so haunting and captivating, he forged a style that was capable of evoking its shivering ambiguities, combining the need to be generous with the need to be true … in all its variety and fullness, and indeed its pain and misery." Joyce needed to escape from both Dublin and John Joyce, but both the city and the father loomed so large that he could escape from neither, except in the act of writing about them.

Like his father, James was always profligate even in the most abject poverty, buying drinks for himself or a hand-painted scarf for Nora when the children's clothes were threadbare or there was no bread on the table. The artist took precedence over son, brother, husband, friend, and father. He worked diligently on his writing, always indefatigable, even heroically disciplined when it came to his art, but he had the energy to entertain other schemes as he worked on stories and novels. In one venture, he got investors to back a plan to open a movie theater in Dublin. At other times, he considered becoming a professional singer or starting his own magazine or engaging in a career as a book reviewer. He pondered becoming an agent for Irish tweeds on the continent and acted for a time as a theater producer in Zurich. He even considered importing and selling skyrockets in Trieste. His brother Stanislaus had little compassion for James's multifarious ambitions—"I take little interest," he said "in the budding *tenorino* that has failed as a poet in Paris, as a journalist in Dublin, as a lover and novelist in Trieste, as a bank-clerk in Rome, and again in Trieste as a Sinn-Feiner, teacher, and University Professor." In the character of such fool's errands, Stanislaus saw his brother taking after the despised father, filled with pipedreams and the old "Irish opium," but in terms of energy and dedication, James was markedly *not* like John. However, reminiscent of his father, James attributed most of his failures to a long list of betrayals—from friends, family, and bureaucracies. Richard Ellmann called this inclination in Joyce "the pleasure of self-laceration," as if he longed for the sort of betrayal that would fuel his fictions. Joyce was a man, it seemed, who longed for betrayal.

In his eagerness to find traitors and unfaithfulness everywhere around him, Joyce had a kinship to Hemingway, living it up to write it down, seeking and finding enemies wherever he turned. As Ellmann says about Joyce, "The fact that he was turning his life into fiction at the same time he was living it encouraged him to feel a certain detachment from what happened to him, for he knew he could reconsider and re-order it for the purposes of his book." Joyce needed exile to accomplish what he wanted to achieve as a writer. His Irish literary forbears—Swift, Goldsmith, Shaw, and Wilde—all left Ireland for a time to find their voices. And Joyce's literary hero Ibsen had left Norway to find the freedom he needed to write about his country. By the time he was eighteen years old, Joyce was already a fervent advocate of Ibsen's iconoclastic realism. Joyce followed Ibsen rather than the writers of his homeland, and he separated himself from Yeats, Lady Gregory, and Synge and the Irish cultural revolution. Someone late in Joyce's career once asked him why he didn't go back to Dublin, and he replied, "It would prevent me from writing about Dublin." That city was the heart and soul of his imagination, and the only way he could reimagine it was from the European continent, safely separated by the miles of Irish Sea and the English Channel.

Joyce sent an importuning letter to Lady Gregory as he was about to head to Paris, a letter that contained both his typical plea for financial assistance and a prideful show of defiance: "I shall try myself against the powers of the world. All things are inconstant except the faith of the soul, which changes all things and fills their inconstancy with light. And though I seem to have been driven out of my country here as a misbeliever I have found no man yet with a faith like mine." Like his fictional surrogate Stephen Dedalus, martyr and labyrinth maker, Joyce was ready to forge the uncreated conscience of his race and suffer for his art. He seemed to have a masochistic inclination that made him relish the opportunity. In Paris, he spent time with John Millington Synge, who was at the outset of his career as a playwright, and Synge offered a sardonic report to Lady Gregory, laced with faint praise: "He seems pretty badly off, and is wandering around Paris rather unbrushed and rather indolent, spending his studious moments in the National Library reading Ben Jonson. French literature I understand is beneath him! Still he interested me a great deal and as he is being gradually won over by the charm of French life, his time in Paris is not wasted.... I cannot think that he will ever be a poet of importance, but his intellect is extraordinarily keen and if he keeps fairly sane he ought to do excellent essay writing."

Until 1913, when William Butler Yeats introduced Joyce to Ezra Pound, the poet whom Gordon Bowker called "literature's own fairy godfather," Joyce had little material success as a writer, despite his unwavering faith in himself. He had struggled mightily for a decade to see *Dubliners* published. At one point in 1912, a jittery printer supposedly burned the page proofs—or at least this anecdote of a fiery death for his manuscript fit the narrative of martyrdom Joyce relished. The more likely truth, according to Bowker, is a more banal story—the pages being cut up and used as packing material. In any case, somehow Joyce got his hands on one set of page proofs and he grabbed them and never returned to Ireland again. Finally, after a decade and a disastrously convoluted series of rejections and acceptances, multiple printers and publishers balking at the threat of obscenity charges, Joyce rejoiced as Grant Richards—who had contracted and then reneged on the deal years before—published the book in 1914.

With the beginning of the First World War casting its bleak shadow, *Dubliners* didn't make a dime. But Joyce's financial luck was beginning to change course. Yeats's generous assistance with literary contacts and

Chapter 3. Joyce and Modern Ireland   63

Pound's strenuous promotion of Joyce's work to magazines and agents and publishers flowed into an ever-widening stream of patronage—Harriet Shaw Weaver, Sylvia Beach, and, over the years, an anonymous roster of wealthy individuals who discovered gratification, if not always intelligible meaning, in seeing a genius's work come to print. Extraordinarily generous patrons like Harriet Weaver gave him the independence to follow his genius, and some readers and critics feel that there was a curse attached to her generosity (more than a million dollars in today's money to give him leave to write)—she gave him the freedom to write his final, unintelligible novel, *Finnegans Wake*.

Joyce spent the years of the First World War, as he did at the outbreak of World War II, in neutral Zurich, the perfect landscape for the detached writer who saw the world conflict as a distraction and inconvenience. His contribution as a citizen of the world was not in battle or politics but in his art. Many would view Joyce's a-political stance as stunningly selfish. Gordon Bowker describes Joyce's feeling as Hitler began his invasion of Europe in 1938—"He was furious that politics in the form of Hitler had been allowed to disturb his creative tranquility and told Colum, 'Let him have Europe!'" For his art, it seems, Joyce was ready to sacrifice everything and everyone, himself included. Edna O'Brien notes some of the sacrifices he made in the writing of *Ulysses*— "twenty thousand hours of labor, his arthritis, suffusions in his eyes and in his brain, having to use charcoal sticks and different inks to see what he had written." He was a man who had to test his sight by trying to count the number of lights on the Place de la Concorde when he went out in the evening, but he still found a way to write every day. Toward the end of the war, the eye troubles that started in 1907 when he was twenty-five years old became particularly pronounced, and the dozen surgeries—iridectomies, sphincterotomies, and capsulectomies—began in an effort to cure his cataracts, glaucoma, and uveitis. In his remarkable account of the genesis and the legal and social shockwaves created by *Ulysses* in *The Most Dangerous Book*, Kevin Birmingham persuasively argues that Joyce's eye problems were caused by syphilis. Given Joyce's regular acquaintance as a young man with prostitutes and his regular visits to Monto, Dublin's brothels' quarter, the diagnosis seems reasonable.

In 1920, Joyce left Trieste, intending to revisit Paris and meet with Ezra Pound, at that time his most recent and ardent fan. He planned to stay a week. He stayed nearly two decades. His arrival in the City of Light was serendipitous, for he met the owner of Shakespeare and Company Bookstore, Sylvia Beach. In 1922, Beach published *Ulysses* under the imprint of Shakespeare and Company when most established

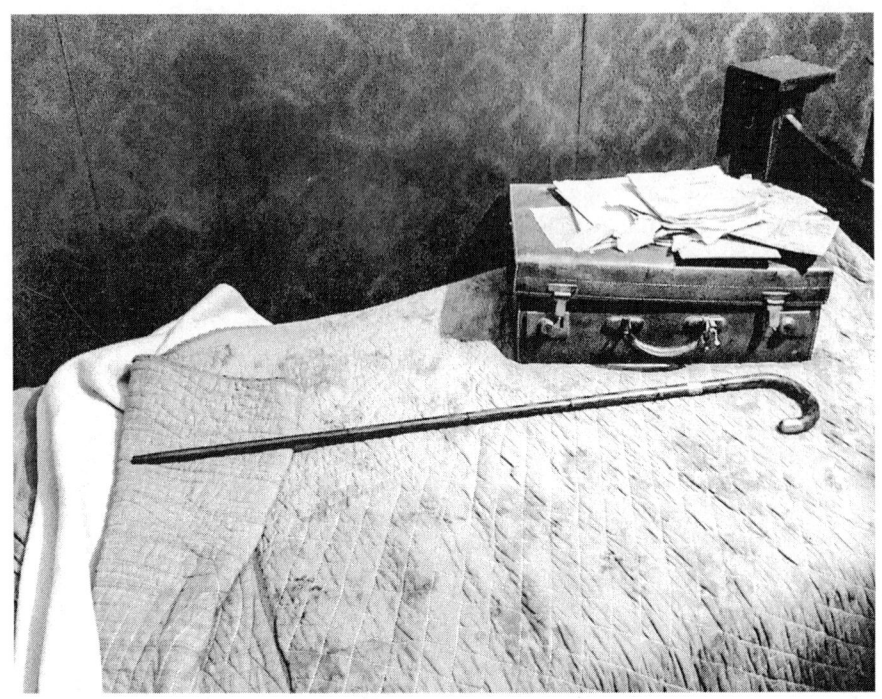

Joyce's bed, James Joyce Centre, Dublin.

publishers shied away in fear of being prosecuted for dealing in obscene material. Beach, the daughter of a Princeton Presbyterian minister, signed on as a Joyce acolyte, and it didn't take long for the author of *Ulysses* to become a Paris shrine for writers and literary pilgrims. Although quiet and apparently often shy, Joyce also thrived on the attention. To one woman who asked him who the greatest living writers in English were, he answered, "Aside from myself, I don't know." He was not prone to talk about literary matters except when the conversation pertained to his own work.

According to Ellmann, Joyce used *Ulysses* to vent his "tireless indignation," to settle scores with friends, family, and enemies. Of course, personal animus was only a small part of the large world of the novel. Even Joyce acknowledged that he was "the foolish author of a wise book." Each one of the eighteen episodes in the three sections of the novel parallels some aspect of Homer's epic poem, and each episode is associated with an hour of the day, an organ in the human body, a color, a technique, a style of writing. For Joyce, the universal was in the particular, the universal a particular shout in the streets, and he sought the extraordinary in the ordinary, the epic in 18 hours and 45 minutes of a

Dublin morning, afternoon, and twilight. In a letter to his now famous older brother, Stanislaus Joyce was later to contrast the difficult *Ulysses* with the impenetrable *Finnegans Wake* in this manner: "You have done the longest day in literature, and now you are conjuring up the deepest night."

Stanislaus had some reservations about what his brother had done with his modern revision of Homer's *Odyssey*, but he read the novel and appreciated its power and uniqueness. On the other hand, Joyce had to read passages aloud to Nora, the closest person to him in his life, for she was not an avid reader. She professed never to have read any of his books. And when he read the passages to her, she offered no encouragement for what she heard. His drinking and careless economy, his self-absorption and single-minded focus on his art, assuredly made him a trial to live with, but he must have found Nora's seeming indifference to his work dispiriting. Joyce and Nora were exquisitely mismatched. As Edna O'Brien summed up the puzzle of their relationship—"Many have been baffled that a man of Joyce's daunting intellect chose and remained constant to this peasant woman. It is beyond these letters, it is beyond propriety, it remains inexplicable as the Eleusinian mysteries." It may have been that she was grounded in a way that kept his intellect, always threatening to become untethered, tied to the earth. She was Molly Bloom and the Wife of Bath, the woman who kept the paradox of James Joyce attached to an ordinary world he might otherwise have lost. Ultimately, he loved and needed her, and she understood him. As she wrote to his sister shortly after his death, "My poor Jim, he was such a great man."

As self-centered and irresponsible as Joyce was, Nora saw that he could also be convivial, witty, sociable, amused and amusing. At parties, he would sing and dance and play the piano. Then again, at home, he could lie for hours face down on the bed contemplating his intricate puns and complicated characters. Depending on his mood, he could be aloof or mesmerizing. She might not have been familiar with the poetry of John Keats, but she had the requisite negative capability. As much as she complained about their financial instabilities and his bouts of drinking and as many times as she threatened to take the children and leave him, she stayed put and stayed loyal. She may have sensed what Edna O'Brien expressed about great writers—"Writers are a scourge to those they cohabit with. They are present and at the same time they are absent. They are present by the fact of their continuing curiosity, their needs, their cataloguing minds, their longing to see into another person, a longing that is increasingly discharged into their work.... Do writers have to be such monsters in order to create? I believe that they do. It is a paradox that while wrestling with language to capture the human condition they become more callous, and cut off from the very human traits which they so glisteningly depict. There can be no outer responsibility, no interruptions, only the ongoing inner drone, rhythmic, insistent, struggling to make a living moment of both beauty and austerity." Joyce had to experience everything in order to write about it, and like a character with Hawthorne's secret sin, he had to distance himself from life to make art of it. He saw the writer as a god, and as a god, he used everyone he knew for his sacred stories and novels, Nora and his children included. Ultimately, his one hero, the one true love in his life, was language.

Surely Joyce loved Nora and his children, too, but he was devoted with a monkish ferocity to his writing. He thought of the intricate illuminations of *Ulysses* as similar to the *Book of Kells*, in his words, "the most purely Irish thing we have." He knew that *Ulysses* had to end with Molly Bloom's 22,000-word stream-of-consciousness soliloquy, her gargantuan eight sentences, her final "Yes." It had to end, Joyce said, with "the most positive word in the human language." The ever-superstitious Joyce, fearful of thunderstorms and dogs and ill omens and always on the lookout for harbingers of good luck, demanded that *Ulysses* be published on his fortieth birthday, February 2, 1922. On that day, Sylvia Beach hand-delivered one copy of the book to Joyce at his Paris flat and the other she placed on display at Shakespeare and Company. It took another decade for the American Judge John Woolsey to declare that the book was not obscene and that the novel could be published and sold in the United States. The statement that Joyce gave to reporters through a friend contained one sentence: "Mr. Joyce finds the judge to be not devoid of a sense of humour."

A year later Joyce started working on his next book, known to everyone until its publication seventeen years later by the title "Work in Progress." That novel, *Finnegans Wake*, he began, in another nod to superstition, on St. Patrick's Day 1923. In *Finnegans Wake*, he exponentially increased the demands he placed on readers' intelligence and patience. His new novel, which would be his last, made *Ulysses* amount to light reading. *Ulysses* gave readers the inner working of the mind awake, the stream of thoughts in the consciousness of his characters. *Finnegans Wake* showed the mind in its dream state and offered a look at the unconscious mind in sleep. He went from a stream of consciousness to a river of unconsciousness, from day to night, from the strange logic of wakefulness to the logical strangeness of sleep. The novel demanded an "ideal reader suffering from an ideal insomnia." Joyce created a language of his own, part English, part Irish, part Italian, French,

Greek—in all, forty languages, according to Joyce's count. But those forty languages don't account for his multilingual puns and neologisms. His most loyal patron, Harriet Weaver, tried to get him to change what she believed to be a disastrous course. "It seems to me," she wrote to him, "you are wasting your genius." Virginia Woolf called the book "a bloated drowned dog ... unintelligible." His old enemy-friend Oliver St John Gogarty sniped at Joyce, calling the novel "the most colossal leg-pull in literature." Vladimir Nabokov, another master of wordplay, later saw it as "a cancerous growth of word-tissue." Even Ezra Pound, to many the voice of high modernism, could not tolerate so much innovation. And, despite Joyce's defense—"In writing of the night, I really could not, I felt I could not, use words in their ordinary connections"— Pound and many other former supporters of Joyce felt that his aesthetic had led him down an artistic rabbit hole. After reading pieces of "Work in Progress," Pound's letter to Joyce in part said this: "I make nothing of it whatever. Nothing so far as I make out, nothing short of divine vision or a new cure for the clapp can possibly be worth all the circumambient peripherization."

When Joyce asked H.G. Wells to help convince the reading public that "Work in Progress" was worth their time, Wells wrote him a compassionate but blunt response about what he called Joyce's literary experiment: "I don't think it gets anywhere. You have turned your back on common men, on their elementary needs and their restricted time and intelligence.... What is the result? Vast riddles.... So I ask: Who the hell is this Joyce who demands so many waking hours of the few thousand I have still to live for a proper appreciation of his quirks and fancies and flashes of rendering? All this from my point of view.... To me it is a dead end.... My warmest good wishes to you Joyce. I can't follow your banner any more than you can follow mine. But the world is wide and there is room for both of us to be wrong." Wells, Weaver, and Pound were part of the consensus, one that even his sympathetic biographer Richard Ellmann expresses: "his genius was a trap from which he did not desire to extricate himself." A trap, Joyce himself, sensed, it seems, when he wrote to a friend calling the book a monster, and although he felt that he had been fated to write it, he had probably been a fool to devote seventeen years to such a strange beast.

Frank O'Connor, fellow Irishman and sometimes admirer of Joyce's work, summed up what he saw as the cul de sac the author of *Finnegans Wake* had entered. "My friend V.S. Pritchett has called Joyce 'a mad grammarian,'" O'Connor wrote, "and I have said myself that his work is a 'rhetorician's dream,'" saying little more than Joyce himself said to his brother when he told him he was interested only in style. O'Connor had his doubts about the direction Joyce's genius was taking him even before *Finnegans Wake*, though. In *Irish Miles*, O'Connor compared Ulysses to decaying Irish architecture: "It was splendid stone-cutting, but I found myself thinking of the chilly English doorway in Graiguenamanagh and sighing. It might be the climacteric of Irish imagination when fantasy breaks loose from brains, and everything is thrown pell-mell into decoration; when we cease to be able to halt ourselves and go on elaborating until no functional basis remains—the point Joyce reached in Ulysses, phenomenal in craftsmanship, the interior poverty beginning to show." Joyce believed, as Yeats did not, that, in O'Connor interpretation of Joyce's effort, "words alone are certain good and that all that happens to human beings can be expressed fully in language. This, as we say in Ireland, is where the ferryboat left him, because it can't. Experience, as older people know, is always drifting into a world where language cannot follow...." For O'Connor, *Finnegans Wake* was a luminous example of "a mind turning in on itself and not caring any longer for the business of communication. I feel it as a sort of disintegration of the material, as though the mind behind had softened from abstraction through pedantry into whimsy." Dear old "doubling Dublin" would be the hallucinogenic heart of *Finnegans Wake*, a riparian nightmare in which rivers would dominate, eight hundred of them named and the River Liffey its central goddess beginning and ending with its "swerve of shore to bend of bay."

The last decade of his life Joyce continued to cry poverty to Harriet Weaver and request advances on investments she had created for him as he continued living above his means, staying in posh hotels, dining at the best restaurants, and sending his daughter to one expensive psychiatrist and mental hospital after another. Besides grappling with *Finnegans Wake* as he struggled with near-blindness, Joyce focused with a love and dedication on his daughter, Lucia, and her accelerating mental problems and her "lightning-lit reveries." The verdict of schizophrenia for her was not one Joyce could or would accept. He believed she had inherited his genius and her outbursts were part of that uniqueness of mind. He also felt that the peripatetic life he had forced on his family had made it difficult for her to function in normal society. And he may have been right about that. The nomadic existence—the multiple countries and dozens of homes—that James Joyce created for his family made John Joyce look like a domestic creature as rooted and stable as a middle-class accountant. Carl Jung treated Lucia but to no avail. What he did see was the similarity between father and daughter. As Richard Ellmann describes Jung's diagnosis: "her portmanteau words and neologisms were remarkable, but [Jung] said they were random; she and her father, he commented later, were like two people going to the bottom of a river, one falling and the other diving." But just as Joyce wanted to believe that Lucia was more genius than madwoman, he wanted to believe that *Finnegans Wake* was a narrative that connected them, that completing the book would save them both. He said, "Sometimes I tell myself that when I leave this dark night, she too will be cured." He hoped that on January 1, 1939, when he "finished finishing" the novel, that both he and his daughter would wake in a saner world.

One thing is certain: the near incomprehensible dream-night of his narrative in *Finnegans Wake* paralleled Lucia's descent into the perplexing world of schizophrenia. In those years, Joyce became the serio-comically sane Lear and Lucia the mad Cordelia. In the background for her mental problems and his physical illnesses, his struggles with *Finnegans Wake* and fear of incipient blindness, were the beginnings of World War II. But, as he had during World War I, Joyce held himself apart, as much as he could, from the war. "I'm not interested in politics," he said. "The only thing that interests me is style." He was a writer, as Gordon Bowker argues, who was "under no obligation to rest content with the English language." Frank O'Connor once said that Irish literature amounted to a tale of two cities, Dublin and London. Embattled and starved and colonized over the centuries, a people who had their language marginalized or erased, their myths mocked and their religion diminished, their sovereignty stripped away, language became a way of regaining a stolen past, a way, perhaps, of forging that conscience Stephen Dedalus speaks about in the conclusion of *A Portrait of the Artist as a Young Man*. The polyglot idiom Joyce created in *Finnegans Wake* was a natural one for an Irish writer for whom the word *was* politics. He was a man versed in many languages, a man living in his own Tower of Babel. When he was with his family in Switzerland, for instance, he spoke English to Nora, and he and Nora spoke Italian to Giorgio and Lucia, and the children spoke to each other in Zurich-German. For him, language, not bombs and bullets, was the way to change the world.

Joyce expected his readers' devotion to his work to match his own. To the critic Max Eastman he said, "The demand that I make of my reader is that he should devote his whole life to reading my works." He may have said it with a smile and an Irish lilt, but he meant it and expected a radical dedication from his readers. At times, he seemed to care less about meaning than he did about the sound of his sentences. The man who had once thought he would make a career as a singer made a novel of sounds, one that ends this way: "Whish! A gull. Gulls. Far calls. Coming, far! End here. Us then. Finn, again! Take. Bussoftlhee, memermormee! Till thousandsthee. Lps. The keys to. Given! A way a lone a last a loved a long the"—he had found the perfect word to end his dreamscape—as he said, "the word which is the most slippery, the least accented, the weakest word in English, a word which is not even a word, which is scarcely sounded between the teeth, a breath, a nothing, the article *the*." No period ends the novel, just a sentence breathing the word *the* back to the opening—"riverrun, past Eve and Adam's, from swerve of shore to bend of bay, brings us by commodious vicus of recirculation back to Howth Castle and Environs."

In late 1940, with the Germans taking over France, Joyce left Paris with his family and headed back to Zurich and the neutrality of Switzerland, where he had been in the flush of youth. Now, ill and prematurely aged, he came back—famous and broken. There, in neutral territory, he died a few weeks shy of his fifty-ninth birthday.

Nine years later I was born in the Bronx and, because of my blond hair and blue eyes, given the nickname Sunny Jim by my Aunt Carrie Regan, who lived with us in our cramped one-bedroom apartment on the Grand Concourse. Jenny O'Pray, my maternal grandmother, had died fifteen years before, and Alfred Hunter had disappeared more than two decades before that, and I wouldn't find any sign of him again until I met Leopold Bloom in *Ulysses*.

Chapter 4

Yeats, Sligo, and the West

"riverrun, past Eve and Adam's, from swerve of shore to bend of bay.... A way a lone a last a loved a long the"
—James Joyce, *Finnegans Wake*

Joyce led me to Yeats and then to John Millington Synge, Frank O'Connor, Seamus Heaney, Edna O'Brien, and the breadth of Irish literature, on a journey across the Irish landscape and through its history. I wended my way from Dingle to Donegal, Dublin to Galway, Cork to Kinsale, Belfast to Portrush, from a slippery hike up Croagh Patrick on a typically wet Irish day to frigid swims in what was once the gentleman's bathing place adjacent to the Joyce Sandycove Tower, the Forty Foot. Those years of travel were a time of discovering Ireland by train and car and foot, and they were also years of reading Flann O'Brien, John McGahern, Roddy Doyle, Anne Enright, Sally Rooney, Paul Lynch, Rob Doyle, Anna Burns, and dozens of others, as I traced the country in its texts.

First, after Joyce, there was Yeats, the poet of as many masks if not more than Joyce himself. In his long career, Yeats moved through the Romantic to the mythic to a hard-edged cultural realism, from a lush idealism to what R.F. Foster called a poetry with a "bleak new edge" or what Edmund Wilson saw as a more plain-spoken verse, "offering a profound and subtle criticism of life." Yeats shifted from the mystical and the occult to faeries, from unrequited love to Irish politics, from the dreamy soughings of his poetry in 1880s and 1890s to the layered honesty and realism of his writing in the 1920s and eventually to the chiseled metaphysical complexity of the poems of his last decades. Richard Ellmann has suggested that the simple, hard, clear poetry that he achieved in the middle of his career, the poetry that Yeats said had "more salt in it," the pared-down simplicity of that poetry, took him a lifetime of experience and revision to discover. In his later years when he discussed his evolution as a writer, Yeats said that for him it had always been "a search for simplicity ... the natural words ... in the natural order."

His voice shifted over the years as, at first glance, did his interests—séance enthusiast and admirer of the occult, mythmaker, writer of autobiographies and self-referential plays, failed lover, wearer of masks, co-founder with Lady Gregory of the Abbey and the Irish National Theater, an ambiguous voice for nationalism, a senator in the Irish Free State. But, as he wrote in *A Vision* and as a careful examination of his writing demonstrates, from the beginning of his career, Yeats had three interests: "interest in a form of literature, in a form of philosophy, and a belief in nationality. None of these seemed to have anything to do with the other, but gradually my love of literature and my belief in nationality came together. Then for years I said to myself that these two had nothing to do with my form of philosophy, but that I had only to be sincere and to keep from constraining one by the other and they would become one interest. Now all three are, I think, one, or rather all three are discrete expression of a single conviction."

Auden once wrote that "art is not life and cannot be a midwife to society." But Yeats was a political figure, and he wanted his writing to alter the culture of his country. The critic Declan Kiberd suggests that idea when he notes that Yeats was one of the foremost poets of de-colonialization because in revising (that is, in re-seeing) the landscape of Irish history and myth, he was a major factor in the repossessing of Ireland. The British critic F.R. Leavis saw that what Yeats accomplished could not have been done by another man in another time: "And it cannot be repeated. No Englishman in any case could have profited by the sources of strength open to Mr. Yeats as an Irishman, and no such source is open to anyone now. No serious poet could propose to begin again where Mr. Yeats began."

For Yeats, poetry was a way of living, a way of being in the world, and even if Auden was right and poetry is "a way of happening, a mouth," he was also right when he said about Yeats that "Mad Ireland hurt you into poetry." A decade before his death, Yeats reflected on the source of his art, foreshadowing Auden's interpretation of Ireland as the catalyst: "Out of Ireland have we come./Great hatred, little room,/Maimed us at the start./I carry from my mother's womb/A fanatic heart." When Yeats died, Ireland, as Auden said, still had her madness and her weather, but Yeats had created a way of seeing the land and the society that seemed new.

A careful look at the Irish Renaissance tells us that the cultural revival preceded and, in many ways, enabled the political revolution that followed—the opposite, for instance, of what happened in America with the likes of Whitman and Emerson following the Declaration of Independence by 75 years. Their call for an American literature came after the invention of America. In Ireland, to an important degree, the literature that Yeats shaped helped invent the twentieth-century political reality of his country. Yeats was wary of violent revolutionaries whose speeches enchanted men's hearts to stone. What he saw as an excess of love and a delirium of the brave led him to wonder what rough beast slouched its way to Bethlehem to be born. He lived his life by the standard of the epitaph he wrote for himself, his poetry casting a cold eye on life, on death.

Yeats Statue, Sligo.

Yeats's grandfather, also William Butler Yeats, was a strictly orthodox minister in the Church of Ireland. He was born in 1806 and died three years before his grandson was born in 1865, but he left him with a DNA that inclined him toward spirituality, if, as Auden suggested, of a silly variety at times. John Butler Yeats, William's son and the future Nobel laureate's father, was born in 1839 and lived into his eighties, and from the beginning until the end of his career influenced the course of W.B.'s life and work. John Butler Yeats seems to have traveled as far as he could from the evangelical influence of his father to become an artist and a non-believer in all religious doctrines. John discarded his faith when he studied at Trinity College in the mid–nineteenth century. When he married Susan Pollexfen, a native of Sligo, he was set to practice law. He married her, he said, because her family had a "genius for being dismal," and he thought such a dour family would give him the gravity and discipline he lacked. R.F. Foster, author of *W.B. Yeats: A Life*, describes the Pollexfens as a clan "drawn to Mysticism and morbidity." Foster wrote, "The Pollexfens lived only for bad news; they refused to show affection, on principle; on their excruciating Sunday dinners they sat all over the house in different rooms, refusing either to go out or to run the risk of meeting each other."

Like John Joyce, John Butler Yeats was a "great talker," garrulous and gregarious, and perhaps he thought the silence of the Pollexfen family, "the most disagreeable people I ever met," might keep him tethered to the earth. But that grounding didn't occur, and he abandoned the law the way he abandoned all organized religion. Two years after William Butler Yeats was born, John started on the path to becoming a skillful but inevitably dissatisfied artist. According to Richard Ellmann, John Yeats could never be satisfied with the art work he produced, and as W.B. Yeats once wrote, "Instead of finishing a picture one square inch at a time, he kept all fluid, every detail dependent upon every other, and remained a poor man to the end of his life, because the more anxious he was to succeed, the more did his pictures sink through innumerable sittings into final confusion." The unfinished paintings scattered about his studio attested to his perfectionism but also underscored his inability to provide for his family. Like the Joyce family under the erratic leadership of John Joyce, the Yeats family under the guidance of John Butler Joyce was a family in constant decline. Even as an old man, living alone in bohemian poverty in New York City, John Butler Yeats kept his unconventional spirit, spending more than a decade before his death working on a self-portrait. According to R.F. Foster, John Yeats had "a determined addiction to failure in his character." His son, Willie, worked diligently against failure in his life as a writer, but he seemed magnetized by failure in his love life.

John Butler Yeats, artist and intellectual, was not the irresponsible reprobate that John Joyce was, but because of his inability to balance business and art, his family was forced to shuttle in an impoverished fashion from London to Dublin to Sligo for much of W.B. Yeats's early life. Whatever stability the Yeats children found in their lives was centered in Sligo. From his mother, Susan Pollexfen, William Butler Yeats inherited a love of the Sligo countryside and a fascination with peasant life and Irish fairy tales and myths. The young Yeats was awkward physically and a slow learner, having difficulties learning to read, and the Pollexfen clan felt, as Ellmann states the case, that the boy was "mentally and physically defective." Yeats sought solace in solitude and dreamed his days away in the Sligo fields and caves. Just as James Joyce had endlessly roamed the streets of Dublin, William Butler Yeats wandered the rocky paths of his beloved Sligo.

Yeats didn't follow in the family tradition and attend Trinity College. According to Richard Ellmann in *Yeats: The Man and the Masks*,

Boat, Rosses Point.

"It was not, as he probably declared, because Trinity College was old-fashioned and uncongenial to his awakening spirit, but because he was unable to meet the entrance requirements in classics and mathematics." If Yeats was dissenting at that time against any entity, though, he was rebelling against his father's rationalist skepticism and against his father's inability to complete what he started. Neither of the Johns—Joyce or Yeats—succeeded at much, but they fathered two of the most diligent and accomplished writers of the twentieth-century. John Butler Yeats was insightful enough to sense that his failure may have helped his son. In a letter to a friend, John wrote, "A successful father is good for daughters. For the sons it is another matter."

John Yeats had revolted against his minister father's Christianity. But W.B., who had as complicated a relationship with his father as Joyce had with his, objected to John Yeats's lack of faith in the unseen and the scientifically unproven and, in opposition to him, gravitated toward fairy tales, myths, astrological musings, and the occult. Caught between his own desire to follow his imagination toward the supernatural and his father's cogent and articulate philosophy of doubt, W.B. spent a lifetime building a vision of the world that attempted to bring the mystical into balance with the real.

Around the time of Parnell's rise to a secular sainthood in his homeland and the Irish Republican Brotherhood's fight for Home Rule, Yeats's mind and heart turned in the direction of nationalism, at least of a literary variety. If Parnell was James Joyce's political hero, though, John O'Leary was Yeats's political saint. O'Leary, a man who had been imprisoned for five years in England and served a long exile in France for participating in the 1867 Irish uprising against England, gave speeches on what the Irish people should value, and his values were akin to Yeats's—an emphasis on Irish geography, history, poetry, and folklore. O'Leary was a political figure aligned to Yeats's instincts, the man he mourned in "September 1913"—"Romantic Ireland's dead and gone/ It's with O'Leary in the grave." Therefore, with what he must have felt was the implicit imprimatur of his political hero, the 24-year-old Yeats published his first chapbook in 1889, *The Wanderings of Oisin*, a narrative poem that opened the landscape of the Irish literary revival.

Up to this point, as one of his friends characterized him, Yeats "had the uncanny faculty of standing aside and looking on the game of life as a spectator." For him, the spiritual life and the imaginative life were synonymous. His belief in that connection led him toward Madame Blatavsky and Theosophy. Occultism, in the form of seances, black magic, supernatural phenomena, and miracles, was another form of rebellion for him against the scientific, materialistic, and rationalistic sensibility of his father. The young Yeats thought of himself as one of the last Romantics, and his mysticism, idealism, and lyricism placed him in the lineage of Blake and Shelley and Keats. Early poems like "The Stolen Child," with its world of leafy islands and slumbering trout, or the melodious "Down by the Salley Gardens," enclosed by weirs and tears, have a brooding, nostalgic music to them. But on January 30, 1889, his life-altering meeting with the beautiful and majestic Maud Gonne complicated his ideas about the relationship between the imagination and action, and his poetry began to take on a more muscular, colloquial, and realistic feel. Even an apparently Romantic poem like "The Lake Isle of Innisfree," written shortly after he met Gonne, shaped his world with a new metaphysical complexity, at its center the yearning to escape, the anticipation of it, not its fulfillment.

He fell in love with Maud Gonne at their first meeting, and that was the moment, he said, that the troubling of his life began. Richard Ellmann said the complication for Yeats stemmed from the fact that he had to decide "which of his two selves should he show to her?" By nature, he was self-conscious, dreamy, poetic, but he admired men of spontaneous action. In part to win her, perhaps, and as a consequence of his own conflicting impulses, he took on the mask of the Irish revolutionary. His dilemma, in a sense, was Oisin's—to dream or to act, to attempt to live forever in art or to accept the inevitable consequences of stepping into the finite world of social and political action. In a sense, this conflict shadowed Yeats throughout his career. Even a poem written shortly before his death—"The Circus Animals Desertion"—talked about the dream that enchanted him, the players and the painted stage and the imagined world of Oisin and Cuchulain, that had dominated much of his life and that it was time for him to "lie down where all the ladders start/In the foul rag-and-bone shop of the heart." Experience, he deeply believed, would lead him back to art. And the imagination.

Maud Gonne, the physical embodiment of Yeats's psychological and aesthetic conflict, was a revolutionary free spirit, a woman who eventually married Major John MacBride, one of the fifteen rebels executed by the British government after the 1916 Easter Rising. Influenced in part by unrequited love, jealousy, and anger concerning MacBride's mistreatment of Maud Gonne, Yeats saw him as a "drunken, vainglorious lout." But even MacBride became part of the "terrible beauty" that Yeats felt was birthed by those men of action in April 1916.

Yeats's encounter with Maud Gonne in January 1889 led him toward three decades of unrequited passion. That meeting and their deep but frustrating connection may have been the psychological and emotional friction point that sparked much of his creativity, what R.F. Foster calls the hopeless love that freed him to write his poetry. As Ellmann sees this part of the poet's life, "Yeats makes a cult of frustration, and courts defeat like a lover." Gonne may have been bad for him psychologically and emotionally but an inspiration for his creativity and a catalyst for his mission to create a national literature. She became his modern Helen, a woman who "taught to ignorant men most violent ways." But he acknowledged the "folly of being comforted" and did not blame her for filling his days with misery, for "what could she have done/Was there another Troy for her to burn?" She was a woman who wanted to change the world by stepping forcefully into it. Yeats's nature led him to imagine her and that change from afar. Gonne figured at the center of one of his oft-repeated thematic connections—the relationship between love and war—an idea crystallized in "Leda and the Swan," which Yeats wrote as civil war broke out in Ireland after the 1916 Uprising. The final couplet of the poem asks the question—"Did she put on his knowledge with his power/Before the indifferent beak could let her drop?"—a question at the essence of Yeats's work and life: where do fate and history intersect with ordinary human experience.

During this era of dichotomies—of Jekyll and Hyde and Dorian Gray—Yeats struggled with his many masks. Dreamer or man of action? Poet or political partisan? Was he to place himself in the world of fairies and mythic heroes or that of politicians and patriots? Imagine the world or join arms with men of action? To a certain extent, the Irish nationalist movement in literature sprang from Yeats's desire to prove himself to Maud Gonne, his Joan of Arc, to show her and himself that he could engage somehow in the fiery business of Irish patriotism. By the late 1890s, Yeats's politics became more thoroughly literary. He joined his idea of Ireland as a potential pastoral socialist utopia to his dream of a national literary movement. He wanted to stitch the spiritual and the political to his artistic pursuits, to preserve "an ancient ideal of life" and carry on four fundamental virtues—"First, honesty amongst friends. Second, courage amongst enemies. Third, generosity amongst the weak. Fourth, courtesy at all times...."

At the start of the twentieth century, with the patronage of Annie Horniman, Lady Gregory and Yeats acquired the building that became the Abbey and the Irish National Theater began. They determined that the subject matter had to be Irish and, as Richard Ellmann says, "Irish in a self-respecting sense; the stage Irishman was banished." Yeats's meeting with Gregory became the start of a lifelong friendship and collaboration. In her, he found an artistic soulmate. Lady Gregory's estate at Coole Park became a haven for him, a place where he found sustenance for his writing, a locus for his imagination reminiscent of his boyhood Sligo. In R.F. Foster's words, "Coole is at once a house and an ethos, standing for a culture fixed at the centre, revolving around established foundations of decorum, commitment, steadiness, and 'pride established in humility.'"

Many of the early plays that Lady Gregory and Yeats wrote or produced were focused on peasant life or Irish myth. When that model was made problematic in 1907 by John Millington Synge's *The Playboy of the Western World*, a play about an imagined parricide and the passions it arouses in the country women for Christy Mahon, the supposed hero, riots erupted in Dublin. Lady Gregory's famous telegram to Yeats explains—"Audience broke up in disorder at the word *shift*." The staunch Irish nationalists were outraged by what they saw as a denigration of Irish womanhood and an upholding of base Irish stereotypes. Sinn Feiners saw Yeats, Gregory, and Synge as symbols of the decadence of twentieth-century Ireland.

Yeats's poems and plays and his activity with the National Theater all played out against the background of the struggle for Home Rule—serving to both record and create history. During this time, his perfect love for Maud Gonne imploded when she married Major John MacBride in Paris. The question that Richard Ellmann asks must have been one that Yeats considered many times: "He was broad-awake and thirty-seven years old, half his life over. What would he do now that his most cherished dream was gone?" His answer was to write poetry

Chapter 4. Yeats, Sligo, and the West

Coole Park.

that struck a balance between the imagination and action, between Platonic and sexual love, between art and life. Richard Ellmann argues that Yeats began to assemble the dichotomies that had roiled his life—"spontaneity against craft, light-heartedness against seriousness, pretense against sincerity, natural mastery against artificial authority ... mask against face." For Yeats, the introspective conflict created something lasting. As he said, "We make out of the quarrel with others, rhetoric. But of the quarrels with ourselves, poetry."

Later, in *A Vision*, he set down his convoluted philosophy, blending the spiritual and the aesthetic, the historical and the personal, in an attempt to understand the history of Ireland and his own private life. It wasn't until 1917, when he was fifty-two years old and he married the twenty-five-year-old Georgiana Hyde-Lees, that Yeats finally, after thirty years of longing, fully accepted that his relationship with Maud Gonne would never come to fruition. A month before he married Hyde-Lees, Yeats proposed to Maud Gonne again and was rejected one final time, and then in an act that seemed desperate, if not slightly incestuous, he proposed to Gonne's twenty-two-year-old daughter, Iseult, who also said no.

Perhaps defying the odds, Yeats's marriage to Georgiana Hyde-Lees was for the most part happy and productive (two children and many poems). Some of Yeats's most powerful poems were written during the

Thoor Ballylee, Yeats Tower.

twenty-two years of his marriage. In the last decade of his life, Yeats drifted into other relationships with women, but Georgiana remained his spiritual partner, the woman who had engaged with him in automatic writing, the woman who remained his down-to-earth helpmeet for nearly a quarter of a century. She ventured with poet-husband into the spirit world and, at the same time, offered him the virtues of safety and domesticity. As Ellmann describes the relationship, "A great serenity came over Yeats as he emerged from the isolation and eccentricity of bachelorhood into peace and harmony."

In 1924, Yeats won the Nobel Prize for a body of poetry that took his personal experience and the tumultuous history of his country and shaped it into dreams. He was a dreamer who discovered a way to enter the world and change its shape—as the co-founder of the Abbey Theater, as a cartographer of the Irish literary movement, as a senator of the Irish Free State, and as a man who cast a steady eye on life and on death, a man who transcended the world in order to participate in it. He labored his entire life to find a path that connected the mythic leanings

Winding stairs, Yeats Tower.

of his mother and the skepticism of his father. Mad Ireland had hurt him into writing poetry, as it had driven James Joyce into fiction. As it did with Joyce, the story of Ireland *made* Yeats the poet. Yeats shaped the story of the country he loved in the same complicated fashion that he recreated the narrative of his love for Maud Gonne.

Poetry, especially that of Yeats, was to be memorized and spoken, I thought from the time I started college, and I still believe that. When I first fell under the spell of his poetry, I started by memorizing "Sailing to Byzantium" because it reminded me that sometimes all we are left with are the stories we put to memory. When I first read that poem, I was young enough to feel I could easily swim in the salmon-falls and the mackerel-crowded seas. It might have been no country for old men; but that sensual music was for me, and for Jo-Ellen. Like the narrator of Yeats's poem, I liked the idea of being drawn into the artifice of eternity, writer becoming text, and text holding its own life and life force. But, then, just married and barely out of my teens, eternity seemed far off and for other people. The tide that was sweeping me away from the Catholic Church and the idea of an eternal reward was drawing me toward art as a new religion, words and stories a different kind of holy scripture. And then I stumbled upon one of Yeats's later poems, "The

Circus Animals Desertion." I was that sea-rider, that see writer, Oisin who would have the chance to live forever, and I would not make the mistake he made and take leave of Niamh. And, in the arrogance of everlasting youth, I was convinced I need not concern myself with ladders because I lived already in the foul rag-and-bone shop of the heart, in the thrum and welter of experience. In the narrow lens that youth offers, I thought I had as much to teach those poems as they had to teach me. In that, I blush to admit, I had James Joyce's arrogance, if not his genius.

Travels in Sligo

> "And I shall have some peace there, for peace comes dropping slow,
> Dropping from the veils of the morning to where the cricket sings;
> There midnight's all a glimmer, and noon a purple glow,
> And evening full of the linnet's wings."
> —William Butler Yeats, "The Lake Isle of Innisfree"

The first time I went to Sligo, in 2015, I climbed Ben Bulben with my friend John McManus, three students, and our bus driver, Sean. The wind blew with an extraterrestrial force as John and I raced each other up the hillside on different routes. John took a path cut up the side of the mountain, and Sean and I marched across the fields, through gorse and blackthorn bushes. John had the steeper climb, but Sean and I, in shorts, our legs bruised and cut, looked the worse for wear as we reached the squat obelisk that declared a hiker had made it to the top of Yeats's mountain. When the students reached us, John and I both claimed to have beaten the other to the top first. John and I still disagree about which one of us had the first glimpse of Yeats's tombstone as we gazed down from the windy summit of Ben Bulben. We each have our own stories that we'll hold to like bull-headed Irishmen.

Sligo called me back. In the early morning during the fall of 2022, Sam Brett, a Sligo local, picked up my friend and photographer John Lawrence and me at St. Jude's Bed and Breakfast in Galway. I had made friends with Sam after he guided my students around Innisfree in 2018, reciting the poem with the island at his back and then walking Rosses Point with us, regaling the group with tales of the Butlers, Pollexfens, and the Yeats clans. Sam is a modern Irish storyteller, his company called Shanakee is located in Sligo.

On this cloud-filled, windy morning, Sam drove toward Thoor Ballylee, the tower that Yeats lived in just a few kilometers from Lady

Gregory's magnificent Coole Park, when he scratched at his short-cropped grey hair and started talking about the Irish connection to the land and the language, how in his country "stories come out of the ground." As he spoke, he opened his phone to some mournful Gaelic music sung by Josephine Begley. He aptly described her singing as keening. "The Irish used to hire keeners," he explained, "to sing doleful tunes during funerals to help with the grieving process. We live in a liminal place on this island. At the edge of the world. Next to death. The land speaks to us. Where does our culture come from if it doesn't come from the land? It's about how we describe it, how we adore it, how we sing to it. Every song that was ever written in Ireland is a love song to the land. Walking the land here is a pilgrimage. And the Irish walk the land telling stories. The sceales, the storytellers, and the seanachies, the carriers of the lore, the poets who collected stories and remembered them, the ones who served the function of keeping the stories of the people were respected as much as the kings."

Thoor Ballylee, once known as Islandmore Castle at Ballylee, a fourteenth-century tower built by the Norman invaders, looks to keep the native Irish at bay. It looks as if it had once been a king's residence. It became Yeats's summer home shortly after the Easter Rising of 1916, a place for him to write the poems and stories he sensed lived in the landscape. He purchased the castle and studio for thirty-five pounds, and it came to be known over the years as the Yeats Tower, and now it is a museum to his memory. Yeats Tower had a magic to it that Seamus

Chair, Yeats Tower.

Heaney appreciated. He wrote about it quite a few times. His friend Andrew Hagan photographed Heaney descending the winding stairs of the castle but was told reprovingly by Yeats, "No, Andy, that's too much." But not for me, who had claim to competition with a Nobel laureate. So, when John took my picture, I just smiled and thanked him.

For Yeats, the West of Ireland was the story at the heart of Irish myth and history. And Sam Brett has the same belief. "Our culture is in our bones," Sam said. "It's in the sacred land, in our bones. We don't invent it. It invents us. Heaney talked about this. The land is our mother, our inherited memory. The bog holds our secrets. In Alaska, they have many words for snow. In Ireland, they have many words for field and road." Sam, then, told the tale of his walking the Camino in both Spain and Portugal. We had that shared experience, for I had traveled that road myself in 2011, but for him his journey in Portugal and Spain was directly connected to Ireland. "Sligo," he told me, "is Shelly's way, the way of the shell. And the scallop shell is the symbol of the Way of St. James, the path to Santiago. Our roads in Ireland—our boreens and

Sam Brett, Innisfree.

bohars—are measured by the length and width of the cow, *bo* in Irish. For us, the land and what lives on it is a holy path, like the tao."

When we left the Yeats Tower and headed the short distance down the road to Coole Park, as if on cue from Sam, a young buck stood in the road blocking our way.

"Oisin," Sam said, and the buck leapt into the woods and out of sight. "Oisin means small deer," he said. "It's our language that connects us to the land, to our history, to the pilgrimage we are on. Yeats knew that. Yeats, along with Lady Gregory and a few others, invented Celticism. He started the Irish Renaissance. And now a new generation of writers and artists are defining Ireland for the next one hundred years."

But for Sam, much of modern Irish literature started with Yeats, and for that reason he wanted to take us back to some parts of Yeats country in Sligo. So, back we went to Innisfree, again for his recounting of the Irish mythological version of the Arthurian legend and to hear Sam recite "The Lake Isle of Innisfree" as the pouring rain turned to mist. Then we went again to Coole Park to marvel at Lady Gregory's estate, what was the Garden of Eden for the Irish literary Renaissance. And, finally to Glencar Waterfall in the shadow of the Dartry Mountains, marching up to view the falls as Sam whispered "The Stolen Child" a few steps behind us—"Come away, O human child!/To the waters and the wild/With a faery, hand in hand/For the world's more full of weeping/than you can understand." Then he pointed us toward Knocknashee, the hill of the faeries and explained that *shee* meant hill. The wind began to howl down the hillside, and for the first time I understood the meaning of the word *banshee*—voice of the woman of the hills. That banshee had spoken to Yeats. And to Sam. I was beginning to hear a voice in the wind myself.

Chapter 5

J.M. Synge and the Aran Islands

> "John Synge ... dying chose the living world for text/And never could have rested in the tomb/But that, long traveling, he had come/Towards nightfall upon certain set apart/In a most desolate stony place,/Towards nightfall upon a race/Passionate and simple like his heart."
> —W.B. Yeats, "In Memory of Major Robert Gregory"

When my Uncle Bob asked me on my fifteenth birthday if I had a string of girlfriends, I blushed to the roots of my blond hair and said, "No, not really." He did his usual: ruffled the bristling edges of my crew cut (growing out into a more suitable style for the mid–1960s), pinched my cheek, and rolled his eyes in disbelief. Then he said, "You'll be the playboy of the western world, I bet, with that blond hair and those blue eyes."

Three years later, I met Christy Mahon, the real Playboy of the Western World. It was the summer of 1968, and I was doing my best to make every pretty girl I met in the Hamptons see my gallant potential, the hero that was hidden from the general public. The Hamptons seemed to me as far away from the Bronx as any corner of Ireland, but in its far easterly location on Long Island somehow felt to me like a straight line to Mayo in Ireland's wild west. When I wasn't reading books or body surfing the Atlantic waves, I worked for a landscaping company as a day laborer scything fields and pruning bushes. I played my part each weekend in the clubs at Dune Road as a confident, worldly man, but back at our rental in Hampton Bays, I was my true bookish self, reading through everything I could find in the local libraries. A beautiful girl a few years older than I was had been reading at the library table across from me. I hadn't had the nerve to speak to her, but that didn't stop me from rifling through the stack of books she had left behind. *The Complete Plays of J M Synge* fell into my lap.

The next day on the beach I read and admired them all—*Riders to the Sea*, *In the Shadow of the Glen*, *The Well of the Saints*, *The Tinker's Wedding*, and *Deidre of the Sorrows*—but it was *The Playboy of the Western World* that I fell in love with, the comedy, the sad yearning, the poetry, the transformation of Christy Mahon from doltish farmer to dazzling hero. Like Christy, I must have reasoned, I could be transformed, far away from the Bronx, and employ the poetry I suspected was in my soul to grow larger than the narrow streets that I felt trapped in near Bedford Park Boulevard and Villa Avenue.

In his 1907 preface to *The Playboy of the Western World*, Synge said that Ireland was a country "where the imagination of the people, and the language they use, is rich and living [a place where] it is possible for a writer to be rich and copious in his words, and at the same time to give the reality, which is the root of all poetry, in a comprehensive and natural form." He went on to say, "In Ireland, for a few years more, we have a popular imagination that is fiery and magnificent, and tender; so that those of us who wish to write start with a chance that is not given to writers in places where the springtime of the local life has been forgotten, and the harvest is a memory only, and the straw has been turned into bricks."

Set in a shebeen in Mayo at the end of the nineteenth century, *The Playboy of the Western World* struck me as all too familiar to me. Michael Flaherty's pub reminded me of Darby O'Gill's in my neighborhood and the Bronx cast of characters who leaned against the bar like painted shadows. Darby's, like Flaherty's pub, was a place where the routine was rarely broken, where I often wondered if I might enter it one day with a new identity and exit as the upturned faces gaped wide-eyed at the daring fellow who had been there and was now gone.

The language of the play was at once recognizable and beautifully foreign, what seemed to me then, and now, the essence of poetry. The Irish idioms and repetitions—"aren't we after making a good bargain" or "It's above at the crossroads, he is"—the words that echoed my mother's and Aunt Carrie's—*skelping* and *scalded hearts*—were theirs and also mine—*he's the spit of you* or *shed a tear for Ireland, won't you?* So, I felt at home and happily lost in a strange land that felt eerily familiar.

Pegeen Mike is the frustrated twenty-year-old daughter of the publican, and she is about to be married to the timid, passionless Shawn Keogh. Enter Christy Mahon, father-killer, diminutive man with a robust soul, Pegeen believes, aligned to the poets, "fine fiery fellows with great rages when their tempers roused." When Christy first enters Michael James's rural pub, he is as diffident and unassertive as Shawn Keogh, his competitor for Pegeen Mike's affection. In this Freudian

Doorway, Aran Islands.

comedy, Shawn, the emblem of the status quo, is under the thumb of his spiritual father, Father Reilly, and daunted by the potent culture of the Catholic Church. In a sense, Christy is the spitting image of Shawn, cowed by his father and his community, that is, until he "kills his father." Once a drudge on his father's farm, Christy has altered his life by, he imagines, murdering his father, in a fit of anger, with a loy. The Oedipal implications are clear and used for compelling comic effect—the son becomes a man by erasing his father. He can only become the playboy of the western world by destroying the domineering father. As Christy says at the end of Act I, after seeing the respect he has garnered for being a man of courage and action, "I'm thinking this night wasn't I a foolish fellow not to kill my father in the years gone by."

The people of the village in Mayo see him as a man of poetic temper and dangerous rage, and he begins to see himself through their eyes, begins to imagine himself into a new identity. The Widow Quin tells him, "Don't be letting on to be shy, a fine, gamey, treacherous lad the like of you" and I heard my mother's voice in our Bronx apartment, "No false modesty now, son, be a daring fellow." It becomes clear to Christy that, as the Widow Quin says, "It's true all girls are fond of courage...." And the way to become the champion Playboy of the Western World was to demonstrate that intrepid spirit, so Christy kills his father a second time and toward the conclusion of Act III, tells the townsfolk, "I'm thinking Satan hasn't had many have killed their da in Kerry, and in Mayo too." And in his final confrontation with his father, he asks him, "Are you coming to be killed a third time, or what ails you now?"

What I realized in reading *The Playboy of the Western World* the first time was that it was not only action that made Christy the hero of the western world, but words, the story he invented for himself and came to live by that transformed him. The townsfolk made him a hero by believing in his story, and Christy, in the course of believing in himself, becomes a poet, finding a newfound power in language. "It's little I'm understanding myself," he says to Pegeen Mike, "saving only that my heart's scalded this day, and I'm going off stretching out the earth between us, the way I'll not be waking near you another dawn of the year till the two of us do arise to hope or judgment with the saints of God, and now I'd best be going with my wattle in my hand, for hanging is a poor thing ... and it's little welcome is left to me in this house to-day." Christy goes from being a dullard to a man whose grief and love for Pegeen Mike rises to the lyrical—"Aren't I after seeing the love-light of the star of knowledge shining from her brow, and hearing words would put you thinking on the holy Brigid speaking to the infant saints...." Christy's transformation from weakling to warrior, his change from slapstick Oedipus to, as some critics have suggested, Christ-figure, Cuchulainn, or Charles Stewart Parnell, comes seamlessly and with an apparent effortlessness that surely wasn't granted Synge as he revised the play over seven years and nearly a dozen drafts.

Christy understands his own power and its source when he says, "If I'm an idiot, I'm after hearing my voice this day saying words would raise the topknot on a poet in a merchant's town...." If words could make Christy the heroic playboy of the western world in Mayo, back in the Bronx I wondered why the right words couldn't transform me as an eighteen-year-old college student who was spending the summer in the Hamptons as a day laborer into the hero of my own life.

Synge's other plays had some of the same humor, if not of the hyperbolic variety of *The Playboy of the Western World*. But some of his dramas offer little more than a glimpse into the unavoidability of tragedy that Synge suggests is the fact of life every human being must face. In one act, *Riders to the Sea* portrays the life of hardship and sorrow that was the Aran Islanders' lot. Death is omnipresent. The sea, which sustains life for the islanders, takes it away as well, as if Synge is asserting that we are all, ultimately, riders to the sea. The islanders are encircled by a treacherous and deadly nature. Maurya, an island woman, loses six men and both of her sons to the sea, and the play ends with her speaking

Stone landscape, Aran Islands.

resignedly to her younger daughter, "May the Almighty God have mercy on Bartley's soul, and on Michael's soul ... and may he have mercy on my soul, Nora, and on the soul of every one is left living in the world."

In *Riders to the Sea* and his final play, produced posthumously, *Deidre of the* Sorrows, where he uses the myth of Deidre and Naisi to dramatize the certainty of time defeating happiness, Synge focuses on the inevitability of tragedy as if he sensed his own imminent and untimely death. In these plays, Synge appears to be chronicling the story of rural Ireland but writing his personal story, as well, working out his own fears, facing the death that closed in on him as surely as it did for Maurya's sons.

Plays like *The Tinker's Wedding* (never performed in Synge's lifetime probably because of the congenial picture of common law marriage and the sordid portrait of the Catholic Church) and *The Well of the Saints* blend the appalling and the ludicrous, leaving the conflicts vibrating between the two extremes. In his preface to *The Tinker's Wedding*, Synge said, "The drama, like the symphony, does not teach or prove anything." Laughter was the key for Synge to an accurate picture of life. In the preface to *The Tinker's Wedding*, he went on to say, "In the greater part of Ireland ... the whole people, from tinkers to clergy, have a life,

Chapter 5. J.M. Synge and the Aran Islands

and view of life, that are rich and genial and humorous. I do not think that these country people, who have so much humour themselves, will mind being laughed at without malice, as people in every country have been laughed at in their own comedies." So, the old couple who are better off blind in *The Well of the Saints* or the venal priest, a "holy man" that could have been imagined by Chaucer, and the bargaining couple in *The Tinker's Wedding* have, as one character says late in *The Tinker's Wedding*, "chosen their lot, and the Lord have mercy on their souls." And, although these plays never achieve the perfect balance of realism and comedy that Synge accomplishes in *The Playboy of the Western World*, the last work Synge completed in its entirety, they have a kinship with his masterpiece. Nora in *In the Shadow of the Glen,* based upon a story Pat Dirane told Synge and he recorded in *The Aran Islands*, is an older version of Pegeen Mike, living an unfulfilled life and trapped in a loveless marriage. Her life is what Pegeen Mike's would have been if she had married Shawn Keogh, shackled to all that is safe and banal, living daily in the shadow of death. The tramp, Patch Darcy, who leads Nora out onto the road, foreshadows Christy Mahon and his wildness. The future life on the road for Patch and Nora may not be easy, but it will not be predictable and suffocating, not the small, constricted life that Pegeen is left with when she fears at the end of the play that she has lost the only Playboy of the Western World she will ever encounter.

* * *

Synge's own life came with a set of merciless ironies. At twenty-seven years old, after giving up on a career in music and the idea of living in France as a critic, he went to the Aran Islands, according to legend, at the encouragement of Yeats who told him, "Give up Paris. You will never create anything by reading Racine and Arthur Symons will always be a better critic of French literature. Go to the Aran Islands. Live there as if you were one of the people themselves; express a life that has never found expression." Whether this legend is pure fact or simply Yeats's desire to rework history into myth, there surely is some truth in the story. Yeats was The Poet when Synge encountered him on the continent, and they had much in common. Synge, like Yeats, was part of the conservative upper middle class Protestant Ascendancy. He was influenced by Yeats, but Synge was his own man, an artist like Joyce who strode beyond influencers. On his three visits to the Aran Islands before he was thirty, Synge found the locus of his imagination, principally on Inishmaan, much as Joyce did in Dublin, Yeats in Sligo, or O'Connor in Cork.

The Aran Islands are a lonely and desolate place, and they must have seemed to Synge at the beginning of the twentieth century even more desolate and lonely than they did to me at the start of the twenty-first. On his first visit to the Aran Islands when he was twenty-seven years old, Synge was already fighting Hodgkin's disease, the form of cancer that would kill him a decade later. I read his book *The Aran Islands* as I waited for the ferry in Rossaveal to take me to Inishmaan for my first visit in 2012. When I stepped off the swaying boat onto the island as if I were stepping out of a time machine, I caught a glimpse of a gaggle of schoolgirls who reminded me of a Joycean sentence from *Ulysses* until I remembered the sentence I was recalling was actually from the Synge book I had read while waiting to cross the bay: "Their red bodices and white tapering legs made them as beautiful as tropical sea birds." The island I explored in the following days was a picture of the hard life, the innocent life, that Synge described in *The Aran Islands*, the desolation, the simple joy, the rain-swept beauty, the keening and music of the howling wind, the raging sea that crashes against the rocks.

The future playwright was born into the Protestant Ascendancy as Edmund John Millington Synge on April 16, 1871, in a suburb of South Dublin. Ah, another odd coincidence similar to the Joycean Alfred Hunter-Leopold Bloom connection, I thought. My grandfather was christened Edmund before he shifted to Alfred, and he was born on the same date as Synge, April 16, five years after the playwright's birth. And to a degree, they were both orphans. Synge's father died of smallpox before John's first birthday. The Synge family were zealous Christians and Protestant landlords, and Synge's older bothers didn't stray from that history, one becoming a proselytizing foreign missionary and the other a land agent in Cavan and Mayo who engaged in a campaign of evictions. John Millington Synge grew up to be a wanderer and an artist who had little sympathy for organized religion or the status quo. He had more in common, he felt, with the tramps of Wicklow or the peasant folk of Inishmaan than he did with land agents or ministers of the Protestant Church.

When he was fourteen, he read Darwin and the seeds of doubt were planted. By the time he was sixteen, as he remembered it, he "renounced Christianity after a good deal of wobbling." He started to look for God in places other than church—in music and art and nature. Eventually, he chose country over God, the Irish language over the Protestant liturgy, the tramp over the landowner, the life of a dramatist over the life of a musician. His first love was the violin, and he hoped to make a career as a musician. After graduating from Trinity, his study of music in Germany taught him he would never achieve the success he sought as a violinist. After his frustrated aspirations as a musician, his time in Paris convinced him that he was not meant to be a critic. Maybe his meeting with Yeats in 1896 helped make him a writer and sent him on the road back to Ireland and toward the Aran Islands to find his true subject matter.

Along with W.B. Yeats and Lady Gregory, he became one of the famous triumvirate of the Irish National Theater. With them, he created the Abbey and its history. Beyond them, he became the great playwright of that theater, eclipsing even the future Nobel laureate in his plays about the myths and manners of Ireland. He started in the shadow of both Lady Gregory and Yeats, but he was always his own man. The first plays of his produced by the Abbey—*In the Shadow of the Glen* and *Riders to the Sea*—made his reputation, but *The Playboy of the Western World* made him famous and infamous. Lady Gregory had her doubts and certain reservations about *Playboy* even though she recognized its brilliance, but Yeats saw it immediately as a masterpiece. In 1907, when it was first produced at the Abbey in Dublin many of the critics and the audience had a different view. On opening night, January 26, 1907, Lady Gregory initially thought they had a great triumph on their hands. She sent a message to Yeats declaring their success, but by the third act, when the audience exploded (with some premeditation, it seems) with boos and catcalls, along with rotten fruit and stink bombs, at the use of the word *shift* in the play, Lady Gregory had to send a revised telegraph to Yeats who was lecturing in Scotland. The perception from the Irish Nationalists and strict Catholics was that the play insulted the culture and institutions they held dear. Arthur Griffin, the Sinn Fein leader, termed it a vile story. The *Freeman's* Journal called the play a "libel upon Irish peasant men and, worse still, upon Irish peasant girlhood." Patrick Pearse, less than a decade from his rush to martyrdom in the 1916 Easter Rising, called *The Playboy* a blasphemy against the people of Ireland. Pearse wanted a sober Cuchulainn on the Irish stage, not a comic anti-hero like Christy Mahon. The Nationalists wanted the stage Irish stereotype erased but they wanted it to be replaced by a heroic cliché. Like Pearse, they wanted a paradigm, not a patricide. For the duration of its run at the Abbey, audiences hissed and yelled over the actors' lines, they catcalled and howled *kill the author*, the only exception in the week-long outburst coming when Theodore Roosevelt showed up as a guest of Lady Gregory and was visibly enjoying the play. Roosevelt's approbation kept the critics momentarily from raising their voices against the play. But once Roosevelt exited, the reaction in Dublin and Ireland went back from silence to vitriol.

The play didn't fare any better with audiences when it traveled abroad a few years later to the United States and was put on in the

Maxine Elliott Theater in New York City. Irish Americans didn't appreciate what they felt were satirical representations of Irish murderers lauded as heroes, Irish peasants as spineless fools, and Irish women as loose and manipulative. So, they followed the pattern established by the Abbey theatergoers and pelted the actors with potatoes and rosary beads, along with the predictable stink bombs. They didn't take kindly to Catholic priests being mocked or their sainted women shown to have human desires. They couldn't accept Pegeen Mike's bemoaning her loss of the only playboy of the western world any more than they could tolerate a few years earlier Nora walking away from her husband in *The Shadow of the Glen* to traipse the hillsides of Wicklow with a tramp.

Molly Allgood, under the stage name of Maire O'Neill, played Pegeen Mike in that first staging of *The Playboy of the Western World*. Synge was sick with the flu and unable to attend the performance or to see his love Molly play the lead role. He had met Molly when she auditioned two years before for a small part in *The Well of the Saints*. She was not quite eighteen, and he was about to turn thirty-four. By the time *Playboy* was produced, they were lovers and, even though they were separated by education and religion and upbringing, they planned to wed in the near future. Like Deidre and Naisi, though, Molly and Synge's story was destined to be sorrowful. They would never have the chance to marry. The cancer that had haunted his life for years would take it when he was thirty-eight. What disease and time couldn't take—what Synge left the world—were a few masterful plays and a timeless nonfiction book about an island that seemed to stand outside of time.

A Separate World—Inishmaan

"There is no language like Irish for soothing and quieting."
—J.M. Synge, *The Aran Islands*

In *Irish Miles*, Frank O'Connor said, "In Ireland you never know what you are letting yourself in when once you ask the way." When I landed for my first visit to Inishmaan with a dozen students in 2012, I soon understood what O'Connor was suggesting. I asked a man the way to Padraig Flaherty's home, the house where we'd all be staying.

"Go up the road until you see Mullen's place on your right. Follow the path to the left until you see Faherty's donkey. The pub is a bit of a ways beyond, and Padraig's house is on the rise there." We walked past overturned curraghs and alongside walled fields of potatoes, past thatch roofs and the curling smoke of turf fires. The air smelled like the incense I remembered from Catholic mass. We sidestepped puddles on

Chapter 5. J.M. Synge and the Aran Islands

Steps, Coole Park.

the stony path, the drizzle changing to a powerful downpour, the raindrops churning down as thick and heavy as hailstones. We had left our suitcases in Galway—so we took our raingear out of our backpacks and marched on looking for a pub or a donkey. The intricate and seemingly endless stone walls on the island could have been invented by the mythological namesake of Joyce's hero Stephen Dedalus, and I suspected, like the original Dedalus, we would have trouble finding our way out of the maze we had entered. We trudged along as the rains came down, making it easy enough for some of us to imagine the island being washed away inch by inch over time until one day it would disappear like a reef beneath the torrent of the indifferent ocean. I imagined the sea spray wearing the limestone cliffs away, columns of salty foam blasting against the rock face second after second, minute after minute, day after day. And then I imagined hungry men climbing the cliffs to reach cormorants and puffins gathered along the ledges. I had read that in centuries past such men were called *Cliffhangers*, engaged in a treacherous business, taking birds from their roosts, snapping their necks like tree branches and stringing a line of them on a rope for an evening meal. I envisioned young men like Alfred Hunter drawn to the far horizon, a view free of all clutter but the rollicking waves. The horizon might have humbled a man like him, made him admit how limited his gaze was compared to the white-capped immensity, or the endless horizon might have made the whole world seem possible and improbable at the same

Cliffs, Aran Islands.

time. It might have made him hopeful or despairing, but it surely would have made a man like him dream of elsewhere.

    I peered down the curving roads that spider-webbed the island, roads barely wide enough for two people to pass each other without rubbing shoulders. I remembered Robert Flaherty's stylized documentary *Man of Aran*, the bursts of red against the graying sky, the women in their dresses, flashing like bolts of red lightning in the dusk. Like Masai warriors on a rocky moonscape. Flaherty's women of Inishmaan had shawls dark as wet limestone draped over their heads. They walked along the shore path, the rocks behind them jutting out, ragged teeth in the mad foaming mouth of the sea. The women carried basket loads of kelp to cover the potato crop or to layer with sand on the rocks to make soil where there was none. Basking sharks, more than twenty feet long, with their backs and tail fins slicing through the water a few yards from the women, made their red dresses appear ominous, hinting at a bloody danger that encircled the whole island.

    "Professor Pearson, there's a man waving to us," one of my students shouted, waking me from my walking reverie.

    It was Padraig, a man in his early sixties with a dark shock of wind-blown hair and a timid smile, and we had found our place, even though I never saw a donkey, a Mullen, or a Faherty along the way. On my first night on the island, I sat against a cold stone wall near Padraig's house and gazed at the now clear sky. I counted seven shooting trails blaze brightly and briefly across the star-cluttered sky. Their fiery particles burned more fiercely than the dim lights shining from the outskirts of Galway to the east. The island seemed to demand that I watch the sky, and not allow my concentration to slip even for an instant, as if I'd miss something important in the thrumming silence and blackness if I turned my eyes away for even an instant.

The island made me feel like a *strainseir*, a non-islander, a word that the people of Inishmaan used to describe a stranger, a word that suggested curiosity rather than foreignness. I liked being a stranger in a strange land, a traveler, an observer by more than inclination, by necessity. The only meaning the landscape had, it seemed to me, was the one I could conjure with my own eyes. When I strolled along the hilltop in the fog, I could see the vague outlines of the intersecting stone walls, and when the fog was too thick to see anything more than a few feet in front of me, I heard the clank of stone on stone as some island man repaired what animals or weather had tampered with. In the distance, I heard the bray of a donkey, a wheezing hew haw that came slicing through the mist.

Maire, Padraig's wife, gave us all a lesson in Irish the morning before we caught the ferry to Galway and then a bus back to the Dublin Airport. A dozen of us sat around her dining room table, the rain hammering against the roof as we repeated the words she taught us. It reminded me of a foreign language class in St. Philip Neri when I was in seventh grade. I was a child again, repeating phrases I barely understood but enjoying the mysterious music of the chorus of voices and the repetitions. It was like a ritual in Catholic Mass, and the chanting lifted the language into ritual.

After the lesson, I told her that I was searching for the story of my maternal grandfather, the elusive Alfred Hunter, and she smiled sweetly and told me, "That's an honorable quest you're on. I wish you well." In terms of specific vocabulary, not much of her ninety-minute lesson in Gaelic has stayed with me, but one phrase she gave me stuck. *An bothar maith. The good road.* That's the road she told me I was on.

Chapter 6

Frank O'Connor and Cork

> "'And what's a-trouble to you, Jackie?' 'Father,' I said, feeling I might as well get it over with while I had him in good humour, 'I had it all arranged to kill my grandmother.' He seemed a bit shaken by that, all right, because he said nothing for a while. 'My goodness,' he said at last, 'that would be a shocking thing to do. What put that into your head?' 'Father,' I said, feeling sorry for myself, 'she's an awful woman.'"
> —Frank O'Connor, "First Confession"

I first fell in love with the short stories of Frank O'Connor when I was a freshman at Fordham University in the Bronx. It was a frigid winter day, and I sat alone at a table in the library, trying to stay warm before my theology class started in a few hours. At eighteen years old, I was far more interested in reading Ken Kesey's *One Flew Over the Cuckoo's Nest*, the *Autobiography of Malcolm X*, Robert Heinlein's *Stranger in a Strange Land*, or Joan Didion's *Slouching Toward Bethlehem* than I was in pondering any Jesuitical syllogisms from my theology class that attempted to demonstrate with algebraic logic that God existed. My drift away from the strictures of the Catholic Church and its ceremonies—from Mass and Communion and Confession—had started a few months before, and that may be why my curiosity was piqued by the title of the story I found by O'Connor—"First Confession." It was not that long ago that I had done my last Confession, and I had no plans to return to do another. Every Catholic boy or girl remembers at six or seven years old the anxiety inducing moment of first Confession. First Confession for most seven-year-olds was a moment of fear that your sins would either not match up to the austerity of the moment or that they would damn you to immediate and everlasting fire and brimstone. O'Connor's story led me back to that moment more than a decade earlier in my life and allowed me to see what a future beyond the Catholic Church might look like.

Chapter 6. Frank O'Connor and Cork

After reading a sentence or two of "First Confession," I knew that O'Connor was the kind of writer I wanted to be. His story was all about voice, and finding a voice, a concept as puzzling to me then as encountering love or defining sin. And finding my true voice was as much of a goal for me as mapping my eventual escape route out of the Bronx. When I read later what the novelist Julian Barnes had to say about O'Connor's work, I flashed back in recognition to my initial encounter with O'Connor's writing. Barnes said, "O'Connor wanted to keep alive in prose, and especially in the short story, what he believed to be at its heart: the sound of 'an actual man, talking.'" Finding my voice, I felt convinced, would lead me away from the Bronx and all it implied, and it would lead me toward all I was seeking—the adventurous future that books promised. In O'Connor's story, I heard my own voice and the sort of voices I needed to pay attention to in order to become the kind of writer I wanted to be. Later in college, I took a job as a taxi driver, not thinking so much about the money I could make shuttling people around Manhattan but rather imagining I was placing myself in the proximity of voices and stories.

For O'Connor, I discovered years later, Chekhov was the prose master and Mozart the musical one, each leading him to the place I wanted my own stories to fall, between comedy and tragedy. "It's a way of seeing things," O'Connor said, "which revokes the tragic attitude without turning into comedy, which says not 'Life is beautiful but so sad' but 'Life is so sad but beautiful,' and this way of seeing things, half way between tragedy and comedy, represents a human norm." Every book I read—from Kafka to Tolstoy—and every job I had during college—from working in the post office to driving a yellow city cab (quite unsuccessfully, by the way, as I was far more a dreamer than a driver)—were for the education of my imagination, an attempt to detect that norm O'Connor mentioned. What I sought in those books and those after school and summer jobs was what Frank O'Connor offered me in "First Confession"—the sound of real people talking, the sound of stories being made.

"First Confession" tells the story of Jackie, a seven-year-old boy who feels, in order to be ready for first Holy Communion, he must tell the priest that he had thoughts about killing his paternal grandmother who has come to live with his family after her husband died. She's an "awful woman," he confesses to the priest. He dreams of getting rid of her, and when the priest asks how he planned to achieve that goal and get rid of the body, Jackie says, "I was thinking I could chop that up and carry it away in a barrow I have." She walks around the house barefoot, eats with her fingers, and gives Jackie's unctuous older sister a penny every Friday. It's too much for the boy to bear.

Of course, this is not a story about a serial killer in the making but a satiric fairy tale about an innocent little boy with a cantankerous grandmother and a jealous and bullying older sister. The story's comic brilliance comes from its being told from the boy's innocent point of view. O'Connor sets up the story so that the reader understands more than the boy does, and that understanding makes the reader sympathize with him at every turn. The priest very quickly grasps the boy's plight after encountering Nora, Jackie's harridan of a sister, and he seems to enjoy every minute of Jackie's First Confession as much as the reader does. Early on, the priest alleviates Jackie's fear that his Sunday school teacher might be right, and he is surely headed for a burning afterlife. Poor Jackie is a victim of a true believer in his teacher, Mrs. Ryan, who, in his words, "talked to us of Hell. She may have mentioned the other place as well, but that could only have been by accident, for Hell had the first place in her heart." Anyone who ever attended a Catholic elementary or high school has encountered one or two Mrs. Ryans along the way.

In a superb bit of slapstick, O'Connor has Jackie, not knowing where to kneel, climb on the armrest of the confessional and then fall out of the booth entirely. Nora slaps him for his misdemeanor and the priest, coming out of the confessional box, hisses at her, "How dare you hit the child like that, you little vixen?" From then on, the priest is on Jackie's side—"Was it coming to Confession you were, my poor man?" he asks him, and the friendship begins. He soothes Jackie's fears by understanding that it's a big burden a boy must carry for his First Confession, and he tells him to wait until the older parishioners have done. Jackie, relieved, thinks, "It only stood to reason that a fellow confessing after seven years would have more to tell than people that went every week. The crimes of a lifetime, exactly as he said."

So, Jackie confesses all—his murderous thoughts about his grandmother, his fending off his sister with a butter knife, and his jealousy of his sister's endowment of a penny each Friday. In an absolution and statement of empathy that the reader understands but that passes far over Jackie's head, the priest says, "'Someone will go for her with a bread-knife one day, and he won't miss her,' he said rather cryptically. 'You must have great courage. Between ourselves, there's a lot of people I'd like to do the same to but I'd never have the nerve. Hanging is an awful death.'" Once he does his duty and warns Jackie of the dangers of butter knives and bad thoughts, the priest takes the unprecedented step of walking him out of the church like an old friend and sending him off with three Hail Marys to say and a sweet to suck on as he strides home with his covetous sister at his side crying out, "'Tis no advantage to

Chapter 6. Frank O'Connor and Cork

anybody to be good. I might just as well be a sinner like you." I remember finishing "First Confession" in the silence of the library, laughing aloud, and thinking to myself, *In its small way, this story is as perfect as Joyce's "The Dead."*

I wasn't surprised to learn many years later when I read O'Connor's narrative about his own life that the story had as much autobiography as fiction to it: "I got my first job through my confessor, a gentle old priest who regarded me as a very saintly boy, and regularly asked me to pray for his intentions. If innocence and sanctity are related, he was probably not so far wrong about me because I once confessed to 'bad thoughts,' meaning, I suppose, murdering my grandmother, but Father O'Regan interpreted it differently, and there ensued an agonizing few minutes in which he asked me questions I didn't understand, and I gave him answers that he didn't understand, and I suspect that when I left the confession box, the poor man was as shaken as I was." When I read "First Confession" for the first time in the Fordham University Library, I knew that boy because I had been him, playing priest in my bedroom at six years old, imagining myself given to a life of service to God as I intoned *Dominus Vobiscum* to my adoring, invisible parishioners and the loving response would come, *et cum spiritu tuo*. But I knew in my heart when I examined my conscience that I was chock full of bad intentions and most of the deadly sins, and I eventually made my way through most of the seven in due course over the years. As a teenager, I found football and basketball and girls, and by then the priesthood became as uninviting as taking a job as a butcher or bank clerk. Like Frank O'Connor, I was determined to transform myself from a book-obsessed dreamer into a writer.

* * *

Michael O'Donovan, who became famous under his penname Frank O'Connor, was born in Cork on September 17, 1903, slightly more than a year before Joyce ran from Ireland with Nora Barnacle. And even though O'Connor eventually escaped from the claustrophobic atmosphere of Cork, a city he declared that threatened to suffocate him, he could no more leave his native city imaginatively behind him than Joyce could forget Dublin. In his posthumously published memoir *My Father's* Son, in writing about his native city, O'Connor said, "Nothing could cure me of the notion that Cork needed me and that I needed Cork. Nothing but death can, I fear, ever cure me of it."

Michael O'Donovan was twenty-one years old when George Russell, known in the writing world under the pseudonym AE, published a verse translation by Frank O'Connor in *The Irish Statesman*. With this

Sheep near Cork.

new identity, Michael O'Donovan blended his middle name, Francis, and his mother's maiden name, O'Connor, to launch his writing career and, perhaps, to separate himself from his father. Michael O'Donovan, the shy momma's boy, the former Irish rebel, a man with little formal education who had schooled himself and become an erudite librarian, had already begun the process of shaping himself into a writer. Taking the name Frank O'Connor was, for him, a declaration of independence, akin to Sam Clemens finding *safe* water and renaming himself Mark Twain. Like Clemens/Twain, the twin personalities of Michael and Frank co-existed for the rest of his life. But, ultimately, the writer dominated every aspect of his experience, and if there was a struggle between the two realities, Frank O'Connor is the identity that survived.

The locus of O'Connor's imagination was always Cork, a river city in the southwest of the country, and next to Dublin the second largest in the Republic of Ireland. His mother, Mary O'Connor, whom he idolized, was raised in an orphanage. The diminutive and demure Mary O'Connor, whom everyone called Minnie, worked as a domestic until she married Michael O'Donovan, a handsome and volatile former Royal Munster Fusilier who had fought in the Boer War. According to her son, she was a fastidious woman, "fiercely undemonstrative in grief or pain," who married, by her son's estimate, the wrong man. Frank O'Connor's story of growing up in the squalid confines of a rental property near Blarney Lane in Cork, in a cabin with a kitchen, a bedroom, and a loft for which his parents paid sixty cents a week, is a narrative that fits seamlessly into the archetypal Irish tale of the nineteenth and early twentieth centuries—a life bounded by the slums, a drunken and often violent father tyrannizing the household, a sainted, quietly suffering mother working as a charwoman to keep them all from starving during her husband's predictable binges, and a young man yearning to escape the claustrophobic culture through writing about it.

The young Michael O'Donovan feared and disliked his father. He explained in *An Only Child*: "I hated every member of my father's family—even cousins I later grew fond of. It was not the people themselves I hated, of course, but drunkenness, dirt, and violence." He tried to distance himself from his father, always calling him "he" or "him" and never "father," hoping, perhaps, to stand safely apart from the man who would brandish a razor at his mother and threaten to "put an end to this!"

Frank O'Connor, nee Michael O'Donovan, as an only child was an anomaly in Irish Catholic society in that century, even if his description of himself as "the classic example of the Mother's Boy" seems to fit the pattern followed by other Irish mothers and sons. His mother doted on him and, when she could, protected him from the scalding treatment of his father. He loved her with a devotion that bordered on the religious as he makes clear in the conclusion of his memoir *An Only Child*: "From the time I was a boy and could think at all, I was certain that for my own soul there was only nothingness.... But I knew that there were souls that were immortal, and that even God if He wished to, could not diminish or destroy, and perhaps it was the thought of these that turned me finally from poetry to storytelling, to the celebration of those who for me represented all I should ever know of God. My mother was merely one among them, though, in my human weakness I valued her most...."

Michael O'Donovan ended his formal education at twelve years old when the teachers at the Monastery of Our Lady's Mount, a school run by the Christian Brothers in Cork, determined he was a dreamer and not a scholar, not a "passer of examinations" and better suited to a trade school. They were wrong, of course, about his genius, but they were right, too: he was a dreamer. Frank O'Connor lurked in the spirit of Michael O'Donovan, waiting to emerge, eager to rail against hypocrisy and lies in every aspect of Irish society. Shortly after he left school, his true self-education began. His father re-enlisted in the army and was gone for two years, and as James Matthews says in *Voices: A Life of Frank O'Connor*, "[O'Connor] burrowed deeper into his own private world; he had given up school but not education." He taught himself foreign languages, became fluent in Gaelic, and memorized passages of texts because he couldn't afford to buy books. He had always been something of an outcast, a bookworm among boys who didn't value reading, a boy who brooded on injustice in a world that valued strength over compassion, a bespectacled dreamer fond of heights for whom "reading was only another form of height, and a more perilous one ... a way of looking beyond your own back yard into the neighbors.'" So, he developed a lifelong habit of finding a perch from which he could watch and listen. For him, there was no alternative to becoming an autodidact because, as he explained in his typical self-deprecatory manner in *An Only Child*, "I adored education from afar, and strove to be worthy of it, as later I adored beautiful girls and strove to be worthy of them, and with similar results." At twelve years old, then, boys' weeklies became his principal form of education, and Michael O'Donovan began to disappear and, through reading, Frank O'Connor began to emerge.

If his equivalent of university experience was the Free Library near Cork City Hall and his inveterate reading in his dimly lit attic, then his post-graduate training was the 1916 Easter Rising and the Irish Civil War that followed in its wake. He fought in his own manner. As he characterized it, he performed "odd jobs" for the IRA and then joined the Republican cause against those who stood for an Irish Free State that allowed for a separate Northern Ireland. He served as a writer and courier for the Republican rebels in the Civil War, and he was captured and imprisoned by Free State forces in early 1923. His internment, which began shortly after his eighteenth birthday, lasted for nearly a year, and became for him what a whaling ship had been for Melville, an inspiration for the stories that would launch his career. His year in prison was, in O'Connor's words, "the nearest thing I could have found to life on a college campus." And, as with many college students who find their years in university altering their old view of the world, O'Connor's internment amounted to the beginning of his perspective shifting from romance to realism, the beginning, he said, of his "grave doubts about many of the political ideas I had held as gospel." He found himself "sick to death of the worship of martyrdom." The boy who had idolized Pearse and Connolly and the martyrs of the 1916 Rising now saw them with a gimlet eye. "Apparently the only proof one had of being alive," O'Connor said of this part of Irish history, "was one's readiness to die as soon as possible: dead was the great thing to be, and there was nothing to be said in favour of living except the innumerable possibilities it presented of dying in style. I didn't want to die. I wanted to live, to read, to hear music, and to bring my mother to all the places that neither of us had ever seen, and I felt that these things were more important than any martyrdom."

While held captive by Free State forces, he taught classes in the

Irish language, a skill he had mastered under the tutelage of his teacher and first mentor Daniel Corkery. His knowledge of the Irish language was another talent that made him an oddity in his own country. As he said in remembering these times, "It was characteristic of Ireland at the time that the mere fact that you spoke Irish could make you be regarded as a freak ... an indication of the extraordinary double life I was leading, a life so divided against itself that it comes back to me now as a hallucination rather than as a memory." In prison, as James Matthews explains, O'Connor "lost his faith in the politics of violence." He had already lost his faith in organized religion and the parochial conservatism of the Irish government. O'Connor often quoted Yeats's remark that no Irish writer was worth his salt until he has lost his faith. What remained for O'Connor were the voices he heard all around him and the stories he felt compelled to write. He was beginning, as he said, "to get a picture of Ireland, the real Ireland, lonely and dotty." And he was determined to draw that picture with a calculated realism.

After the Civil War ended and upon his release from imprisonment, with the help of Daniel Corkery, O'Connor took a job as an apprentice librarian. After two years, he found a permanent position as a head librarian. For a self-educated, book-obsessed young man from the slums, this was like winning the lottery, presenting him with a job that paid good money and gave him access to all the books he could read. When he was twenty-five, he moved to Dublin and held the position of chief librarian at the Pembroke District Library for a decade. The year before he had moved to Dublin, he had published the poetry translation in the *Irish Statesman* under his pen name. In 1928, at age twenty-five, he crossed into a new world. As James Matthews explains it, "Michael O'Donovan came to Dublin as Frank O'Connor, to conquer it, to save Irish literature; he succeeded to the extent that he became, within a few years, notorious in Dublin as the slightly abrasive conscience of Irish literature." Over the next four decades, neither his candor nor his courage ever faltered.

From early on, as the young writer masquerading as a librarian, he wrote stories as if his life depended on it, and as Matthews says, "already the marks of the typical O'Connor story had begun to emerge: simple and colloquial diction, brisk dialogue, and a layering of tragic and comic emotions." Two years after he arrived in Dublin, he received a telegram from the *Atlantic Monthly* accepting his story "Guests of the Nation," and Frank O'Connor, the writer, was on his way. During his time in Dublin, AE continued to be a father figure for him, albeit of the New Testament variety, but William Butler Yeats took on the role of the Old Testament father, a bit more distant and feared but no less adored.

As Matthews interprets it, "Of his three literary fathers, Corkery A E, and Yeats, it was Yeats who made the most lasting personal impression on Michael/Frank.... Yeats and O'Connor quarreled endlessly because they were too much alike. O'Connor spent his entire life fighting one Irish dragon after another, vacillating, as Yeats had, between idealized image and real fact; but unlike Yeats, who strove to bring life into a unified whole, O'Connor grasped life in bits and pieces."

O'Connor's insights found their way into the variegated portrait of Irish life he put into his many short stories. He wrote two novels, but his genius and his legacy rests in his short stories. In this, Frank O'Connor intersects with his younger colleague with the same surname in America, Flannery O'Connor, both born, it seems, to see the world in brilliant miniatures. Like her, Frank O'Connor may have perceived that, in James Matthews terms, "things that look monstrous when seen too close appear quite normal when viewed from afar."

On April 1, 1938, because of health concerns and in order to devote himself to his writing and administrative work at the Abbey Theater, Frank O'Connor retired from the Irish Library Service. Like his father, always watchful of his money and a man he "had more in common with than I liked to admit," Frank O'Connor retired with an annual pension of seventy-five pounds and a determination to support himself as a writer, following Yeats's advice that he should "write as if he were shouting to a person across the street." Not dissimilar to the advice Flannery O'Connor offered herself—"To the hard of hearing you shout, and for the almost blind you draw large and startling figures." In his stories, Frank O'Connor also offered a tragicomic view of life, if not the same explosive variety as Flannery, and he always wrote with a clarity and passion that Yeats's advice implied. For a number of years, he also gave himself to the cause of shaping the direction of the Abbey Theater, becoming, after John Millington Synge, Lady Gregory, and William Butler Yeats, one of the great driving forces in that cultural phenomenon. Eventually, as he had quit the library service to preserve his life as a writer, he stepped down from his duties at the Abbey Theater. In the last sentence of *My Father's Son*, he describes the moment, "At once I resigned from every organization I belonged to and sat down, at last, to write."

In 1943, his first *New Yorker* story—"News of the Church"—was published, the first of dozens to appear in the magazine over the next quarter of a century. As O'Connor's writing career began to explode, his personal life started to implode. After a long romance with a Cork woman that ended unhappily for O'Connor, he had an affair and lived with Evelyn Bowen, a Welsh actress married to the British actor and

Chapter 6. Frank O'Connor and Cork

View from the window of Frank O'Connor's boyhood home.

drama critic Robert Speaight. It was the sort of scandal that put O'Connor beyond the pale for many in his home country. After he married Evelyn and had two children with her, he began a relationship in England with another woman, Joan Knape. When Joan announced that she was pregnant, O'Connor, caught between England and Ireland, between mistress and wife, opted, as he usually did, to be candid. He told Evelyn about Joan's pregnancy, and in a spirit of goodwill that beggars understanding, Evelyn invited Joan to live with them in Ireland. Baby in tow, Joan came to stay in Dublin with O'Connor, Evelyn and their two children, and Franks' mother, Minnie, making for a ménage that conservative Ireland could never sanction.

Within a few years, O'Connor divorced Evelyn, now with three children by him, and separated from Joan and their son, Oliver, and married Harriet Rich, a young American woman twenty years his junior whom he met while lecturing at Harvard. With Harriet, he had a daughter, Hallie Og, and lived in the United States and Ireland for the next decade and a half, finding a way to step aside from his father's example as a distant, violent father and volatile husband. As one of O'Connor's associates said, "Michael is the architect of Frank's chaos." Surely, with his penchant for honesty, O'Connor saw that this was true, and he struggled in his last decade to join the writer and the man, making sense of the contradictions he saw in himself. And, as James Matthews makes clear, there was a world of oppositions in him—"He was arrogant and self-conscious, poised and nervous, tentative and dogmatic, friendly and spiteful. He fought against censorship and pietistic restrictions his entire life and yet held very conventional views on manners and morality." As he himself said of O'Casey, "His weaknesses as a writer were his strengths as a person, and vice versa.... He had no religion, but he possessed great faith, the moralist's faith, the savagely indignant faith of Swift."

On March 10, 1966, Michael O'Donovan died in the country he both loved and loathed. Although he lived much of his life in England and America, he was an Irish writer to his marrow. As Julian Barnes said of O'Connor, "To write about Ireland ... meant to write about the longing for departure, the pain or pleasure of absence, and the mixed blessings of return." O'Connor wrote about his native country because he knew "to a syllable how everything in Ireland can be said." His stories may have been inspired by events that happened in America, or they may have been tales with English backgrounds. People told him stories and he listened, just waiting for the right moment to transform them into narrative art. Whatever the source or the catalyst for his tales, he put all of his stories into an Irish idiom and onto an Irish landscape. The writing of Frank O'Connor, the many voices in his stories, as he suspected they would all along, have survived.

* * *

In college, in the weeks after my initial encounter with "First Confession," I gave short shrift to my school assignments as I immersed myself in O'Connor's stories. "My Oedipus Complex" struck me as a tale that could have been spoken by the narrator of "First Confession," maybe a prequel to it, recited by the same boy a few years before his First Communion. "My Oedipus Complex" is another autobiographical fiction that employs the delicately balanced point of view of a young child's perceptions but an adult's idiom, a double consciousness that aligns candor and comedy in the rhythm of each sentence. As happened with O'Connor's father, in "My Oedipus Complex," the narrator has returned from the war and intruded on his peaceful life with his mother. Initially, like a character in a fractured fairy tale, the young narrator goes to bed each night and prays for his father's safe return, until his prayers are answered—"Little, indeed, did I know what I was praying for!"

In the frank thoughts that only a child could utter, the narrator notes his mother's happiness at her husband's return. The boy sees it differently: "I saw nothing to be pleased about, because, out of uniform, Father was altogether less interesting, but she only beamed, and explained that our prayers had been answered, and off we went to Mass to thank God for having brought Father safely home."

The conflict for the boy is simple: his father is intruding on his territory and forcing him to share his mother's attention. In a wonderful piece of irony, the boy says, referring to his father, "I had never met anyone so absorbed in himself as he seemed." The narrator feels at a disadvantage because his father is able to read the newspaper and entertain his wife with the news of the day. "I felt this was foul play," the narrator complains. "Man for man, I was prepared to compete with him any time for Mother's attention, but when he had it all made up for him by other people it left me no chance." His ploy of interrupting his father's recounting of the news of the day merely compels his mother to scold, "You must be quiet while Daddy is reading, Larry."

That settles it for young Larry: "Either Father or I would have to leave the house." The child zeroes in on the main conflict—his father wanted to sleep, and he wanted to talk. Both wanted the attention of the woman of the house. In the end, in a perfect denouement, a new baby is born and both father and son are pushed to the sidelines, where their only comfort, and a bony comfort it is, rests in each other's arms.

Both "First Confession" and "My Oedipus Complex" have what Julian Barnes described in O'Connor's work as the hysterical clarity of a child's absolutism of eye. O'Connor's darker stories have the same clarity but with shadows of irony and moral ambiguity. When I read "The Man of the World" in that college blitzkrieg through Frank O'Connor's work, I was reminded of some of Joyce's early stories. "The Man of the World" comes with its own sort of epiphany, less knotted but as emotionally resonant as Joyce's ideas in "Araby," "The Sisters," or "An Encounter." The shame that the narrator, Larry, feels for going along with his older and more experienced friend's voyeuristic spying on a married couple renting a nearby place unnerves him. His breaking into their private world, watching them, not having sex as his friend Jimmy suggests they will, but innocently praying in their bedroom makes it a "moment everything had changed for me." He is transformed from the watcher to the watched and realizes the meaning of the shift. "I had felt someone else watching us," he says, "so that once we ceased to be the observers and became the observed. And the observed in such a humiliating position that nothing I could imagine our victims doing would have been so degrading."

Like Joyce's *Dubliners*, O'Connor's collections of stories sit readily within the structure of childhood, adolescence, maturity, and public life. Many of O'Connor's stories—"The Man of the World" or "My Oedipus Complex," for instance—fit into the category of adolescence and maturity and strike the reader with a Joycean sort of epiphany. His war stories usually move beyond childhood and adolescence and dramatize a more complex loss of faith and innocence. His most famous tale of the Irish Civil War, "Guests of the Nation," echoes back to Erich Maria Remarque's novel *All Quiet on the Western Front* or Orwell's essay "A Hanging." Like those works, "Guests of the Nation" depicts the absurdity of war and government-sponsored execution. There is no valid legal or military reason to kill the two English prisoners in the story, Belcher and 'Awkins, and Bonaparte, the Irish rebel guard, knows it. The scene where the gregarious and loquacious Englishman and his colleague are put to death is as heartbreaking as the image of Orwell's Hindu prisoner sidestepping the mud puddle in Burma as he is led toward the gallows to be hanged. For Bonaparte, "somehow the picture of the two of them so silent in the boglands was like the pain of death in my heart." And the final sentence that the narrator leaves us with is an unequivocal, and thus not exactly Joycean, epiphany—"And anything that ever happened me after I never felt the same about again."

O'Connor's stories of maturity are typically wry and realistic, often debunking myths of Irish affability and sociability. "A Bachelor's Story" depicts the narrow-hearted and unforgiving Archie Boland, vengeful as Othello but not as passionate, and "The Mad Lomasneys" portrays the beautiful and whimsical Rita Lomasney and her quietly steadfast suitor, Ned Lowry. This is the story of a quiet man, but it is far more complicated than the representation of Irish romance one will find in *The Quiet Man*. For every ounce of Rita's erraticism, Ned offers a pound of stability. But the true joy of the story is that there is no stability, only eccentricity. Rita falls madly in love with a priest, even though the reader knows from sentence one that Ned Lowry is the man for her—"Ned Lowry and Rita Lomasney had, one might say, been lovers from childhood." As she admits to herself about Ned later in the story—"She might be ugly and uneducated and a bit of a chancer, but the best man in Cork—the best in Ireland, she sometimes thought—wanted to marry her, even after she had been let down by another man." The reader's Dickensian expectations—that Rita and Ned will finally land in each other's arms—never comes to fruition. On an inexplicable whim, she marries another man, and true to his own eccentric form, Ned "behaved in a decorous and sensible manner. He didn't take to drink or break the crockery or do any of the things people are expected to do under the circumstances." Instead of playing the milquetoast Irish Othello like Archie Boland, Ned buys the couple a very expensive clock as a wedding present.

When Ned starts to date another woman, the pregnant Rita, with her puzzling and compelling lack of logic, gets jealous, but that doesn't stop her from asking him, "Would Senorita What's-her-name ever let you stand godfather to my footballer, Ned?" Then, she tells Ned and her sister Nellie that she married Justin because he was the first man to show up at her house one rainy day. "I think I half hoped you'd come first," she tells Ned. "Justin came instead." Ned remains stoical until Rita's admission that "If you'd come earlier, I'd probably be asking Justin to stand godfather to your brat." Rita taunts him to speak what's on his mind, but all he can do is savagely flick his cigarette into the fireplace. And O'Connor tells the reader in the final sentence, "A month later he married the senorita." As with many of O'Connor's stories, this one shows his interest in the turns in character over the twists in plot.

With "In the Train" O'Connor portrays the choral voice of an Irish village, who in their opposition to the legal machinery of the state have determined to save an accused murderess from the court system in order to enact their private punishment—ostracizing her from the community. "In the Train" is a character study of a society—a group of policemen, the local poteen maker, a sergeant's unpleasant wife, a rambling drunkard, townspeople and rural folk, all ready to impose their own penalty without a trial, all ready to pronounce the woman guilty even though the narrative never firmly establishes her guilt. The question of what has happened to Irish society and its age-old values is at the heart of "The Long Road to Ummera" too. Reminiscent of Faulkner's *As I Lay Dying*, O'Connor's story is a portrait of a woman, Abby, who demands of her insensitive and business-like son, Pat, that in her final days she be taken back to her home ground in Ummera by the ancient long road. Mother and son struggle with one another, the value of ritual and memory are pitted against modern practicality and progress. Abby becomes a symbol of an Ireland that has died but refuses to be forgotten. She shuffles up the road, a shapeless lump of an old woman in a plaid shawl, "faded to the colour of snuff." Her puffy eyes are "screwed up in tight little buds of flesh and her rosy old face that might have been carved out of a turnip was all crumpled with blindness." It's hard to imagine that this desiccated little country woman could outmaneuver her businesslike son from Cork, but she does. In the end, her body is brought back to Ummera, and her son announces to her remembered landscape and the roofless family cabin, "Neighbors, this is Abby, Batty Heige's daughter, that kept her promises to ye at the end of all."

O'Connor confronts some Irish myths and a few myths about the Irish in "The American Wife" and "Darcy in the Land of Youth." In "The American Wife," the titular character, Elsie Colleary, idealizes Irishmen who for her seem "more manly" than their Irish-American counterparts at home. American men, she feels, "let their wives boss them too much." She finds the right man in Tom Barry, proposes to him, marries him, and, with each of their successive babies, three children in all, Elsie tries to get him to move to America. After Elsie leaves again for America, this time permanently, with their three children, Tom stays behind and lives with his sister—"To all appearances, they are happy enough," the narrator says, "as happiness goes in Cork," the place Tom will never be manipulated into leaving.

In "Darcy and the Land of Youth," Mick Darcy, working as a clerk in an English war factory, is O'Connor's modern stand-in for Oisin, and his apparently promiscuous English girlfriend, Janet, is the contemporary version of Niamh. Right from the start of the story, O'Connor announces his intention of wrestling with the plot and themes of the ancient tale by foregrounding the myth—"One of the few things Mick Darcy remembered of what the monks in the North Monastery had taught him was the story of Oisin, an old chap who fell in love with a fairy queen called Niamh and went to live in the Land of Youth." Janet, O'Connor's stand-in for Niamh, shocks Mick with her free-spiritedness—"she had more or less told him that she expected him to be her lover, and he had more or less told her to go to hell...." Mick finds it difficult to deal with "the shock of realizing that a girl he cared for had lived with other men." When Mick returns to Cork, in a way he is like Oisin shaking off what feels like a hallucination. The clerks and servant girls and the familiar Western Road of Cork "were like a dream from which he had wakened so suddenly that he had not even realized that he was awake." Back in Cork, in the banal real world of his past experience, Mick suddenly remembers "the story of Oisin that the monks told him, and it began to have meaning for him. He wondered wildly if he would ever get back or if, like Oisin in the story, he would suddenly collapse and spend the rest of his days walking up and down the Western Road with people as old and feeble as himself, and never see Niamh and the Land of Youth."

With a deft comic touch, O'Connor simultaneously holds up and undercuts the myth of Oisin—"You never knew what powerful morals the old legends had till they came home to you. On the other hand, their heroes hadn't the advantage of the telephone." So, Mick heads back to

Chapter 6. Frank O'Connor and Cork

England and Janet, and rejoices after the consummation of their affair at becoming "at last a man of the world," only to find out that Janet is more conventional than he thought. The Land of Youth becomes for Mick the Land of Adulthood and Marriage. Mick "would have liked to remain a man of the world for just a little longer, to have had just one more such awakening to assure him that he had got rid of his inhibitions, but clearly it was not to be." Mick's story was more like Oisin's than he had, perhaps, first imagined. As Richard Ellmann has said of O'Connor's work, "His stories preserve in ink like amber his perceptive, amused, and sometimes tender observations of the fabric of Irish customs, pieties, superstitions, loves, and hates," and his friend W.B. Yeats's remark could readily apply to him, "Being Irish, he had an abiding sense of tragedy, which sustained him through temporary periods of joy."

O'Connor Country

> "Towns and cities are just like human beings.... Cork ... it's the most important city in the world."
> —Frank O'Connor, BBC Interview, 1961

> "In my boyhood there were never more than two real roads out of Cork."
> —Frank O'Connor, *Irish Miles*

In early October of 2022 in late afternoon, John Lawrence and I got on the Dublin train to Cork in the impressively old world and modern Heuston Station in Dublin, what used to be called Kingsbridge Station, reminding me of the mysterious neighborhood a few blocks from mine in the Bronx of my boyhood. The train ride took two-and-a-half hours, quickly exiting the grey-hued south Dublin suburbs and passing along lush green rolling hills dotted with sheep and cows. Brightly painted farms stood in the shadows of the Wicklow Mountains to the east and the Slieve Bloom Mountains to the west. The sky was grey, but everything else in the world seemed an impossibly undiluted green. As the train rocked me into assorted daydreams, I thought of the strange encounter between the young Frank O'Connor and the famous James Joyce in Paris. O'Connor asked Joyce about a painting he had hanging in his hallway.

"Cork," Joyce said to him.
"I know my city," O'Connor replied, "I mean the frame."
Joyce's answer, "Cork."
Although I don't know exactly what to make of that anecdote, I love

what it seems to imply about both Joyce and O'Connor, their Irish sense of place, of humor, of language.

Frank O'Connor once said of his boyhood home, "Towns and cities are just like human beings...." He may have meant they have their own distinct personalities, their carefully held secrets, their dreams, fears, histories, and ways of expressing themselves. By that standard, the first impression that Cork gives to a stranger is of a handsome and talented friend who, with humility and a fair amount of good grace, accepts his status as Ireland's second city. Cork is a slightly smaller and grittier version of Dublin, a city where everyone appears to be under thirty years old. The streets and restaurants are filled with young people, streaming along the streets and hills and bridges. The city is an island between two channels in the River Lee. Corcaigh is the Gaelic for marsh and the Irish name for Cork, and like a cork it floats up and down in the proximity of that marshland. It is a city encircled on three sides by breath-catching hills and the fourth side by the Irish Sea, a city made for escape artists, and most escape artists start practicing for their future by being inveterate walkers. O'Connor, like James Joyce, was such a rambler, and he took pleasure in the hills of his town—"the up and down of it on the hills as though it had been built on a Cork accent." And it is no coincidence that O'Connor associated the very contours of the Cork landscape with the sound of its people's voices. It was the sound of voices that led him to the stories he needed to tell.

And Cork is a town of tales, tall and short. On the train from Dublin to Cork, we sat next to two Irish Rail train men, Damion O'Regan and Evan Corkery. "No relation to Daniel Corkery," he said to me. The two-and-a-half-hour train trip flew by because the four of us spent the time trying to make sense of the phenomenon of Donald Trump and the incomprehensible rise in nationalism in many parts of the world. Evan was even-tempered and rational enough to make me want to move to Ireland immediately. Damion had a pleasant, goofy smile, and he might have been as coherent as Evan, but I never understood one word he said. His thick accent and whispered delivery, combined with the rattling of the train, made his words a gurgle of sounds that could have been lifted from *Finnegans Wake* for all the sense I could make of them. So, I returned his goofy smile for my own and nodded in agreement with everything he said.

James McKeon, a Cork native and local historian and biographer of O'Connor, met us the next morning to come with us as we made our way through Cork to O'Connor's boyhood home. With what was becoming my unusual talent for choosing people who had recently undergone surgery, James had just gotten out of the hospital a few days before our visit and he required a walker. With the help of Will, our cab driver, we got the walker in the boot and slid James into the front passenger's seat. I was getting a bit nervous about calling Sam Brett in Galway to say we would see him tomorrow. I was concerned that I might jinx him.

The walker and the recent hospital stay didn't seem to daunt James. He turned out to be an enthusiastic and knowledgeable, if physically limited guide. He pointed out the school Frank O'Connor went to when he was a boy named Michael O'Donovan, a school that was far down the many hills from his house. I asked Jim, who had tried unsuccessfully to get a bridge named after O'Connor, if the city of Cork had named any streets or buildings in honor of their most famous writer. If there were any statues or festivals, perhaps, as there were for Joyce in Dublin or Yeats in Sligo.

"No, no," James said. "They put up a plaque for O'Connor," he paused for effect and laughed. "But they put the plaque on the wrong house."

They finally got it right, though—8 Harrington Square on Ballyhooly Road had a plaque on it that said, "Frank O'Connor lived here." His neighborhood reminded me of Frank McCourt's description of his street in *Angela's Ashes*—dozens of diminutive row houses squeezed together high above the center of the city.

As we drove along the winding streets, Will asked Jim with a patent Irish redundancy, "Is it up there, is it?"

"It's there all right, it is," Jim said answering with the same poetic repetition, pointing to a tiny place with a brightly colored wreath adorning the front door.

I rang the bell twice and was about to leave when the door swung open and Ann, the owner for the past half of a century, opened the door with a beautiful megawatt smile.

"Come in, come in," she said. "It's a small house with a big heart. Come in, won't you?"

The current owner of O'Connor's boyhood home.

The living room, which might have been ten feet by ten feet, was crammed with dolls and teddy bears and family photos. There were pictures of her daughter's wedding day and one of her own, and it was clear that her daughter was her spitting image and that Ann, still appealing, had been a beautiful woman in her day. There was also a photo of her son in his twenties with his rugby team. He had died a few years before in the army. "He's gone to heaven now," she said.

When Ann took us upstairs to see the two bedrooms, one that had been O'Connor's and the other that had been his parents, I started to feel that, by comparison to O'Connor, I had grown up in magnificent, near-palatial splendor in my family's one-bedroom apartment in the Bronx. The room that had been O'Connor's parents—and Ann's and her husband's when they were raising their children, was smaller than the living room and had enough crucifixes to ward off a legion of Satans. She looked at another photo of her son and said again, "He's gone to heaven now. I miss him every day."

She took us into another room, even smaller, maybe eight feet by eight feet, and said, "This was my daughters' room. We made up the living room into a bedroom for my son. And this was Frank O'Connor's room when he was a boy." She pointed to the skylight window and smiled. "He used to climb out of that window and sit on the roof and dream. That's where his stories started, I guess."

We went down the narrow, low-ceilinged staircase and she showed me the backyard, what amounted to a sort of open-air storage closet. When we walked the fifteen or twenty feet to the front door, she gave me a hug and I wondered sixty seconds later if she were going to let go. She smiled up at me radiantly and pointed to a lens on the outside wall. "I tell the neighbors, 'Don't have an affair or you'll be caught on camera. Frank O'Connor may not be watching any more, but I can."

I headed back down the hill to catch the bus, thinking O'Connor wouldn't have appreciated all the crucifixes in his old house, but he would have smiled at the camera. And he would have relished everything about Ann, including her brilliant smile and warmth and the way her accent rolled like the very hills of his town.

Chapter 7

Edna O'Brien—
A Country Girl in the West

> "I thought that ours was a land of shame, a land of murder, and a land of strange sacrificial women."
> —Edna O'Brien, "A Scandalous Woman"

I had been a professor of creative writing for a number of years when I first encountered the novels of Edna O'Brien, starting with *The Country Girls* trilogy, a cultural watershed in Ireland, a series of novels published in the 1960s that gave voice to modern women's sense of frustration and offered a candid gaze at their sexual longing and psychological yearnings in a world dominated by men in government, the Catholic Church, and the home. I read all of her novels that I could find in the bookstores in Norfolk, Virginia, but it was the graceful collections of stories by Edna O'Brien that entranced me. In their mastery of form, they reminded me of the work of her Irish contemporaries John McGahern and William Trevor.

The first story I came upon was "Irish Revel," published two years after her breakthrough with *The Country Girls*, and it recalled for me both Chekhov in its deceptive simplicity and apparent objectivity and Joyce in the carefully calculated ambiguities of "The Dead." "Irish Revel," her first story published in *The New Yorker* and originally titled "Come into the Drawing Room, Doris," came out when she was thirty-one years old. The story has what John Banville called "the combination of immediacy and sympathetic recall." Like Banville, I was drawn into the story for its "delicacy and fond humor" but also for its "portrait of the grossness and cruelty of country life." The story, which comes to the reader from the point of view of an innocent and romantic young woman, Mary, a girl longing for an imagined love, an English painter, John Roland, who offered her some attention when she was a few years younger. As the story opens, Mary has been invited to a party at the

Commercial Hotel in town, and she goes with the unsupported hope that she might re-engage with her artist/lover.

Mary is a dreamer and goes off on a bicycle to the party in a black lace dress that her mother doesn't even want her to wear to Mass on Sunday, but Mary also has a realistic dimension to her nature—"For as long as she could remember, she had been pumping bicycles, carting turf, cleaning out houses, doing a man's work. Her father and her two brothers worked for the forestry, so that she and her mother had to do all the odd jobs—there were three children to care for, and fowl and pigs and churning. Theirs was a mountainy farm in Ireland, and life was hard." The other girls at the party turn out to be, for the most part, snide and uncompassionate. The men prove themselves to be shallow and vulgar. Mary's disappointment is two-fold—John Roland, predictably, does not attend, and she is not so much invited as a guest but expected to act as a serving girl and then as a dance partner for the older men at the party. Her ultimate disappointment may come when she heads home and wonders if all parties—all dreams—are so much less than she would have imagined. The final sentence of the story struck me with a sadness and recalibrated hope reminiscent of Gabriel Conroy's in "The Dead"— "She was at the top of the hill now, and could see her own house, like a little white box at the end of the world, waiting to receive her."

In an early story like "Irish Revel," as with her later stories, O'Brien does what Deborah Treisman, fiction editor at *The New Yorker*, suggests the writer does consistently in her career—"She puts women's sexuality on the page and then those pages were banned in Ireland." Treisman sees "Irish Revel" as a fractured Cinderella story without a happy ending but, perhaps, with a "moral ending," where innocence may not be fully lost, as Mary sees the value and comfort of home. The writer Rachel Kushner offers a similar insight, saying that O'Brien "treats

Cyclist in Galway.

her characters with the utmost precision and sympathy for what it means to have a dream and then have that dream shattered." As both Kushner and Treisman imply, O'Brien's Ireland of the 1950s and 1960s was a man's world in which women had to struggle to access their own fancies and dreams in much the way that Mary and the other city and country girls in "Irish Revel" had to labor to find their way in the world amidst a flurry of confusing signals.

Many of O'Brien's stories are concerned with the disappointments of love and with the impossibility of not rushing in the direction of what may be an inevitable disaster. A good number of her stories deal with young women having complicated affairs with older married men. "The reason that love is so painful," one of her characters claims, "is that it always amounts to two people wanting more than two people can give." For Joyce, Dublin is the heart of paralysis. For O'Brien, Dublin and Ireland in general hold the dark heart of frustrated dreams.

O'Brien underscores the smallness of Irish country life in many other stories—"The Connor Girls" and "The Rug" dramatize the backbiting in small towns, the striations between Catholics and Protestants, the jealousies and the constricted expectations in communities, and the deep-seated grudges in families. Stories like "The Creature" and "The Doll" struck me like dark fairy tales about people living "on that last tightrope of hope" existing in "that stagnant, godforsaken little place" that is O'Brien's Ireland, a darkly comic, brutal, cloudy landscape that somehow she is always able to imbue with light, her characters never losing "the desire to escape or the strenuous habit of hoping." That strenuous "habit of hoping" that her characters—women in particular—struggle with wears them down, making them lonely and often dissatisfied.

O'Brien's relationship to Ireland is a bit like Faulkner's with Mississippi, a delicate balance of fondness and disgust. In "Old Wounds," a character who may be voicing O'Brien's own feelings wonders, "Why, I asked myself, did I want to be buried there? Why, given the different and gnawing perplexities? It was not love and it was not hate but something for which there is no name, because to name it would be to deprive it of its truth." John Banville, in his introduction to O'Brien's Selected Stories, gets to the heart of things, "Edna O'Brien mourns for the plight of her wounded women and at the same time celebrates their exuberance, their generosity and, ultimately, their indomitable spirit." What she may want for her characters is what she wants for herself—"to live our lives as they should have been lived, happy, trusting, and free of shame." For me, O'Brien described the older women in my life I had most admired—my mother, Dorothy Hunter, and my mother-in-law,

Mary Louise Kennedy. They could have been models for her characters in their generosity and joy, in their compassion and exuberance of spirit, in their indomitable spirits.

For O'Brien, the frailties and addictions of love—its confusions and terrors—are always better than emptiness. Like Faulkner, she will choose grief over nothingness. She chooses eventful life and love rather than the safety of inaction, a security that resembles death. When the narrator of "The Love Object" records her fears, the reader might be eavesdropping on O'Brien's own anxieties—"all my life I feared imprisonment, the nun's cell, the hospital bed, the places where one faced the self without distraction, without the crutches of other people—but sitting there feeding him white sugar, I thought, I now have entered a cell, and this man cannot know what it is for me to love him the way I do, and I cannot weigh him down with it, because he is in another cell confronted with other difficulties." The narrator clings desperately to painful happiness with her married lover because to let it (and him) go would eradicate all her joy and pain, leaving her with nothing—"and nothing is a dreadful thing to hold on to."

*　*　*

O'Brien was inspired by the work of James Joyce, so it was not a surprise to me when in the course of a few months reading everything she wrote, I picked up a copy of her rapturous and gem-like biography of Joyce. Like him, she spent most of her adult life outside of Ireland but observing it (as she did Joyce in her succinct biography) with a lynx-like clarity. Her view is often dark and pessimistic but always she gives life to the inner lives of girls and women.

In her 2012 memoir, *Country Girl*, Edna O'Brien said, "Places are at the heart of writing," and the people and places of her small island have been at the heart of her stories from the beginning of her career. She was born ten days before Christmas in 1930 outside the village of Tuamgraney, in County Clare in what may have amounted to the typically fraught Irish family. As she wrote about her growing up in rural Ireland and the shadowed stone house, Drewsboro, she was raised in, "We were all lonely in that house, lonely and sometimes at loggerheads." Her father had what has been stereotyped as the Irish habit of drinking and the anger that often came with it, and when he was in his drying-out periods in the Cistercian monastery in Roscrea, Edna felt free and alive. This desire to have the father disappear and to have her mother's love to herself she held in common with her countryman Frank O'Connor. "Those lulls while he was away," she said in her memoir, "were the happiest times in our house, my mother and I baking, cleaning windows

Chapter 7. Edna O'Brien—A Country Girl in the West

inside and out, and once, as I remember, mastering the intricate recipe for queen of puddings, which, when it came out of the oven with its crest of lightly burnt meringue, seemed to levitate from the oblong Pyrex dish."

What O'Brien struggled against as a teenager and later as an adult woman, wife, mother, and artist were the endemic aspects of Irish culture—a society awash in alcohol and the Catholic Church, battling sexual repression and silence, caught in historical grudges and repeated violence. It was borne on O'Brien from the time she was very young that she came from "fierce people and that the wounds of history were as raw and vivid as the pictures on … packs of cards." Her story was Stephen Dedalus's, history being a nightmare from which she wanted to awaken. She went to school at the Convent of Mercy in Loughrea in County Galway, and later in Dublin she attended the Pharmaceutical College of Ireland. As a child, she had her "daft ambition to be a writer" and then in convent boarding school, like many introspective Catholic school boys and girls in Ireland and elsewhere, she considered the religious life. "There were morning prayers," she writes about that convent education, "evening prayers, vespers, supplications, contritions, psalms, and versicals…. The flames of Hell seemed as real as the turf burning in the fire…. Hell was far more real to us than Heaven. Heaven was golden and vaporish." In her remarkable love story "Sister Imelda," she writes about the mutual affection a schoolgirl shares with a young nun and how that relationship led the main character toward considering the convent for herself. But that story, like many others in which young women—or older ones—fall dizzily in love with one man or another, is a tale of frustrated love, ending with the narrator saying, "I knew that there is something sad and faintly distasteful about love's ending, particularly love that has never been fully realized." As a young woman, O'Brien imagined herself as a bride of Christ in much the way a young man like James Joyce may have envisioned himself at one time as a soldier in Christ's army. Like most of those who imagined they had a religious vocation or had a visceral fear of hell, O'Brien discovered that the temptations of the world were too exciting to dismiss and perhaps worth risking hell in the long run. She became "ravenous. For food. For life. For the stories I would write."

* * *

As a young woman in Dublin, she drifted away from pursuing a career in pharmacy for the community of poets and playwrights and novelists and for the life of a writer. It was in Dublin, during her four years working as a pharmacist's assistant, that she discovered "the great gods of Irish literature and embraced what she called the two intensities—writing and reading—that came to mark the rest of her life. She bided her time in that chemist's shop, 'training for a profession,'" she said, "that was not my chosen one, but convinced that I would meet poets and that one day I would be admitted into the world of letters." She saw Siobhan McKenna perform the part of Cathleen Ni Houlihan in Yeats's play and decided to be an actress until a brief and disastrous audition cured her of that ambition.

In her autobiographical first novel, *Country Girls*, she describes exchanging the strictures of the Catholic Church and Ireland's patriarchy for the sovereignty of the artist who follows her own moral compass. As the biographer and critic Stacy Schiff explains, O'Brien's break for freedom was "headlong and noisy." In 1959, she married the writer Ernest Gebler, fled to the Isle of Man, and hid from her family in the home of the writer J.P. Donleavy. It was her husband who opened a subscription for her in the library in Dublin, where she devoured all the most recently published books and, as she says, "so, in truth, began my real apprenticeship as a writer." Eventually she moved to London with her new husband.

In 1960, when she published her then-controversial *The Country Girls*, a novel banned in her home country for what many readers and church officials considered the sexual explicitness and the shocking rebellion against conservative Catholic values, she told the story of Kate and Baba, two young women fleeing the restrictions of rural Ireland for the relative freedom of Dublin and London, where they seek to create larger lives for themselves. O'Brien followed that book with the other two fictions in what became her trilogy about Kate and Baba, *The Lonely Girl* (1962) and *Girls in their Married Bliss* (1964). The Country Girls trilogy and many of her other books ran afoul of the Irish Censorship Board.

O'Brien's life mirrored—or recorded—her own evolution as a woman and a writer. Kate's precipitous marriage to an older man was Edna O'Brien's, as well. Art imitated life or life imitated art—Kate's rebelling against her upbringing and running off to Dublin and her marriage to an older, controlling man in the trilogy ran a parallel course to the implosion caused by O'Brien's rebellion, escape, and marriage to the jealous and resentful Ernest Gebler. Gebler was a man O'Brien describes as readily wounded by any writing success she had. Each of her triumphs would "incur a hefty entry" in his logbook of resentments. After her divorce from Gebler, O'Brien lived, in Stacy Schiff's characterization, "at high pitch and full taboo-defying tilt." Her memoir details years of parties and a number of affairs in which the guestbook looks like a Who's

Chapter 7. Edna O'Brien—A Country Girl in the West

Who in Arts and Entertainment in the twentieth century—Robert Mitchum, Sean Kenney, Richard Burton, Marlon Brando, Leslie Caron, Marianne Faithful, R.D. Laing, Jane Fonda, Laurence Olivier, Gore Vidal, Hillary Clinton, Gunter Grass, Norman Mailer, Samuel Beckett, Gore Vidal, Philip Roth, Bill Walton, Al Pacino, Thornton Wilder, Robert Mapplethorpe, Jackie Onassis, and Sean Connery. Amidst the whirl and fury of her new freedom, she fought to regain custody of her two sons from her manipulative and vengeful ex-husband and to write the books and plays that would define the liminal world of a woman coming of age in the mid–twentieth century. For many critics and readers, Edna O'Brien became a model of incautious honesty and fierce, poetic feminism. For others, she became a "bargain basement Molly Bloom."

As Schiff says, "O'Brien was notorious before she was famous." *The Country Girls* was excoriated from the pulpit, burned in public meetings, and went unread in O'Brien's own family. In Schiff's words, "Essentially, O'Brien does for Ireland what her great friend (without benefits, she insists) Philip Roth did for Newark: she scandalized it, then put it on the map."

At twenty-nine, she had written *The Country Girls* and helped alter the conversation about women in Ireland. She has continued to do that over a career of more than six decades. A woman of great ambition and vitality, she celebrated her 90th birthday by giving a witty and thought-provoking lecture at the Abbey Theater in Dublin as part of the T.S. Eliot Series.

The Wild Wild West of Ireland

> "Flaubert's mother said that his love of words had hardened his heart. Could that be true? Could that be true?"
> —Edna O'Brien, *Country Girls*

I'd often wondered since my boyhood days in the Bronx if my love of reading had been my escape then or if it had separated me from the world as much as connected me imaginatively to it. That question, that nagging doubt, perhaps, had been part of the catalyst that sent me pushing into the world, always into new worlds, to prove to myself that a love of books and words and stories had not hardened my heart but, rather, opened it. That books were an integral part of experience, not a separation from it. The world was another book, an enigmatic story, always the same, always shifting its meaning, like a great novel or poem. The west of Ireland and the landscape of Edna O'Brien's novels and stories

Edna O'Brien's childhood home, Tumagraney.

embodied that mystery for me. Many times over the years I had roamed western counties like Clare, Galway, Mayo, and Sligo and had fallen in love with the damp, cruel, wind-swept beauty of the landscape and the elliptical smiles of its people. They reminded me of O'Brien's description of many of the Irish villages she knew growing up—where "many restless souls reside dreaming of a different destiny," the places where "pity is a luxury and deliverance a thing of the past."

The first thing you notice in the West of Ireland are the stone walls that lace the landscape, joining and separating people and animals. One field of vision. Many discrete fields. A Druidical landscape, ancient and mysterious, carrying a language foreign and familiar at the same time. The cuts on the rock like ogham, carrying a message that only the ancients or the well-versed could translate. That made the reggae music—Bob Marley's "Let's Get Together"—pulsating from the bus I rode from Cork to Galway feel a bit like an otherworldly memo. And when the music played again that night when I sat in the back of Keogh's Restaurant near the Spanish Arch, I wondered if I were being told something I had better pay attention to. The lyrics played—again incongruously in what to all appearances was a traditional Irish pub—"Is there a place for a lonesome sinner?" And then when I passed near the Spanish Arch on the way back to my hotel, there was a poster picturing Che Guevera and calling him an hijo of Galway, I knew that I better keep my eyes and ears open, that "There ain't no hiding place among the kingdoms of love, yes."

So, the next morning when Sam Brett picked up John Lawrence and me to drive us around Galway, Sligo, and parts north, I watched and listened with my whole heart. Sam was a bit late to pick us up at St. Jude's Bed and Breakfast on College Road in Galway, but I was just grateful, given the fact that I seemed to be bringing bad luck to writers and guides in Ireland, that he had not recently had surgery, and he wasn't limping. Sam is a third-generation Irish storyteller, a seanachai, in the old tradition and a man who knew Irish writers, history, and the landscape and culture they blossomed in or ran from. Sam is a man of many talents and interests—wood sculptor, historian and storyteller, amateur literary scholar, sailor, boat builder, and owner of a company—Shanakee Adventures, situated in Sligo.

Two days before we arrived in Galway, John Lawrence and I had gone to the Abbey Theater to see O'Brien's latest play, *Joyce's Women*. That play, she said, was the best way she had been able to find to depict James Joyce, her ultimate hero for six decades. She decided that the way to bring him to life was to depict the principal women in his life—his mother, May, his mistress, Nora, and his patron and financial savior, Harriet Weaver. The play had some good moments but seemed strained to me but going to the Abbey in Dublin is like going to the Globe in London: it always feels

Edna O'Brien's childhood home today.

like a special event. I didn't learn anything new about Joyce or about any of his women, but Nora's closing line in the play underscored something I thought was true about Nora and Edna O'Brien, as well—"I was hard, but I had to be."

    Sam seemed to have a clear insight into what that life might have been like during O'Brien's time. "My mom was that country girl in Edna O'Brien's books," he said. She was part of that generation and told me about. She survived the oppression of the Catholic Church and the culture it created. I guess I was the last generation that faced their reign of terror. They're history now, those priests and nuns. "Cheers to them, eh?"

    Edna O'Brien's home life might have been hard at times, but the landscape around her house in Tumagraney was lush and stunning, in its own world but not more than a good walk from the rows of stores in Scariff town. O'Brien's home looked much as it had when she was a girl growing up, a long, narrow road surrounded by fields and farms. The new owners had given the place a fresh coat of paint and a new door. My guess was that they had probably done a major renovation inside, too. No one was home, though, so I wasn't certain. When I knocked on the door, a dog barked lazily inside as if he were greeting me, not trying to scare me away. I waited for a few moments and waved hello to the dog. Then I decided to walk away, imagining the house as it once had been when O'Brien lived there. The two donkeys in the pasture in front of her home place made it easy for me to visualize her still there, a country girl changing the shape of the world she lived in.

Chapter 8

Seamus Heaney and Northern Ireland

"The cold smell of potato mould, the squelch and slap/Of soggy peat, the curt cuts of an edge/Through living roots in my head...."
—Seamus Heaney, "Digging"

"Silence is the job. It's the great thing, silence...."
—Sebastian Barry, *The Whereabouts of Eneas McNulty*

Seamus Heaney was that rarity among great writers—by most accounts, he was generous, loving, and profoundly content in his marriage and family life. He was respected and loved by many of his fellow writers. He had taken seriously, it seems, John McGahern's advice on how to deal with envious or belligerent peers—"implacable courtesy." And when that didn't work for Heaney, he took the other Irish tack—"an unspoken 'Well, fuck you too, buddy.'" For the most part, though, Heaney left the rage and animosities unspoken. Often, it seems, among great writers the opposite is true: implacable courtesy is not a typical character trait, and the unspoken gets pronounced loudly and often. The usual biographical narrative portrays artistic success springing from a troubled childhood, and it's invariably attached to intemperate behavior. Often, the landscape of an eminent writer's biography is scarred by interludes of Byronic drinking, drug use, infidelity, and mean-spiritedness. R.F. Foster's summary of Seamus Heaney's life and career, like many other contemporary accounts, paints the picture of a man who made a triumph of both living and art. For Foster, Heaney had a personality and worldview that "guided him through a life of extraordinary success, enabled a radiantly happy family life, and made him universally loved." Foster notes the "achieved fullness of his life," and describes the connection the poet had to his country. "It was reflected," Foster says, "in the extraordinary outburst of national grief in Ireland—and, indeed, elsewhere, but especially in Ireland. For example, at the All-Ireland Gaelic football semi-final in Croke Park, a crowd of eighty thousand people stood and applauded for two minutes in homage after the announcement of his death. His unforgettable funeral in Dublin, where Paul Muldoon delivered a heartbroken and heartbreaking eulogy, was a genuinely national occasion."

In his eulogy, Muldoon underlined Heaney's vitality, his lack of pretension, his generosity of spirit, his big heart, his sense of humor. "We remember," Muldoon said, "the beauty of Seamus Heaney—as bard, and in his being." Heaney took the vocation of the poet as a solemn charge, but he also took his commitment to his wife, Marie, their three children—Michael, Christopher, and Catherine—and his community as a sacred part of living.

I came upon the poetry of Seamus Heaney when I was deep into my own writing career, happily married and a father to three sons, and I often thought I might have been too stable, too happy, too blessed, to write the sort of stories I had admired for decades. I began to pay close attention to Heaney and his work after he received the Nobel Prize in 1995. The committee described his work as mastering a "lyrical beauty and ethical depths, which exalt everyday miracles and the living past." I discovered in his poetry the "consummate simplicity" that R.F. Foster found in his work. Like Heaney, I felt at home in the poetry of Robert Frost, "the primal reach into the physical," what Heaney described in his conversations with Dennis O'Driscoll in *Stepping Stones* as "a covenant with the reader, an openness, an availability." And, as Heaney acknowledged, a wizardry, "a ratification of the impulse toward transcendence."

The Giant's Causeway.

Chapter 8. Seamus Heaney and Northern Ireland

I became fascinated by the poet and the man, his seeming ability to make living and writing not merely coexist but nourish one another. The deceptive clarity he achieved without ever losing hold on the sort of mystery that makes a piece of writing stay new with each reading took my breath away. He achieved, in R.F. Foster's words, "a feeling for syllable and rhythm, penetrating far below the levels of conscious thought and feeling, invigorating every word." Heaney accomplished for me what he alluded to in his reading of the poetry of Czeslaw Milosz and Joseph Brodsky. Like their poetry, his offered the chance of an awakening similar to what he described to Dennis O'Driscoll—"A populace that is chloroformed day and night by TV stations like Fox News could do with an inoculation by poetry. Obviously, poetry can't be administered like an injection, but it does constitute a boost to the capacity for discrimination and resistance." Heaney went on to say that "a good poem holds as much of the truth as possible in one gaze." In that gaze, poet and reader can find, as Heaney explained to Charlie Rose, a redemption, a discovery of something lost or forgotten.

I read Heaney's works in the order he wrote them, *Death of a Naturalist* first, dazzled by the poet's ability to bring the past to life and make it resonate with unspoken questions and truths. He brought me to tears with "Mid-Term Break," the narrative poem about the death of his three-and-a-half-year-old brother, Christopher, in a traffic accident. Christopher, his hand held by an older brother, was near a bus stop close to his home when he saw some of his siblings across the roadway. He extricated himself from his brother's grasp and dashed into the road and right into the path on an oncoming car. "Mid-Term Break" is as much about the narrator of the poem being thrust into the inscrutability of adulthood as it is about the tragic death of a child. At the time of his brother Christopher's death Heaney was two months shy of his fourteenth birthday.

"Mid-Term Break" describes Heaney's being called back from boarding school to attend his brother's funeral and, for the first time in six weeks, to see his brother, now in his coffin, "No gaudy scars, the bumper knocked him clear./A four-foot box, a foot for every year." The poignant clarity of the last two lines, the rhyme not diminishing but highlighting the sad incongruity of life, convinced me that this was what art should accomplish—a way of saying that stood in the clear light of day but remained in the shadows, as well. For me, "Mid-Term Break" called to mind Robert Frost's "Out, Out—," speaking powerfully and enigmatically at the same time about the tragedy of a young person's dying. Like many of Heaney's poems, "Mid-Term Break" begins where he liked to start—"in the ground of memory and sensation."

I was born a city boy, but my instinct had always been to escape the cityscape of the Bronx to what I imagined was the serenity of the country. In "Death of a Naturalist," Heaney reminded me of what it was to be a boy stepping away from the apartment buildings and city streets to wander along the banks of the Bronx River. The Botanical Gardens near my apartment building on 198th Street could have been Heaney's "flax-dam [that] festered in the heart/Of the townland." The lush details of the poem—bluebottles, dragonflies, butterflies, the nimble-swimming tadpoles—all reminded me of the wonder I felt exiting the crowded subway stations and avenues of my Bedford Park neighborhood to find myself alone in what felt to me as a boy like the primeval forest. But by the time I read "Death of a Naturalist," I was like that retrospective narrator at the center of Heaney's poem, I had changed and knew that nature was not simply benign, and I understood that boy's feelings when he "sickened, turned, ran" from the great slime kings and from the spawn that would clutch his hand if he dared to dip it into the clotted water.

As with many great poets, Heaney can be found in the silences in his poems. He is the poet of all Ireland, but he is truly the bard of the North, the poet I associate with the landscape of my grandfather. Alfred Hunter's County Armagh is not far from Heaney's County Londonderry, separated by not much more than Lough Neagh. The lake is the largest in Ireland—twenty miles long and nine miles wide—but by American standards not a daunting size or distance. The Heaneys and the Hunters may have passed each other on a market day in the crowded streets of Derry. As Alfred Hunter was arranging his

Statue of red Hugh O'Donnell, Donegal.

disappearance from Armagh and Ireland, Seamus Heaney's ancestors were likely watching their world begin to be dismantled before their eyes in revolution and civil war.

Heaney knew rural Ireland, and he lived through the violence of the mid– to late–twentieth century. In chronicling the Ireland he knew, in writing about the conflicts between the burdens of celebrity and the obligations of art, he became the natural heir to William Butler Yeats. Like Yeats, throughout much of his career, Heaney struggled to negotiate the slippery and rocky path between being a prominent public figure and a private, fiercely independent writer. This tension, as R.F. Foster points out, is at the heart of much of Heaney's work—the conviction that the poet must acknowledge the Yeatsian "pure joy of things not indentured to any cause" while remaining aware of the way that poetry is a political act. Even in one of Heaney's earliest and most loved poems, "Digging," which appeared in his first volume in 1966, *Death of a Naturalist*, the poet strives to find a connection between past and present, looking to discover a language that allows the poem to find its place in the world and, at the same time, be on the outskirts of limiting current events. In a sense, the poem is a love letter to Heaney's father, the country man, "By God, the old man could handle a spade./Just like his old man." Heaney's grandfather, by the poet's account, could cut more turf in a day than any man on Toner's bog, and Heaney's father had followed in those footsteps. But as much as the poet admires the skills of the men of his father's and grandfather's generation, as much as he is enamored of country things, he has taken another path, one that requires an office and a pen rather than a farm and spade. And his poet's pen, as the opening two lines announce, is connected to the violence of the world of Northern Ireland in the 1960s—"Between my finger and my thumb/The squat pen rests; snug as a gun."

Heaney found his mythos in memory and the natural world. His sister-in-law, the writer Polly Devlin, pointed to the rural temper of his work: "Seamus not only knew to his bones these country ways and vanished words that resounded with usage; he used them as echo chambers, made them necessary memories." Heaney knew the country ways that I suspected my grandfather must have known, even though Alfred had left Ireland for good nearly three decades before Heaney was born on April 13, 1939, on the family farm in Mossbawn, a townland within the triangle shaped by the villages of Toome, Castledawson, and Bellaghy. Alfred Hunter's life, of course, was not Heaney's. Alfred Hunter of Armagh was orphaned early, and the idea of home for him must have come to seem an elusive dream. Heaney, on the other hand, had a supportive, loving family, and despite moments of sadness and tragedy, his childhood and adolescence, as Dennis O'Driscoll says, "had its Edenic dimensions." Heaney lived on his family's farm near the northern edge of Lough Neagh. Sometime after his brother Christopher's death, his family moved a few miles north to the village of Bellaghy, where the poet is now buried.

Heaney's much-admired father, Patrick, was raised by his uncles to be a farmer and a cattle dealer. As a friend and biographer Hugh Mulrooney points out, "The picture we see of Seamus Heaney's father is that of a strong silent man who has carved out a place in a disappearing world." That disappearing world was to become the center of Heaney's poetry early—and often late. Heaney's mother, Margaret McCann, came from a family of linen mill workers. And, on that 40-acre farm and in that single-story, thatch-roofed house without electricity and running water, mother and father from divergent backgrounds sowed the seeds of love and discipline and decency in their large family and helped make the natural world the landscape and theme of many of their oldest son's poetry.

If the two worldviews, the urban industrial linen mill experience of the mother and the rural history of his father, created any conflict in Heaney, he joined the two experiences by becoming a writer, a man of the world but a man who remembered the past, the natural world, and allowed them to speak to the political and social realities of the present. Heaney memorialized his country background, particularly in his earlier poems. The picture that Heaney left for posterity was, in R.F. Foster's words, "a small Derry farmhouse, a cattle-dealing father, a much-loved mother and aunt presiding jointly over the domestic world; the routine of beasts, crops, and land; horses and carts, candles and oil lamps, an outdoor privy, mice scrabbling in the thatch above the children's beds at night, a world already becoming archaic in his youth." Heaney was a countryman in the city, a rural boy in the academy, and a Catholic in the Protestant North. Hugh Mulrooney, remembering Heaney as his former colleague, suggested as much when he wrote, "He always described himself as a man from County Derry and never used the Londonderry label."

Heaney proved to be a brilliant student, and his love of reading and writing was fostered by an intelligent family of farmers and schoolteachers who placed a high value on education, even if the farmhouse was not awash in books or bookish talk. His Aunt Sally was a teacher, and it was in her house that he "got a feel for books—she had a bookcase with sets of Hardy and Kipling...." His achievements in school seemed preordained, and his success in primary school led him, at twelve years old, to win a scholarship to St. Columb's College, a Catholic boarding

Chapter 8. Seamus Heaney and Northern Ireland

Derry.

school in Derry. His characterization of St. Columb's reminded me of my own high school experience at Mount St. Michael Academy in the Bronx—"the usual monastic regime, Mass in the morning, masturbation at night, classroom in the day-time, the study-hall/scriptorium in the evening. Cold-water shaves, cold weather playgrounds." There was a kinship between Derry and the Bronx, I realized, and a Catholic upbringing and education were part of a culture that one could step away from but never leave behind.

Upon graduating from St. Columb's, Heaney received a full scholarship to Queen's University in Belfast and graduated with honors in 1961. He had a natural affinity for teaching and became a schoolteacher at St. Thomas's Secondary Intermediate School in Ballymurphy in Northern Ireland. St. Thomas's was the kind of school I understood well, similar to my first jobs as an English teacher in the New York City public school system after I graduated from Fordham University. The way Heaney described St. Thomas it could have been a portrait of JHS 113 in the Bronx, my first teaching job. "St. Thomas's was what they called in Britain a secondary modern and in Northern Ireland an intermediate school," Heaney said in an interview. "Set up to provide secondary education for those who didn't make the grade to grammar schools via the eleven-plus exam. Set up for 'non-academic' pupils. No Latin, but woodwork and metalwork ... all Catholic and nearly all from the big desolate housing estate at the top of Whiterock Road."

I remember enjoying my first year teaching at JHS 113, as Heaney seemed to enjoy his at St. Thomas's Secondary, but I understood perfectly when he said he was fulfilled "to some extent, but not overwhelmingly." I felt that our experiences starting out as young teachers were compatible—my school, like his, "looked like an open prison, it had railings, steel window frames, tiled corridors—H-Block architecture." There were some brilliant students and teachers but more often than not, like Heaney, I encountered "oafs and gobshites." So, I followed in Heaney's path, even though I had no knowledge at that time of his road toward the writing and university life. If I had the courage at twenty-one years old, I would have tucked my degree under my arm and headed for a garret in Greenwich Village and started writing a novel. Instead, I first headed to the University of San Francisco to study for a master's degree and then on to Penn State to work on a Ph.D. in American literature, a safer road for a middle-class kid who was the first one in his family to graduate from college. For that matter, even my college experience at Fordham had a distinct middle-class tint to it: I received a four-year scholarship from the International Brotherhood of Electrical Workers, my father's union organization in New York.

Heaney left St. Thomas's behind and became a lecturer at St. Joseph's College of Education, a Catholic secondary school in south Belfast. Within a few years he had joined the faculty of the English Department at his alma mater, Queen's University. In 1965, he married Marie Devlin, described by R.F. Foster as "dazzling," and within a few years had three children and an expansive social life of writers, artists, and professors, the Heaney home becoming a center of hospitality in Belfast.

Heaney's first collection of poems, *Death of a Naturalist*, was published in 1966 by the highly respected Faber and Faber. The themes in his first volume would inhabit much of the work that followed—the violent history of his country, the carapace of protective silence, the sense of Ireland's rural past disappearing, the question of where a poet should stand amidst the complications of the world. The bog would become one of his central metaphors, pointing toward history, both its protective and destructive features, the bog standing as a place for hiding memory and violence and a means of preserving them. The bog would reappear in his poetry, an image representing the soggy tangle of Irish history and cultural myth and communal memory. Through his poetry,

Chapter 8. Seamus Heaney and Northern Ireland

he would dig into that complicated story for the next five decades. The bog in a poem like "The Grauballe Man" would become his image of the inescapable past—*the slashed throat, the cured wound, each hooded victim slashed and dumped.*

From 1970–1971, Heaney took a position for a year as a lecturer at UC Berkeley during a time when America was exploding, and Berkeley was the epicenter of the political and cultural upheaval. I moved to Berkeley in June of 1971 with my own dazzling bride and worked on my MA in English at the University of San Francisco across the bay. I realized some years later that it would not have been farfetched to think I could have strolled past Heaney as he walked down Telegraph Avenue in the direction of Moe's Books or Sproul Plaza and campus. Heaney's description of his time in Berkeley could have served to describe mine as well coming from the gloomy grey-streaked skies of the Bronx. Heaney said, "It was the first time we'd lived for any length of time outside Northern Ireland. The first time we lived in the sun." About his first lectureship at Berkeley and his initial visit to California, Heaney remarked: "what Californian distance did was to lead me back to the Irish memory bank...." As California led him back to Ireland, it led me eventually in the same direction.

A central question for many of Heaney's critics and readers over the years has been a similar one that Yeats often faced: whether or not he evaded taking a political position in his poems. Some critics relentlessly accused Heaney of standing aloof from the tragedy of Irish violence. This was an accusation that Heaney implicitly leveled against himself in "Punishment." In speaking directly to the girl in the poem who was tortured and killed for a sexual transgression, the poet exclaims, "My poor scapegoat,/I almost love you/but would have cast, I know,/The first stones of silence./I am the artful voyeur."

The question at the heart of the matter, and in Heaney's own words, was how to resolve "the conflict between detachment and solidarity, between being an activist and an artist, a poet and/or a propagandist." He came to believe that "poetry just being useful is a bigger sin than just being pleasurable." It was an issue that he faced with a combination of transparency and artfulness, it seems to me, in "Casualty," his poem about the 1972 murder of his friend, the pub-loving Louis O'Neill. O'Neill, a small farmer and eel fisherman, had been a regular customer in Heaney's father-in-law's public house in Ardoe, and as Heaney explained in speaking about the poem, O'Neill was "the kind of level-headed, low-key, humorous countryman I always feel at home with." Heaney went on to say that his "friendship with Louis was special because of that unforgettable summer morning when I went out on

Lough Neagh with him and another companion to lift the eel lines. So when he was killed in that explosion, I knew I would have to write something, but wasn't sure how it could be done." The murdered man, one of the many revenants in Heaney's poetry, was "blown to bits," out past curfew on the night of the funerals for Bloody Sunday when the British "shot dead/The thirteen men in Derry." O'Neill's name is never given in the poem. The murdered man remains anonymous, just a fisherman who drank like a fish, a man with a "quick eye" and a "deadpan sidling tact." He stays anonymous and innocent, killed because he swam "towards the lure/Of warm lit-up places." A blameless victim who might ask the poet, an educated man, to puzzle him the answer to the question at hand: Why? Heaney ends the poem asking his friend, the "dawn-sniffing revenant," to "question me again." And the implicit question also becomes *How*. How can a poet find a path between tribal politics and poetic integrity? Where is the logic or decency in these anonymous killings? As the sly and shy fisherman Louis O'Neill might have said to the poet, *Puzzle me the right answer to that one.* And the answer Heaney may have arrived at is another question: "Who's to know/How to read sorrow rightly, or not at all?" This question he strove to answer over his career, seeking to "hold in a single thought reality and justice."

Heaney is not necessarily a sanguine poet, but he is a compassionate one, and rosary beads and human love infiltrate his verse as well as memories of the farm and descriptions of the natural world. As he says in one of his later poems, there's always the chance that the poet can find a way to make "hope and history" rhyme. Or, as he underlines in "The Harvest Bow," *The end of art is peace*. Heaney searched with the devotion of an ancient fili for a way to make poetry relevant and true at the same time. He took it seriously but had a sense of perspective and humor about his vocation, about what poetry is and what it can accomplish. "The image I have," he said, "is from the old cartoons: Donald Duck or Mickey Mouse coming hell for leather to the edge of a cliff, skidding to a stop but unable to halt, and shooting out over the edge. A good poem is the same, it goes a bit further and leaves you walking on air."

In 1972, Heaney quit his lectureship in Belfast and moved his family to Glanmore in the Wicklow Mountains in the Republic of Ireland, a move criticized by those who felt the most important poet in Northern Ireland should stand his ground in the north, making his poetry and presence a political statement about the horrors of the sectarian hostilities. When he moved to Wicklow, he worked as a freelance writer, doing book reviews and essays and radio scripts along with his poetry. Shortly after the shift to Wicklow, Heaney registered his sons in school there, and the headmaster listed his occupation in the administrative documents as *file*. Heaney didn't demure. He had accepted his role as full-time poet. In 1976, Heaney took a position as the Head of English at Carysfort College in Dublin, moving with his wife and three children to Sandymount, not far from where Joyce briefly resided in the Martello tower in Sandycove. With a Joycean wink, Heaney described his new home—"Now I live by a famous strand/where seabirds cry in the small hours/like incredible souls." Joyce's shade seems to have stayed with him in Dublin, finding its way into "Station Island" to utter the Irish poet's revolutionary cry, "The English language belongs to us." Heaney was well aware of his double life as writer and teacher, artist and family man, Northerner in the Republic, and Irish poet who wrote in the English language.

And when Heaney wasn't in the capital of the Republic, he was in the United States, taking part-time professorships at Harvard and elsewhere. In 1982, a few years after I graduated from Fordham University, Heaney gave the commencement address at Fordham in the form of a 46-stanza poem. Both teasing and avuncular, the poem brought up some of the questions that Heaney wrestled with during his career: "Poetry even, that I love best,/Was put severely to the test/In recent years/By guns in streets, bombs on the tracks/Human flesh in plastic sacks...." He alludes to the hunger strikes and the murders in Derry and Belfast and then takes the graduating class at Fordham back to a time before the first college was built on earth. "Men of knowledge," he says, "were sacrosanct" and druids and seers had influence in the world. And the world that Heaney cherishes is not all academic and artistic. He tells the Fordham graduates that he is the eldest of nine children, and he has siblings who are farmers, others who teach school, tend bar, work as domestics or on construction sites, and family members who toiled in linen mills or on the railroad. In his admiration for people who work the land or toil with their hands, in his cherishing of "the ordinary miracles and the living past," Heaney remarks, "So part of me half stands apart/Beyond the pale of books and art/And is not moved" until writers and poets and professors can "justify their place/And win their rights and keep face/Until their value for the race/Is really proved." Heaney's poems are flooded with images of the natural world—blackbirds and bogs, riverbanks and marigolds, skunks and dragonflies, frogs and otters. The value of his poetry, the value of all great poetry, may be in the witness it pays to the world around us, observing what we've lost sight of, making note of ordinary miracles before they disappear.

Heaney's books kept coming, his readership grew, and, for the most part, the critics held steady in their praise, and the honors culminated in the 1995 Nobel Prize for literature, placing him with three other Irishmen—W.B. Yeats, George Bernard Shaw, and Samuel Beckett—who had won the prestigious award for a lifetime achievement in the twentieth century. What the Nobel committee made clear is what many critics and readers had known for a long time—Heaney's poetry offered a rare blend of poignant clarity and skillful suggestion. His poetry was emotional without being sentimental, seeming to rise from the wisdom of both Wordsworth's "emotion recollected in tranquility" and Frost's definition of a poem's beginning as "a lump in the throat" and transforming itself into thought and language.

Heaney wrote more than two dozen books of poems, plays, translations, and assorted prose. His realization that "the successful achievement of a poem could be a stepping stone into your life" became a philosophy that allowed him to create art out of life and, by the accounts of family, friends, and colleagues, life out of art. The main tension that he saw in Dante's life and poetry was at the heart of his, as well—"two often contradictory commands: to be faithful to the collective historical experience and to be true to the recognitions of the emerging self." The implicit questions in his life and work were the ones cited by R.F. Foster—"what is poetry for, and how does it earn its place in the 'real world'?" Heaney answered those questions for me when I first read his poems, and he continues to answer them for me today.

He died on August 30, 2013. He was on his way to the hospital to be operated on for a ruptured arterial blood vessel. In a text message to his wife a few minutes before he died, Heaney sent her a Latin phrase—*Noli timere*—"Don't be afraid."

According to the playwright Tom Stoppard, "Seamus never had a sour moment, neither in person nor on paper." For me, he is the poet who fulfills the promise he alluded to in his late poem "Postscript"—to "catch the heart off guard and blow it open." To be able to write poems that can accomplish that without sacrificing family, friends, or loved ones is a miracle itself.

North by Northwest

> "Compose in darkness./Expect aurora borealis"
> —Seamus Heaney, "North"

On Saturday, November 27, 1909, when he was twenty-seven years old, James Joyce walked the streets of Belfast with two Italian businessmen in an unsuccessful attempt to find a location for a cinema they

Chapter 8. Seamus Heaney and Northern Ireland

wanted to open in the city. Clearly, Joyce was no businessman, and it didn't take long before he went back to thinking about Alfred Hunter, the man who had assisted him during a night of drunken revelry in Dublin. The cinematic dream never worked out for Joyce, but he turned the ghost of Alfred Hunter into the soul of Leopold Bloom, one of the most memorable characters in the modern novel.

The shade of my own Alfred Hunter following me, I found myself in Belfast in 1985, the specter of car bombs and knee-cappings hanging in the air. I had parked my rental car on a street in the heart of downtown Belfast, and a soldier, a rifle slung over his shoulder, ran up and ordered me to move it—or it wouldn't be there when I returned. That night I read an old newspaper and saw that the day before I arrived, June 14, 1985, the IRA had exploded a thousand-pound bomb in the center of the city.

In the fall of 2022, I stopped long enough in Belfast only to smell air and get the sense that the city had a new vitality post–Heaney, post–Troubles, and in the middle of Brexit. We drove into Derry, where Heaney had spent his high school days, instead. I still couldn't tell the Protestants from the Catholics, and I pondered again the question I once asked a history professor at Trinity about the religious/social divide in parts of Northern Ireland I associated with Alfred Hunter and Seamus Heaney. *How did they know a James from a Seamus?* The professor's answer was similar to one I read in a Heaney interview years later: "Everything in Northern Ireland sends a signal." Everything—given names and surnames, street addresses, school ties, accents, school affiliation, friends—marked individuals as Protestant and Catholic. What was invisible to me became a subtle clue to people on one side or another of the religious-political chasm. That was true of the Belfast I saw in 1985, and at that moment in history, it led to marginalization and violence. The subtle distinctions between Catholics and Protestants were still alive in Derry, I was sure, and the demarcations still existed, but the threat of violence had faded. And the surface of the place seemed peaceful enough until you raised your eyes to the many signs around of past strife and violence.

John Lawrence and I spent a night in Sligo and then planned to wend our way through Derry, a city of slightly more than one hundred thousand people, a city of competing IRA murals and Unionist signs, a town that had either come to terms with its past or refused to let anyone forget. I knew the universe was trying to tell me something in the Sligo hotel where we had breakfast when Mary Black's "Columbus" followed by Cat Stevens' "Father to Son" came over the speakers. They were the songs I had heard in the Youghal pub on my first trip to Ireland thirty years before with Jo-Ellen. And when I was leaving the restaurant to

Scull crew on the River Lagan, Belfast.

take my suitcase to the car, Mary Black's "Only a Woman's Heart" came on to remind me that Jo-Ellen was at home waiting for me and that I was no Alfred Hunter, thinking about leaving my family behind. We stopped briefly at Drumcliffe Churchyard on our way out of Sligo and listened to a cacophony of crows screeching in a cluster of sycamore trees as the mist began to clear over Ben Bulben. It seemed reasonable to give a nod to Yeats, one Nobel laureate, as we headed toward the most recent Irish poet to receive the honor. As we stood in front of the swan handles bedecking the wooden church doors in front of what had been a sixth-century monastery, a community for both locals and pilgrims, founded by St. Columba. In the late sixth century, St. Columba illegally copied a manuscript by St. Finnian. Holy men or not, in the hills and valleys of Ben Bulben they fought over the rights to the manuscript and many died in what has come to be known as the Battle of the Books. The king ruled that St. Finnian had been in the right and that "To every cow its calf, and every book its copy." So, in the case of what might be one of the first literary thefts on record, Columba fled, as did Oisin and Niamh, to the island of Iona off the coast of Scotland. There Columba did his penance for his copyright theft and built a monastery that would bring as many to Christianity that had died in the battle he had caused. Ireland takes its books seriously and always has, it seems.

Chapter 8. Seamus Heaney and Northern Ireland

Drumcliffe with Ben Bulben in the background.

Sam Brett then drove us along the Mullaghmore Peninsula with a view of Classiebawm Castle with Donegal Bay behind it and Ben Bulben in the distance. It had been the summer home of Lord Mountbatten, assassinated in 1979 at the height of the Troubles by the IRA, his ship blown up within sight of both Ben Bulben and his beloved castle. When Sam stopped for John to take a photo of the castle, his truck got "bogged" in the soft ground, and we couldn't make it budge. Sam's perpetually serene face and calm demeanor revealed a momentary crack. His eyes narrowed and his lips pursed until an Irish woman and her three male companions helped us place rocks from a stone wall under the tires and pushed the vehicle back into the road out. We thanked them and Sam drove off toward the Unionist North.

"We're the Western Gael!" Sam shouted. "We're tired of our whole colonial history. Even Joyce and the eastern intellectuals. Fuck Joyce and the rest. The new Ireland will come from the West. The Irish Renaissance will come from the West!" With that, he spent the next two hours recounting the Battle of the Bogside in August 1969 in Derry and how that protest sparked the decades of bombs and killings of the Troubles in that city, Belfast, and elsewhere on the island, the civil rights

Mullaghmore Peninsula.

morphing into a war. He talked about Bloody Sunday as if it had been yesterday rather than 1972.

"We didn't have any bombings in Sligo," he said, gazing at the mural of a young Bernadette Devlin that had been painted on the side of a building in the shadow of the Derry walls, her eyes focused on the future, encouraging the protesters at the Bogside in 1969, "but we were part of the same story. The same angry silence. In Sligo, the motto has always been 'say nothing until you hear more and then say less.'"

Anger and silences—Sam's and perhaps Alfred Hunter's and those at the heart of Irish culture—were on my mind as we pulled into Seamus Heaney's HomePlace in Bellaghy, a museum dedicated to his life and work. There's no sense of anger or silence in his poetry or in the images that describe his life. The museum, a few miles from the farm where he grew up, seems a love letter to a man respected and well loved. Images of the poet, his father and mother and siblings, his wife and children and friends merge with audio and video of Heaney's interviews and readings. Heaney once said that the calling of the poet was to be of service, "to ply the work of the individual into the larger work of the community as a whole." It appears that he is remembered for that.

On my first and only view of Armagh, the landscape was cloaked in fog, and Heaney's poem "Follower" rattled in my head, the word

Chapter 8. Seamus Heaney and Northern Ireland 143

grandfather substituting itself for *father*. Like Heaney, I sensed my ancestor Alfred Hunter "stumbling/Behind me ... refusing to go away." I was on the train south, and an emerald-green field, as precisely bisected as an English croft, glistened with dew and shone in the light of a rainbow. And I heard Heaney's voice, "If you have the words, there's always a chance that you'll find the way."

Chapter 9

Writers of the New Ireland

The population of Ireland today is around five million people. In the seventeen decades since the Great Famine, it has never come close to the eight million people that populated the country in the mid–nineteenth century. It's a new world, though, not the impoverished, priest-ridden country of Daniel O'Connell or James Joyce, nor the misogynistic stronghold that Edna O'Brien struggled against, and different voices have arisen to chronicle and question this modern Ireland. Irish literature is experiencing another renaissance, offering a dark, comedic, non-parochial picture of Europe's westernmost island.

Contemporary writers like Tana French, Lisa McInerney, and Benjamin Black paint a picture of an Ireland having difficulty untangling itself from the post–Celtic Tiger greed and the drug-induced alienation and carnage of its teenagers. McInerney depicts a society of misfits in the post-crash Cork. Her first novel, *The Glorious Heresies*, published in 2016, follows a fifteen-year-old drug dealer Ryan Cusack around town in his interactions with his alcoholic father, terrifying gangsters, sex workers, and a club-wielding grandmother. It's a picture of twenty-first-century Cork that is reminiscent of Tony Soprano's New Jersey.

Benjamin Black (aka John Banville) reaches back to the mid–twentieth century in his Quirke series, which is set in what some readers might have imagined as a more benign Ireland of the 1950s. Quirke often deals with corruption in the upper atmosphere of the Catholic Church. Beginning in 2006, Banville, who has been described as a "literary polymath—somewhat in the line of Graham Greene," wrote seven Quirke mystery novels under the pseudonym Benjamin Black about a Dublin pathologist turned amateur detective. In 2021, Banville published *April in Spain*, a Quirke mystery under his real name. *April in Spain* is a mystery that circles back to his 2010 novel *Elegy for April*, highlighting the patriarchy and toxic silence that permeated the island in the mid–twentieth century.

Tana French, the author of eight books, is best known for the six novels

Chapter 9. Writers of the New Ireland 145

in her mesmerizing and popular Dublin Murder Squad series. In the six books in the series, French creates a mythos, minor characters in one story becoming protagonists in another, detectives migrating from center stage to the background from one novel to another. Most of her detectives are loners, and most are lonely, often haunted by secrets from their own pasts as they struggle to unknot the twisted truths of the present. For example, Mick "Scorcher" Kennedy, the Dublin Murder Squad's top detective, tries to solve a grisly triple murder in *Broken Harbor*, a murder that brings him face to face with his troubled younger sister, his own past, and his mother's suicide. At one point in the story, Kennedy seems to sum up French's overall view of the Irish economic boom, its crash, and grim consequences for the country. "I can remember this country," Kennedy says, "back when I was growing up. We went to church, we ate family suppers around the table, and it would never have even crossed a kid's mind to tell an adult to fuck off. There was plenty of bad here, I don't forget that, but we all knew exactly where we stood and didn't break the rules lightly ... people smiled at strangers, people said hello to neighbors, people left their doors unlocked and helped old women with their shopping bags, and the murder rate was scraping zero."

Broken Harbor, like other novels in the Dublin Murder Series, shines a light on the shadowy suburban ghost estates created by the economic rise and fall of the Celtic Tiger in the early twenty-first century. In the novel, awash in images of predatory animals, the half-abandoned estates serve as a metaphor for a loss of innocence and a turn towards modern madness, and Detective Kennedy realizes that Ireland was turning feral. He says, "Everything that stops us from being animals is eroding, washing away like sand...." Kennedy wants to believe in what he feels is a set of values that once existed in his life and in his country. But, as in French's other novels, Ireland has become a place blind to its past and headed toward a national malaise. "The ultimate predator in the story," as the critic Shirley Peterson says, "is the Celtic Tiger itself."

Past and present get twisted and entangled in French's plots, as they do in Irish life, it seems. The town of Broken Harbor was in early times Breadcadh and now in the twenty-first century the developers shapeshifted it into Brianstown, ancient fishing village transformed into holiday spot for the middle class and now a housing estate cum ghost town. But in French's stories, the past can't be repressed, and in *Broken Harbor* Detective Kennedy's mother's suicide stalks him into the present, his sister's visible mental illness is a mirror of his invisible one, and Pat Spain's escalating madness is a twin to his wife's dangerous delusions. Everyone—detectives, criminals, and bystanders—thrives on silence and repression. When Jenny Spain says, "nobody knew ... at least we had that [and] we had the chance of getting back up and doing great again," she may as well be speaking for every character in the book and for the communal code of the Irish. As Maureen T. Reddy makes clear, "If French's novels ask, 'who are the Irish now, in the twenty-first century' ... the answers they suggest are far from reassuring." And for any reader of *The Irish Times*, drug deals, corruption, and grisly murders are not a new story.

As cheerless as the image of modern and contemporary Ireland suggested in the mysteries and social commentaries of Benjamin Black, Lisa McInerney, and Tana French, for many readers Rob Doyle, one of the group of groundbreaking contemporary young Irish writers, creates an even more savage world in his fiction. In his visceral 2014 novel *Here Are the Young Men*, he paints a deeply troubling picture of the cultural unraveling going on in Ireland today. Doyle chronicles murders in *Here Are the Young Men*, but the novel is less a murder mystery than it is a warped Irish *Catcher in the Rye*, a narrative about a group of alienated and angry young Dubliners whose lives seem less lived than mediated through Facebook and Instagram. In their attempt to find a meaning in the emptiness of their day-to-day existence, no longer anchored in the religious or cultural beliefs of their parents, this group of teenagers drifts into drugs and alcohol and throwaway sexual relationships—and the story ultimately erupts in what feels like a mythic madness, a ritualistic murder that is both frightening and somehow strangely sanguine.

With echoes of *A Clockwork Orange*, Doyle's *Here Are the Young Men* chronicles the brutal tale of four young men and their occasional girlfriend—Matthew, Rez, Kearney, Cocker, and Jen—a tribe of seventeen-year-olds, having just completed their Leaving Certificate Exams, on the verge of graduating from secondary school, and struggling to find a path forward in a world that makes little sense to them. They are the alienated children of the Celtic Tiger with little sense of hardship, history, or past values. The narrative shuttles between the first-person point of view of the protagonist, Matthew Connelly, and the third person perspective focused on his friends, Rez and Kearney.

To one degree or another, each of the characters subscribes to Matthew's opening lines in the narrative—"If it's not broken—I chanted silently in rhythm to our steps—then break it. If it's fixed, break it again, break it more, wreck it. Wreck everything, and for no reason whatsoever...." Just before the story opens, a classmate they all knew—Stephen Harrigan—hanged himself in one of the doorways of their school classrooms. And in this existential drama and for these alienated young adults, suicide is always a viable option. As Cocker explains to Matthew,

"'But, like, what if that's it, though, that's what's in store for us? he said.' 'I mean, like, maybe he did it that way as a sort of warnin or whatever. Like to say, Youse lads will be finished school in just a week or two, and look, here's the way it goes after that, this is the fuckin final destination or whatever. Ye know what I mean? Like a warnin.'"

In the prefatory page of *Here Are the Young Men*, Doyle offers a gambit similar to the one used by Tim O'Brien in *The Things They Carried*, blending the possibilities of fact and fiction, saying, "This is all true. We did these things. This is all reality." Like Tim O'Brien, Rob Doyle suggests the connection between story truth and happening truth, between actuality and the imagination, is real, an aesthetic and philosophical stance he pushes even further in his second and third genre-bending books. For instance, in his third book, *Threshold*, he offers an even more directly self-referential series of tales in which he says, "my life was the research for the book I was writing about my life, which was many books, would justify that life." Like a twenty-first-century Hemingway with an Irish accent, Doyle described living it up to write it down. And even if *Here Are the Young Men* is not a documentary truth it is a record of the spirit of the Dublin he grew up in during the Celtic Tiger and its aftermath. Matthew's father is at a loss to understand his son's behavior and asks him, "Do ye not realize how lucky ye are?" His father, who grew up in Ireland's more difficult economy, can't fathom his son's indifference and lack of direction. "Look at all the opportunities that are out there, waitin for ye," he says. "This country has never had more money in it than it has now. Jesus, we used to be hardly any better off than a Third World country.... And now our economy is the envy of the bleedin world, and all you and your mates do is sit there mopin."

Matthew Connelly, the main character in *Here Are the Young Men*, and Rez, his introspective friend, yearn for some sense of meaning beyond drugs, alcohol, pornography, and masturbation, but, also, beyond the road to success mapped out by their teachers and parents. God is dead for them, the church is defunct, school is a sham, work is empty. Their form of transubstantiation, as they utter "Body of Christ, Amen" and smirk, comes not as they place the sacred host on their tongue but a tab of Ecstasy. Their companion Kearney, though, revels in the meaning he finds in misogyny and cruelty. He is a Dublin version of Flannery O'Connor's Misfit; the only proof he can find for his existence is in causing others' pain. Kearney daydreams about mass murder and imagines inventing sordid, violent video games, and those games are more real to him than everyday life. The adrenaline rush of rape and brutal violence makes Kearney feel alive. He contemplates, for example, developing a game titled *Orgasm of Hate*, in which people play out their genocidal fantasies about killing individuals in the homeless and elderly communities. Eventually, that game becomes real life entertainment for Kearney.

Kearney's alienation's is sociopathic, an extreme form of the isolation felt by Rez and Matthew. The question that Rez asks Matthew may be a pertinent one for many in his generation: "I mean, what does it really mean to you to be Irish? I mean, like, growin up in the suburbs, which may as well be anywhere, and watchin American films and English telly and English football, and everyone you're supposed to look up to, all they go on about is cars and mortgages, and they are supposed to be the most important things in life. The property ladder. Jesus. And now we're supposed to race out there and join the fun?" The story Doyle presents to his readers has much in common with the one Tana French, Lisa McInerney, and Benjamin Black offer. It's a portrait of an Ireland that has lost a hold on its past but has failed to make sense of its future.

* * *

Kevin Barry, the author of three highly accomplished collections of stories and three distinctive novels, seemed to be trying to outstrip Joyce in terms of the itinerant life of the writer. By some accounts, he lived in seventeen different addresses before his fortieth birthday. Born in Limerick and now a permanent resident of a former police barracks in Sligo, Barry has, with a wink, described himself as a "raving egomaniac" who won't be satisfied until he receives the Nobel Prize. One thing is certain: he is not a writer who repeats himself. Nor does he plan to. In a 2015 interview with Dan Sheehan in *Electric Lit*, Barry said, "I think you should always be trying to change. I really hate this idea of the writer who finds a voice, and then writes in that voice for forty years."

Barry has an element of Flann O'Brien in him, and James Joyce and Frank

Rob Doyle.

O'Connor, as well. Ultimately, though, he is suis generis. At nineteen years old, Barry worked as a cub reporter in Limerick. Later, he worked as a columnist for the *Irish Examiner*. He has won a host of awards, one the *Times* EPG Short Story Award, the biggest monetary prize in the world for a single short story. His first book, the futuristic gang saga *City of Bohane*, set in the mid–twenty-first century, won the International Dublin Literary Award in 2013. The novel is grounded in a mythical town in Western Ireland, but Bohane is actually based upon Porto, Portugal, where Barry was spending a holiday when he came up with the idea for the narrative. Barry said that *City of Bohane* was written in Technicolor and influenced by American television, where he claims that the best long-term fiction is being written right now. *City of Bohane*, a wild, enigmatic, dystopian novel, rocked the world of Irish letters when it came out in 2011. Barry has the reader riding the swells of Irish slang in an otherworldly city that could be present-day Cork or Limerick or Dublin. Bohane is a place where "Aggravators were on the prowl from the flatblock circles of the Rises and the ozone of danger was a sexy tang on the air." It is a truly Irish place where headwinds take "schelps" at characters' heads and the rains come slantways "off the hideous fucking ocean, and the grapes nearly frozen off us, and dirty ice caked on top of the puddles, and we are not happy, exactly, but satisfied in our despair." Barry's language in the novel has some of the invented force of Joyce's *Ulysses* and perhaps even leans in the direction of *Finnegans Wake* at times, that is, if *Finnegans Wake* had any inclination at all to speak with some narrative clarity to the reader. With *City of Bohane*, Barry exploded on the scene.

Two novels—*Beatlebone* in 2015 and *Night Boat to Tangier* in 2019 followed, each book slipping the moorings from the novel it succeeded. "I get bored with repetition in life and in art," Barry has asserted. He sees himself in the tradition of tradition breakers—in the company of Irish writers like Laurence Sterne and Flann O'Brien, in the clan of writers who created "some fucking mad stuff." He's put together some mad stuff, surely. The novel *Beatlebone* could be defined a novel, a collection of essays, a memoir, or a pastiche of all three forms. Whatever term critics and readers use to define *Beatlebone*, Barry achieves his goal of bringing the reader into the heart of a tall tale, nudging him toward the edge of believability, "where the reader is thinking to themselves 'ah c'mon, no fucking way … but maybe.'" After all, the story may sound preposterous—that until the day he died John Lennon owned a hippie island—Dorinish—in Clew Bay off the coast of County Mayo, but it's true. Lennon bought the island for about $2,000 in 1967 and in the early 1970s invited the King of the Hippies, Sid Rawle, to establish a commune there. In *Beatlebone*, fact and fiction, history and legend, all merge into a story that could be seen as Barry's Portrait of the Artist as Young Man. If *Beatlebone* points towards Barry's West and the conflict between celebrity and authenticity, and *City of Bohane* points south and toward an apocalyptic future, then *Night Boat to Tangier* moves the reader East and in the direction of an eerie naturalism that recalls an Irish writer Barry admires—Samuel Beckett in *Waiting for Godot*. In *Night Boat to Tangier*, Maurice Hearne and Charlie Redmond, two down-on-their-luck Irish gangsters, former drug traffickers seeking a new trade, wait like Didi and Gogo lookalikes in the Spanish port of Algeciras for Maurice's estranged daughter, Dilly, to walk through the ferry terminal shaking her dreadlocks into the night air. As with Beckett's play, Barry's novel is a waiting game, and neither God nor Dilly is scheduled to show up and give any meaning to the character's lives. Barry portrays the loss of love and its opposite—not hate but death.

Barry's darkly comic and sometimes phantasmagorical style can be found in *City of Bohane*, *Beatlebone*, and even in the more stripped-down *Night Boat to Tangier*. But his three collections of stories—*There Are Little Kingdoms* (2007), *Dark Lies the Island* (2012), and *That Old Country Music* (2020)—show the influence of one of Barry's favorite American writers—Flannery O'Connor—and her aesthetic—"To the hard of hearing you shout, and for the almost blind, you draw large startling figures."

The sense of tragicomedy that permeates Flannery O'Connor's work struck me as pervading the first collection of Barry's stories that I read—*Dark Lies the Island*. Barry's collection, published in 2012, approximately one hundred years after James Joyce's *Dubliners*. Playfully but significantly, *Dark Lies the Island* works as a homage to Joyce's collection about Ireland at the end of the nineteenth and at the beginning of the twentieth century. "Across the Rooftops" is a case in point. "Across the Rooftops," set on a Cork rooftop in the early morning, as a young man struggles mightily to negotiate a first kiss with a young woman he has been interested in for some time. This is not exactly the un-named narrator of "Araby" and the unattainable Magnan's sister, but, despite the one hundred years separating the stories, they are mirror images of one another. As with other tales in *Dark Lies the Island* such as "Wifey Redux," "Beer Trip to Llandudno," and "Ernestine and Kit," "Across the Rooftops" comes angling across the century as a wink and a nod homage to Joyce's *Dubliners*. The main character in "Across the Rooftops" is older than the narrator of "Araby," but he is equally adolescent in how he internalizes his anxiety over his imagined relationship with the beautiful object of his desire. The young male narrator of "Across the Rooftops" is paralyzed by indecision, imbuing each potential move as if it were a life-altering moment—"I thought about maybe kissing her shoulder. How would that be for a move? It would be the work of two seconds—a lean-to, a planting of the lips, a withdrawal. And a shy little glance to follow." He is willing to talk to her "about everything except the space between us." Every natural instinct reshapes itself into an overthought calculation. Every gesture becomes an opportunity for second-guessing and hesitation—"Maybe I should just ask, I thought. Can I kiss you? How would that sound?"

Like the adolescent narrator of "Araby," the narrator of "Across the Rooftops" creates an alternate world in his head, a world that calcifies the romantic moment—"You're killing this stone dead," the girl says. And when the kiss finally occurs, it's too late. The moment has been lost, and the narrator is left in a plight similar to the protagonist in "Araby"—gazing up shamefacedly into what he sees as his own bleak future. For Barry's character, there is no Araby—just what's in store for him. His eyes may not burn with anger and anguish as they do for the narrator of "Araby," but a gull does descend to the edge of a church roof and "the mad stare of its eye was vivid and comical and a taunt to me." So, in the adolescent overcalculation of the significance of the moment, the narrator of "Across the Rooftops" says, "I looked out across the still, quiet city, and I sat there for hours and months and for years. I sat there until all that had been about us faded again to nothing, until the sound of the crowd died and the music had ended, and we all trailed home along the sleeping streets, with youth packed away, and life about to begin." As with "Araby," Barry's homage in "Across the Rooftops" suggests two compatible readings—one about a painful loss of innocence and the other an equally painful refusal to shed that innocence.

"Wifey Redux," the second story in *Dark Lies the Island*, works as both a pitch-perfect satire of the perfect Celtic Tiger nuclear family and as a tongue-in-cheek homage to Joyce's "The Dead," the story of a marriage accosted by the past. The first sentence of "Wifey Redux" makes both the tone and direction of the story clear. The narrator explains, "This is the story of a happy marriage but before you throw up and turn the page let me say that it will end with my face pressed hard into the cold metal of the Volvo's bonnet, my hands cuffed behind my back, and my rights droned into my ear...."

In the hands of a less-skillful comic writer, "Wifey Redux" could have ended up a hot mess of Freudian winks and eye rolls. On the surface, the unreliable narrator, Jonathan Prendergast, and his wife, Saoirse, have won life's lotto—when they met, Jonathan was a handsome

Matt Dillon type, and Saoirse was exquisitely beautiful, with a bone-China complexion, heartbreaking green eyes, and "an outstanding arse." Three years into their marriage came their beautiful "mantle-piece pretty" daughter, Ellie. And by the time Ellie is seventeen years old, with the same sexy lisp as her mother, the edges of the happy marriage have frayed. Jonathan couldn't lose his civil service job unless he stood naked on the office copier, their house looking out at the bay at Dun Laoghaire has octupled in value since they purchased it, and they have every knick-knack and gewgaw of Irish upward mobility. Beneath the surface is another story entirely. Jonathan's waistline has expanded, as has Saoirse's arse, their beautiful Ellie is a superficial spoiled brat, Saoirse has developed as suburban Pinot Grigio habit "that would knock a fucking horse," and Jonathan has intermittent crying jags and a direct line to his psychiatrist, Dr. Murtagh.

The true story of the Celtic Tiger fairy tale is between the lines and in the parentheses of Barry's tale—"our beautiful, perfect daughters emerge into a perfect facsimile of how our beautiful, desirable wives had been, back then, when they were young. And slim. And sober." So, the Kierkegaardian sense of despair is there, albeit in the typical, unacknowledged Irish manner. Enter Aodhan McAdam, handsome as a movie star, with his blonde, floppy hair and "eight million quids' worth of dental work" and a physique that suggests he has been "raised on prime beef and full-fat milk," and the fuse is lit. The narrator, incrementally driven mad by Aodhan's "orthodontic beam" each night at their front door, is pushed slowly toward the cliff's edge by the thought of his daughter having sex with the hunky Aodhan. "Even saying the horrible, smug, hiccup syllables of that fucker's name," Jonathan moans, "makes me retch." But it's the illiterate graffiti scrawled in the rain shelter near the Dun Laoghaire Pier announcing Ellie's mastery of the oral arts and Aodhan's later dumping Ellie that send Jonathan flying over the edge and straight to the Do-It-Right Warehouse where Aodhan works on Saturdays. There, with the crack of a face slap and some choice words, Jonathan leaves Aodhan, a crying child "ashen-faced and limp" with the fear of Biblical fatherly retribution. Jonathan's final symbolic gesture—the one that compelled the Gardai to show up in the parking lot to arrest him—is to buy a ladder and a hammer and take down the exclamation point in the Do-It-Right! sign. In smashing the exclamation point, Jonathan is examining "lost fields, lost kingdoms, a lost world—and I was serene as a bird riding the swells of morning air over those lost fields."

As in Joyce's "The Dead," "Wifey Redux" is a story about the myth and reality of past love invading a relationship in the present. Aodhan, an Irish name that means *fire*, is the catalyst for the white heat of the conclusion, Jonathan's figurative immolation in the Do-It-Right parking lot. Jonathan's threatening of Aodhan and his smashing of the symbolic exclamatory mark of the Celtic Tiger suggests that the first step toward authenticity is demolishing false gods when we come upon them.

In an interview, Barry once said, "Irish people are great talkers. We love the sound of our own voices. Contrarily, then, sometimes we say very little.... It can take years to figure out the meaning of an Irish conversation. It can be ten years later that we found out what she actually meant." This insight sheds some light on "Wifey Redux," with its unreliable narrator, in which what is not said is always bubbling like truth just beneath the surface of the comedy. As Barry has explained, the essence of the narrative is there, under the surface: "that's where you find your stories and your drama." Barry stands somewhere between James Joyce, who wanted to put all words on the page, and Samuel Beckett, who sought to take most of the words off the page, and sees himself more in the mischievous and roguish tradition of Flann O'Brien, and "Wifey Redux" may amount to a homage to "The Dead" if Flann O'Brien had taken on the subject matter of perfect romance remembered and recalibrated.

Barry is fond of quoting Harold Pinter's line, "Don't ever give them what they think they want," and in "Ernestine and Kit," another potentially twisted homage to *Dubliners*, specifically to "An Encounter," Barry surely does not offer the predictable. As with his allusions to Joyce's other tales from *Dubliners*, in "Ernestine and Kit" Barry shows that in one hundred years since Joyce's collection of stories, Ireland has become a darker, more unpredictable island. Joyce's story "An Encounter" locates itself in the landscape of sexual abuse and pedophilia. "Ernestine and Kit" initially appears to be an innocuous tale of two matrons in their sixties who are on a day trip through the fairs and festivals of North County Sligo on a fine early summer day. Their interest in the weekend crowds as they enjoy their jaunt seems innocent enough until it becomes clear that Kit and Ernestine raise the malevolent stakes in Barry's portrait of present-day Ireland. At first, Kit and Ernestine seem harmless, merely caustic and judgmental, but before long they reveal themselves to be psychopaths, their bizarre blend of xenophobia, racism, and animosity compelling them to steal toddlers from those they consider to be undeserving parents. With a sly narrative dexterity, Barry reshapes the story from one about two eccentric retirees to a chronicling of sadistic malevolence. From Joyce's early twentieth century suggestion of sexual deviance in "An Encounter" to Barry's portrait of a child's violent kidnapping in the early twenty-first century, the representation of the island has gotten darker.

When Kevin Barry talks about the Irish writers who influenced him, he often mentions Flann O'Brien. "Kit and Ernestine" may harken back to O'Brien's dark humor, but the story may have even more in common with the American writers Barry admires—Saul Bellow, Philip Roth, and Flannery O'Connor. In particular, Barry has argued that Irish writers have a lot in common with writers of the American South in terms of weaving the rhythms and accents of speech onto the page. "The surreal humor of the West of Ireland," Barry has maintained, "is close to that of O'Connor's South." In that respect, Kit and Ernestine could have been literary cousins to O'Connor's the Misfit, Manley Pointer, Mrs. Shortley, or Tom T. Shiftlet. Barry's twenty-first-century Ireland goes a step farther into the darkness beyond Joyce's *Dubliners*. One reviewer has characterized Barry's fiction as "heartbroken people up in the hills." Barry's response: "That pretty much covers it." Barry's contemporary Ireland, summed up in the titular story of the volume, "Dark Lies the Island," is a place awash in the internet and chat rooms, populated by privileged and indifferent parents, and suicidal teenagers who cut themselves "for the red vibrancy, for feeling."

The main character of "Dark Lies the Island," Sara, floats through a gap year after passing her Leaving Certs, but she is actually hiding out in the family's pretentiously modern holiday house near Clew Bay in County Mayo. Her father, a successful architect, spends his time enjoying tapas in Spain. Her mother is in France with her breast implants and her new husband. Sara is left to face her demons and the darkness of the twenty-first century along Ireland's West Coast. And, although Barry never reveals the exact nature of Sara's epiphany, she does find the courage to throw all the knives from the house into the darkness and discovers a way to find peace or at least a way to face the suicidal emptiness—"She closed her eyes and allowed the world without to fade, for a small while anyway, and for half a minute, and then a whole one—and then more—there was something just a little like sleep." In Kevin Barry's world, there are drugs and malevolence, unrequited longing and failed marriages, there is a tragi-comedy akin to Flannery O'Connor's and a dizzying satire related to that of Flann O'Brien. Barry's "Dark Lies the Island" moves the reader beyond Joyce's *Dubliners*, the paralysis becoming a chokehold. The priest-ridden island taking on even more ominous shadows. The only escape for his characters: the ability to face the darkness and laugh when the pain rises to an incomprehensible level.

One rainy night in October of 2022, I got to talk to Kevin Barry in what has become the new person-to-person in the twenty-first century. Kevin and I were supposed to meet either for tea or for a morning swim at Rosses Point, one of Yeats's favorite places to walk and meditate. But

Chapter 9. Writers of the New Ireland

Kevin Barry.

Kevin's wife had scheduled a vacation to Spain on the day we were to meet, and we talked via Zoom. My hotel room in Sligo had no internet—so I had to station myself in the lobby with my laptop, and I could not help feeling a bit like one of the characters in *Night Boat to Tangier*. Hotel customers floated by me like ferry passengers, and I perched on a stool a few miles from Kevin's barracks station home in Sligo. Kevin sat in a rented house in Spain, a tired but accommodating smile on his face, his hands occasionally combing through his wild hair, making it stand up in even more fantastic patterns than were typical for him as he talked about Irish culture, literature, and the place of his books in it all.

I asked him about *Dark Lies the Island* working as an homage to Joyce's *Dubliners*. "Even though it came around one hundred years after Joyce's collection, I wasn't thinking of a nod to *Dubliners*," he said. "So much of writing fiction rises from the subconscious. The same place that dreams come from. And maybe as the writer you're the last person that the meaning comes clear to. So, I suppose, Joyce may have been dancing around in my subconscious." I wondered if there were any contemporary Irish writers who didn't have Joyce dancing in their dreams and nightmares.

"It was actually around the time of *Dark Lies the Island* that County Sligo started to come into my writing a little bit," Barry went on, "the first flicker of it at least. My immediate environment began to infect the work. I was someone who grew up in the suburbs and lived for a long time in cities. And then suddenly I was in the dark countryside. And that started to seep into my work. When I started to write fiction in my twenties in Cork City, I stayed a million miles away from Joyce and Irish literature. I didn't think about being an Irish writer. I was obsessed by the great American Jews—Philip Roth and, above all, Saul Bellow. I loved the vitality of their style, the mix of low and high on the page."

He paused, his hand shooting up to take his headband off and rake his hand through an untamed patch of graying hair. "It was only years later that I came to Irish writing by reading the great John McGahern. I read *Amongst Women*, and the description of the bitter old father sitting in front of the fire twirling his thumbs around one another—there was a shock of recognition, *Oh, fuck, that's my father!* I had that oily sense of discomfort you get when you read someone who's writing so close to home. Then the writer who really appealed to me in Irish writing was Dermot Healy, a writer associated with County Sligo. His work like a world that was closer to me than McGahern's. Then, of course, there was Flann O'Brien and the great Irish tradition of mischievous, roguish narrative, a tradition that goes all the way back to Laurence Sterne. I didn't get Beckett at all when I read him in my twenties, but I do now. I never consciously go to my desk and say I'm going to do some Irish writing, but you can't avoid it, now can you? Your personality finds itself directly on the page. I consider myself, by and large, a comic writer. It's a very Irish comedy, very dark, black. When I write, an inky dark comedy comes out. The tint of the humor is funereal. I'm always talking about Irish funerals, and what happens outside the dead house where the body is laid out. There are always these little clusters of men and women making crack. Laughter in the dark, you know? The Irish can't deal with reality. And that's the sort of humor in my books, a kind of *if you don't laugh, you'll cry* humor. Also, Irish writers can't resist the lyrical impulse, the lyrical note. I've tried resisting it in my work, to barb it, you know. To take the piss out of it. Now I'm becoming more relaxed with the lyrical impulse as I grow older. I figure it's there and it's going to come out."

Two of Barry's influences as a short story writer came from the American South—Barry Hannah and Flannery O'Connor. "Irish writers have a lot in common with American writers from the South," he said. "We face some of the same difficulties on the page—rendering those idioms can look fuckin' ripe, even over-ripe. We're writing for the hard of hearing, we are. The world's in bad shape, you can't deny it, but Ireland may be more temperate than America. I think the current inclination in Ireland is to make it like Scandinavia. We have big problems, though. This island is radically overpriced. They're killing the golden goose very quickly. I think that Ireland is one of the worst places that a writer could be based." He laughed. "Bar all the other places. I love to come back to the Shannon River and the West of Ireland. It's rainy and it's morose, but we are still a nation of readers. People here still take books seriously. And that might make them more open-minded than people in other parts of Europe. And with all the lurches toward intolerance we see in Europe and around the world, you can't help but worry. But there may be cause to hope in Ireland with writers like Rob Doyle and Paul Lynch and Sally Rooney."

Chapter 9. Writers of the New Ireland

Barry's next book will not be set in Ireland but in the copper mines of Butte, Montana, in the 1890s. However, the characters will be Irish immigrants, and Barry will be rendering the idioms, using dark comedy as a way of seeing and seizing the world, shouting for the hard of hearing, and allowing the lyrical to settle on the page with a barb.

* * *

Sally Rooney, a self-described Marxist, started as an Irish star and soon became a world phenomenon. Her first two novels in 2017 and 2018—*Conversations with Friends* and *Normal People* (both adapted into BBC TV series)—hurtled her to fame when she was still in her twenties and barely out of Trinity College, where she got an undergraduate degree in English and an MA in American literature. Her third novel—*Beautiful World, Where Are You*—came out in 2021. Critical applause has run a parallel course to her growing readership—both for good reason. Rooney pays meticulous attention to the details of everyday experience, and she has the ability to make ordinary moments in the lives of her Millennials shimmer with significance. In prose that is never overwrought or self-conscious, Rooney transforms what could be seen by some as post-teenage whining into matter that for many readers is both deeply important and compelling. Critics have talked about the fierce clarity of her prose, the acute and sophisticated psychological portraits, her insights into what it means to be young today.

Her first novel, *Conversations with Friends*, tracks the convoluted relationships among two twenty-one-year-old Trinity undergraduates—Frances and Bobbi—and a thirty-something married couple—Melissa, an established writer, and Nick, a moderately successful stage and screen actor. Frances is an aspiring writer and, with Bobbi, performs her poems on stage. Melissa recognizes their talent as writer and performer, and the narrative knot tightens as she invites the two undergraduates into the complicated and privileged life she leads with Nick. Bobbi and Frances, once lovers themselves, are drawn respectively toward Melissa and Nick.

The protagonist of the novel, Frances, is a wry witness to everything and everyone around her, and her observations—as with her friend Bobbi's—are intimidatingly and self-consciously smart, as if, like Rooney herself in her early twenties and the number one debater on the European continent, they were college disputants who seamlessly fit into Rooney's characterization of the debating world—"College university debating requires a particular intersection of personal qualities," she once wrote. "You have to enjoy talking out loud in front of people. You need to have a taste for ritualized, abstract interpersonal aggression." That statement came from Rooney's essay "Even if you beat me" in the spring 2015 issue of *The Dublin Review*, but it could have as readily been uttered by Bobbi or Frances in *Conversations with Friends* or one of the introspective and smart-tongued characters in Rooney's later novels. Many conversations in Rooney's novels come across as debates, ideas articulated with a force and humor that can be daunting and enthralling in the same instant.

Frances in *Conversations with Friends* is simultaneously appealing and annoyingly self-consumed. She may very well be Rooney's portrait of herself at that age—"Most of the things I did when I was nineteen," Rooney wrote in her essay about her stardom as a debater, "were motivated by a desperation to be liked." Frances, like Rooney who writes about her medical scare caused by occasional fainting spells, has a moment where she is forced to face the fragility of her own health. In addition to her endometriosis, Frances cuts herself "to feel." Frances is not alone in her uncertainty, her disconnection from the world, or her inclination to depression. Nick, the luminously handsome thirty-two-year-old married man who falls in love with her, may be kind and gentle and have a capacity for unconditional sympathy, but his wife often sees him as pathetic and "pathologically submissive," and he does demonstrate moments of zombie-like docility.

Frances, similar to the other significant characters in *Conversations with Friends*, is looking for a way to live authentically and joyfully in a world that makes little sense to her in terms of politics and economics and human interaction. Toward the conclusion of the novel, when Frances's affair with Nick seems to have imploded, in speaking of her current relationship with Bobbi, suggests what her search may amount to—"Each of our gestures felt spontaneous, and if from the outside we resembled a couple, that was an interesting coincidence for us. We developed a joke about it, which was meaningless to everyone including ourselves: what is a friend? We would say humorously. What is a conversation?" Put another way, she appears to be asking: what is love? what is meaningful human interaction? Rooney's answer to those questions is always riveting and often quite funny, as when she meditates on her confused feelings of guilt and lust as far as Melissa and Nick are concerned: "Does he respect Melissa more than me? Did he like her more? If we were both going to die in a burning building and he could only save one of us, would he certainly save Melissa and not me? It seemed practically evil to have so much sex with someone who would later allow you to burn to death."

The relationships in the novel—Bobbi with Melissa, Frances with Nick, Nick with Melissa, and Bobbi with Frances—make for what seems an impossible knot, a sexually-charged Word document. But, as Rooney

Chapter 9. Writers of the New Ireland   159

intimates toward the end of the novel, maybe not so impossible and maybe a conversation that can transcend emails and texts. "You can love more than one person," Bobbi tells Frances, but it's not clear that Frances believes in that possibility until the final four words of the book when Frances tells Nick, "Come and get me," and the writer suggests that maybe there is more than one kind of love, "an alternative model of loving." Perhaps, there are many ways of defining healthy, tender human relationships, and Frances may be uttering more than another witty remark when she says, "To love someone under capitalism you have to love everyone. Is that theory or theology."

Toward the climax of the novel, Frances steps into a church to pray that the pain she is experiencing will subside. She prays and then she faints, "an activity that has become normal for her." She is unused to prayer and not accustomed to experiencing epiphanies, but she has one nevertheless. "When I opened my eyes," she says, "I felt that I understood something, and the cells of my body seemed to light up like millions of glowing points of contact, and I was aware of something profound." Like many revelatory moments, this one disappears, but it leads Frances toward accepting the fact that the impossible complication of love may be possible after all. Ultimately, *Conversations with Friends* provides no answers, though, but to imply that although their relationship may be doomed, Frances and Nick will find a way to continue being together—at least for the time being, like characters in play by Beckett, they wait.

Despite the postmodern trappings of Instagram, texts, sexting, and sharp-edged conversations played out in emails, Rooney's realistic novels of manners have more in common with Jane Austen than they do with Thomas Pynchon. Even Rooney acknowledges that her books are "basically nineteenth-century novels dressed up in contemporary clothing." There is also a Holden Caulfield sensibility to many of her characters in their alienation from middle-class values and hypocrisies. Rooney has been called the "Salinger for the Snapchat generation"; however, Lauren Collins in *The New Yorker* argues that making too much of the Salinger connection would be a dangerous oversimplification—"Her characters are let down by the adult world, but intrigued, too, and maybe galvanized. Their default attitude is a raised eyebrow. They fear they may be the biggest phonies of all." Rooney's characters are unequivocal in their views about Fascism ("No one who likes Yeats is capable of human intimacy") or Marxism (believing passionately in Socialism as many of them continue to live the privileged life granted to them in a capitalist society), and even though they hold often entrenched opinions about politics, art, culture, and all sorts of human hierarchies, they struggle for a way to live with decency and compassion in a world that Lauren Collins described where "the expectation of caring for others no longer obtains, in which it's easier to wreck a home than to own one." In this fractured and unfair world, Rooney's characters decry the imbalances in capitalism but a number of critics, like Christian Lorentzen in the *London Review of Books*, have pointed out that those same characters "skate to the top" of the very systems they denounce.

The two novels following *Conversations with Friends* do not extend the perimeter of Rooney's work, but they may deepen its resonance. In this respect, pushing deeper into the same territory, Rooney may share some DNA with Flannery O'Connor. Rooney's characters, like O'Connor's, come from the same family tree, bear common traits, and her thematic concerns remain recognizable in all three books. *Normal People* offers an analogous dynamic to *Conversations with Friends*—Connell being the handsome, universally-liked, sensitive high school insider, and Marianne being the plain, albeit brilliant, outsider who longs to connect with him and, despite her claims otherwise, her peers. Connell in *Normal People*, Nick in *Conversations with Friends* and Simon in *Beautiful World, Where Are You* share the same genetic code of decency and thoughtfulness. But for their own depression and insecurities, their own exertions to find their place in the world, they would be one-dimensional heroes. Connell is thoughtful and honorable, and he likes Marianne, eventually falling in love with her, but he is also a self-conscious teenager who is reluctant to be outed as the boy who is dating someone outside the circle of the anointed at their school. All of Rooney's principal characters want to be "normal people." They want to fit into the crowd and not obsess over their singularity and loneliness. The main characters all struggle with the emptiness they feel engulfing them, and they suffer from a confusion that often deteriorates into masochism and misunderstanding. Marianne, especially, seeks to lose herself into "normality" by being dominated. In secondary school, Connell is accepted and popular, and Marianne is a pariah. Those roles get reversed when they go to Trinity, where Marianne becomes admired and desired, and Connell strains to find his place. When it comes down to essences, though, Connell, like Nick and Simon, is humble and loving, patient and considerate. And all the male protagonists remain to one degree or another like the female protagonists, outsiders. Nick, Connell, and Simon all have a passivity to them. They are all gentle souls, so handsome they become sex objects (this may be Rooney's ironic wink at the patriarchy), and readers often locate her male characters somewhere on the continuum between the inert and the saintly, between the phlegmatic and the heroic.

Chapter 9. Writers of the New Ireland

In a similar vein, Rooney reimagines the similar female protagonists in her three novels—all radiantly clever and introspective, all troubled loners who desire love and acceptance but fear what such acceptance might do to their identities. Unlike the men, none of the female protagonists are beautiful—or at least their beauty initially goes unrecognized by the crowd. Their searing intelligence is both their blessing and their curse, like Marianne's "cold, interpretive eyes," both a way of dealing with the world and a way of deflecting it. Marianne, like other female protagonists in Rooney's fiction, wants to shed her suis generis status and cling to it as well. There are other patterns in Rooney's fiction. Fathers are often alcoholics, violent, or absent. Mothers, other than Lorraine Waldron, typically have but a fragile understanding of their daughters. Bisexuality is often the desire du jour. No relationships are without dark passages and switchbacks. There is no one road to love. Art does not change much in the world, but what else, her main characters often wonder, in their discussions of economic and political inequities, is there to do but engage in conversations and pursuits of the artistic sort? Economic success is typically something that these characters say that they care little about, but like a boon and a plague it comes to them anyway. The main characters are horrified by the unfairness in the world, but they rarely go beyond the aesthetics of conversation and push into the realm of political action. Unlike "normal people," Rooney's most admirable characters are damaged souls on the periphery of things, but they see the world with a laser-like clarity. Ordinary facts—how a cup of coffee is lifted to the lips, how an unspoken gesture breaks through a silence, how what is not said becomes louder than what is said—take on a luster for them (and thus for the reader). The commonplace vibrates with meaning. When seen through the eyes of Frances in *Conversations with Friends*, Marianne in *Normal People*, or Eileen in *Beautiful World, Where Are You*, the everyday world becomes memorable and worth considering in its minutest detail. What her main characters see—after much self-absorption and self-reflection—is that there is a way to save one another, as Marianne saves Connell and he saves her—"He brought her goodness like a gift, and now it belongs to her."

All of Rooney's books appear to tread a line close to the autobiographical, but *Beautiful World, Where Are You* strikes at the heart of what her recent rocket ride to fame might have felt like to her. In reviewing *Beautiful World, Where Are You*, Christian Lorentzen quoted some lines from Norman Mailer that might be pertinent to Rooney's literary ascent. "We wanted to change the nature of American life," Mailer declared. "None of us ended up as heroes; we ended up as celebrities."

Alice Kelleher in *Beautiful World, Where Are You*, is a twenty-nine-year-old novelist whose huge success has sent her into a tailspin. Like Rooney, Alice fell into fame and fortune without ever desperately seeking either. At twenty-four years old, Alice signed a book deal worth two-hundred and fifty thousand dollars. With the fame came a nervous breakdown, hospitalization, and an escape to the countryside in Ireland where she meets Felix, another damaged soul, coming to terms with his mother's death, his own addictions, and a dead-end job in an Amazon.com-like factory. The novel traces her relationship with the rough-edged Felix Brady and, through emails and texts, her deep friendship with Eileen Lydon. Eileen is an editorial assistant making twenty thousand a year, and she responds to Alice's complaints about the burdens of fame in an understandable manner—with the same eye roll and smirk that many readers may feel are the appropriate responses to the trials and tribulations of some of Rooney's privileged characters.

Beautiful World, Where Are You, like *Conversations with Friends*, is about an entangled foursome—besides Alice's negotiating her way through fame and into some kind of an authentic relationship with Felix, there is Eileen's long-standing connection to her on-again, off-again lover Simon Costigan, a policy adviser for a non-profit. Simon is five years older than Eileen and her devoted friend since childhood. In essence, Simon is a cross between Connell and Nick—handsome and humble, compassionate and unselfish, but, typical of Rooney's male protagonists, quietly troubled. Once again, in *Beautiful World, Where Are You*, Rooney creates a Jane Austen–like novel of manners but with a twenty-first-century filter—phone sex and philosophical emails, gender fluidity, a precisely delineated sexual encounter every dozen pages or so, and a yawning existential abyss that the characters all face. The emails that shuttle back and forth between Eileen and Alice give Rooney the opportunity to meditate on the political and social landscape of the twenty-first century, allowing her to be a novelist of manners and ideas at the same time, permitting her to emit some Marxist thunder in the course of her study of the relationships between men and women. At one point, Eileen declares that "our political vocabulary has decayed so deeply and rapidly since the twentieth century that most attempts to make sense of our present historical moment turn out to be essentially gibberish." Her theory, both funny and thought-provoking, is that "human beings lost the instinct for beauty in 1976, when plastics became the most widespread material in existence."

Early in the novel, offering her own take on our plastic planet, Alice writes to Eileen bemoaning the socio-political unfairness she sees in day-to-day life: "This lifestyle for people like us! All the various brands of soft drinks in plastic bottles and all the pre-packaged lunch deals and confectionery in sealed bags and store-baked pastries—this is it, the culmination of all the labour in the world, all the burning of fossil fuels and all the back-breaking work on coffee farms and sugar plantations. All for this! This convenience shop!" Perhaps too much of a self-absorbed liberal oversimplification—especially when she goes on to say, "People ground to death in the most horrific ways, children, women and all so that I could choose from various lunch options, each packaged in multiple layers of single-use plastic." A lot of the email seems about her and, despite her critique, she buys lunch anyway. For Alice, the twentieth century amounts to one long question that never got answered.

Both Eileen and Alice, and Simon and Felix, for that matter, are desperately seeking a way to live in the world with compassion and decency even as they recognize, as Eileen says, that "it seems vulgar, decadent, even epistemically violent, to invest energy in the trivialities of sex and friendship when human civilization is facing collapse. But at the same time, that is what I do every day." They all have a political and social conscience (even the outwardly cynical Felix shows his community conscience in the end), and the guilt associated with not being able to do the practical work that might change the world. Eileen sums up what might be a generational point of view for many young Irelanders—"...when we should have been reorganizing the distribution of the world's resources and transitioning collectively to a sustainable economic model, we were worrying about sex and friendship instead. Because we loved each other too much and found each other too interesting. And I love that about humanity, and in fact it's the very reason I root for us to survive—because we are so stupid about each other."

The plight of Alice, who speaks to the successful writer's predicament, appears to echo Rooney's own—a sincere Marxist inclination attached to a dizzying capitalist success in publishing. Despite, or perhaps because of, her stunning success with her books and film adaptations, Alice is unhappy and finds her life difficult—"...although it's nothing, it makes me miserable, and I don't want to live this kind of life. When I submitted the first book, I just wanted to make enough money to finish the next one.... People who intentionally become famous—I mean people who, after a little taste of fame, want more and more of it—are, and I honestly believe this, deeply psychologically ill." It is not difficult to read such a statement as Sally Rooney's contemplating her own predicament.

Alice goes on to wonder, "Whose interest does it [a writer's fame] serve? It makes me miserable, keeps me away from the one thing in my life that has any meaning, contributes nothing to the public interest, satisfies only the worst and most prurient curiosities, and serves to arrange literary discourse entirely around the domineering figure of the 'author,' whose lifestyles and idiosyncrasies must be picked over in lurid detail and for no reason." For Alice and the other characters in the novel, the beautiful world seems to be a chimera. The question, as voiced by one of the characters, becomes "...humanity on the cusp of extinction [and] here I am writing another email about sex and friendship. What else is there to live for?"

The answer that the novel ultimately suggests is one similar to Keats's—beauty, truth, and goodness are all one. In *Beautiful World, Where Are You*, through Alice and Simon, Rooney shines a light on Christian values and says directly—"whatever is beautiful leads us toward a contemplation of the divine." And as the novel concludes there is a moment of homage to James Joyce's "The Dead." At a house party where the foursome have landed, Felix sings "The Lass of Aughrim," the same tune Gretta Conroy listened to Bartell D'Arcy sing at the Missus Morkans' annual Christmas dance party, the same tune that brought the past back to her with a nostalgic power. Like D'Arcy's, Felix's voice has a tonal purity, "rising to fill the quiet and then falling very low, so low it almost had the quality of silence." As Alice watches Felix's slim figure in the slanting light, her eyes fill with tears, and Rooney writes, "For some reason, because of some prior association the melody brought to her mind Alice's eyes filled with tears as she watched him." Eileen stands apart from the others watching them and "out of the window, the sky was still dimming, darking, the vast earth turning slowly on its axis." For a writer who seems to despise William Butler Yeats, Rooney shows an affection for Joyce in this passage. The only piece missing in the scene is "the snow falling faintly through the universe and faintly falling, like the descent of their last end, upon all the living and the dead."

Just as the singing of "The Lass of Aughrim" brings an epiphany for Gabriel Conroy, Felix's singing seems to announce a shift in perspective in *Beautiful World, Where Are You*, and the novel ends with an Austen-like unambiguous assertion of beauty and love. Alice and Felix have made a life together, and Eileen and Simon live happily together. Eileen is pregnant, and she says, "having a child is simply the most ordinary thing I can imagine doing. And I want that—to prove that the most ordinary thing about human beings is not violence or grief but love and care." In the ordinariness of their lives, all four characters seem to have found something beautiful and good. The beautiful world, the characters find, is right in front of them. They discover that all they have to do is open their eyes to see it.

* * *

A writer like Paul Lynch often looks to the past to make sense of the present. Published in 2013, his first novel—*Red Sky in Morning*—with echoes of William Faulkner and Cormac McCarthy, traces the tragic story of Coll Coyle, a tenant farmer in Western Ireland in the early 1830s. Coyle kills Desmond Hamilton, the malignant son of his landlord, an act of unthinking violence that changes Coyle's life and that of his family. Coyle has little choice but to run—across Ireland and eventually to America. The demonic foreman on the Hamilton farm, John Faller, could be a scion of Cormac McCarthy's Judge Holden in *Blood Meridian* or the blood-curdling Anton Chigurh in *No Country for Old Men* or even the relentless tracker, Lord Baltimore, in *Butch Cassidy and the Sundance Kid*. Alan Cheuse, in an NPR review, fairly calls Lynch's villain "the infernal faller," a Lucifer in the flesh, a twisted killer reminiscent of Flannery O'Connor's Misfit. The fallen Faller tracks Coyle like a mythic hound out of hell, the foreman's hatred and cruelty so exaggerated that he steps outside ordinary evil to suggest EVIL itself, something beyond comprehension, something undeniable and inescapable.

Before he became a full-time novelist, Lynch was a respected film critic for the *Irish Times* and other newspapers. The language in his first novel, *Red Sky in Morning*, and the three that follow is dense with torqued adjectives and poetic twists in the dialogue and description, but Lynch's cinematic inclinations are also on full display. While keeping the clarity and an adrenaline-fueled cinematic forward motion, Lynch consistently pushes the boundaries of his prose in a way similar to McCarthy, Joyce, and Faulkner. Like them, Lynch struggles to reinvent language, to reshape it, aligning Irish melodies with the rhythms of sentences in English. Lynch's prose style has an archaic feel to it, a whisper of Old English, as if the *Beowulf* poet had been influenced by the history of American Westerns. Characters are "arm-hauled across the room," "a knife-cut of light" slices from the open door, "youngers" creep over the floorboards, someone's hand is "a night orchid on the latch of the door," people "sly-watch" plates of meat, and "wanty hands" are held out in supplication.

By his own account, Lynch labors over his sentences, rewriting some of them fifty times, ending up with a style one critic called, "bold, grandiose, mesmeric." Surely, his carefully calculated prose style has a high post-modernist character to it—pushing majestically into the past to find Ireland's story in the 1830s of *Red Sky in Morning*, the post–World War II era of *Black Snow*, and the mid–nineteenth century recounted in *Grace*—except for his most recent novel—*Beyond the Sea*—a narrative as elemental and cut to the bone as Hemingway's *The Old Man and the Sea*. Unlike Lynch's first three novels, *Beyond the Sea* is not set in Ireland, nor does it have any of the rhythms and accents of Irish speech. The plot of Lynch's fourth novel is loosely based on the true story of the Salvadoran fisherman Jose Alvarenga, adrift for 14 months after his boat got caught in a storm in 2012. Alvarenga survived but his 23-year-old crewmate Ezequiel lost hope and starved to death. Lynch follows the basic outlines of Alvarenga's incredible story in a way reminiscent of what Stephen Crane did in fictionalizing the actual events of his own shipwreck in "The Open Boat." And, as with Crane, Lynch manages to transform a news story into a universal tale of friendship and endurance and love.

Lynch's achievement in his four novels to date is astounding, but his masterwork is *Grace*, his third novel, published in 2017. *Grace* portrays the Great Famine in Ireland with a ferocious poetry and a documentary realism. The sequel to *Red Sky in Morning*, *Grace* recounts five years in the life of Coll Coyle's daughter. The story starts with the teenage Grace, at the outset of the Potato Famine, as Sarah Coyle shears her daughter's hair with a knife in order to send her, "this girl pale-skinned, fourteen, still boy-chested," into the world to get work as a young boy. Sarah also realizes that her lover, Boggs, has recently cast a lecherous eye in her daughter's direction, and to save her from him, she is willing to send her into the equally treacherous world. When Grace heads out on the road, a teenage girl turned Don Quixote, her twelve-year-old brother, Colly, not yet born when Coll Coyle ran from his home and left his family behind, follows her. Colly, the spitting image of his dead father, serves as a Sancho Panza, offering practical advice and comic relief, to Grace's Quixote.

Paul Lynch in his home office.

Grace heads out from Donegal a few days before Samhain, the night of the dead, in the company of pookas and ill omens. It isn't long before Boggs tracks them down and attempts to drag Colly back to the farm. Grace levels Boggs with a rock from a nearby stone wall, but like Christy Mahon with his father in *The Playboy of the Western World*, she can't make him stay dead. Colly and Grace leave their home in Blackmountain behind and head into the wilds of Donegal. Colly is hardly ever silent, "gushing as if rivered with words," and after he drowns trying to stop a dead sheep from floating away, he is less silent dead than when he was alive. Colly is a spouter of riddles, and his last, and clearest, riddle while he is alive comes when he is trying to plan out how to retrieve the dead sheep from the river—"What is always traveling but stays put, has a bed but canny be slept in, and a mouth that never eats nothing?"

Grace is now alone, a fourteen-year-old girl disguised as a boy and headed into the landscape of a disastrous famine. Grace "squints at the faroff but there is nothing but bogland." Lonely and lost, she looks for solace and strength in Colly's voice in her head. He becomes Grace's alter-ego, shuttling back and forth between being her mentor and tormentor. As Grace roams through the streets of Donegal Town, passing beggars, who seem to her like shades, their eyes like wolves, she is accompanied by the voice and presence of Colly. In a moment of mistaken identity reminiscent of the experiences of Huck Finn, Grace is taken by a group of cattle herders to be the young boy they were waiting for to start the drive. Among them Grace meets the handsome, buck toothed Embury Soundpost, the leader of the drive and a man whose profit making during the Great Hunger will turn ruinous for him. As they drive the cattle across the countryside, Grace witnesses some of the effects of the famine—"what she sees makes her feel both sickened and fearful." How the boy stands on the verge like something whispered. Closer still and she can hardly look, for there is something so awful about him. Colly calls him a monkey but clearly he is not. It is not his tattered clothing Colly refers to, the stick shape that makes it seem something within the child is broken. Nor is it the hair thinning on his head that makes the boy of perhaps five years old appear like an old man in miniature. "It is the fur on his face. The fur of a half animal. The fur of a cat. The fur of a mule. The fur of a boy who has had the gab taken out of him by the pooka. For sure it is the fur of hunger."

Treachery turns the cattle drive into a ruin, and Grace is forced to wonder if she is a female version of Oisin—"If I go home to Blackmountain," she says, "it will turn out that hundreds of years have passed. I'll go in the door and turn into an old woman and fall dead on my feet. Nobody will ever have heard of me"—and this prophecy will not be far from the truth. She travels across apocalyptic Ireland, "the moon candling the stonework" as she meditates on "what she has seen, the road now so full of troubles you can hardly look at it." Starvation has changed her entire world, and she is forced to sleep in haylofts and churches, barns and ditches. People refuse to help others, scared to death of the famine plague—"The customs are dying out," Grace thinks, "because the people are frightened." Grace, following in the footsteps of her literary ancestors—Odysseus and Huck and the sixteenth-century Grace O'Malley from Irish folklore—encounters an array of characters in her picaresque wanderings. One, Blister, a clownish wise man, offers her one piece of insight, his final rule, as she heads out into the darkness—"There aren't any rules. Hup! Things are getting worse now. The country is starving. The world is going to fuck. The old times are done for, do you know what I mean? We're going into the getting-worse part."

Eventually, Grace becomes a bog road worker, and she is befriended by John Bart, a handsome young man with a crippled arm and a penchant for using his knife blade. He protects Grace by fending off two would-be rapists, and the two take to the road together, compelled to steal oats from horses and leftovers from dogs' bowls. For Bart, Grace is a wonderful enigma, and when they become highway robbers, he makes explicit the Grace O'Malley reference and notes that she is like the pirate queen of Connaght. Bart is brave and resilient, but Grace's courage and endurance ultimately outlast his. Grace, like the legendary queen, survives most of the men she encounters in her journey—Colly, Boggs, Embury, McNulty, even the ghost of her father, lost in America, killed in a railroad massacre in Duffy's Cut near Philadelphia in 1832, an actual historical event in which fifty-seven Irish railroad workers, many stricken with cholera, were executed by fearful locals. "Wake up, the voice says. It is the voice of her father and she feels herself being gathered into his power, the smell of him uniquely, that ancient smell, old as the world is and brought to her from so long ago, and he is shadow and he is voice and he is the deepest hum." This moment in which Grace imagines the voice of her father connects *Red Sky in Morning* to *Grace*, links the inhumanity of Coll Coyle's eviction in the early 1830s and his mistreatment in America to the tragedy of the Potato Famine in the mid- to late 1840s, and suggests that the governmental ineptitude and political indifference joined the two realities inextricably and made possible the moral collapse of the Great Hunger in Ireland.

Grace's career as a highway robber does not last long. Their gang kills a husband and wife, and one of their gang, McNulty, is beaten to death by a posse of farmers. Bart is destroyed first by McNulty's torture and then famine fever, and Grace is taken for dead, lifted from an open grave by a religious cult figure, given only the name Father. She survives the misogyny of the cult and Father's mind-control, too. She finds her way through the darkness, the famine, through the underworld, and, unlike her father or the other men she traveled with in her long pilgrimage, she makes her way back to Blackmountain and the light. A five-year journey has led her back home, where she finds a man, Jim Collins, who "stands ample in easy kindness." She has found a way to believe in the future for her and Jim and the child that will soon come. She "begins to feel a shift inside her as if a great light were shining through her, a light reaching into the dark ... like sunlight passing through water...." The resilient fourteen-year-old Grace has become the indomitable nineteen-year-old woman who has returned like Odysseus or Ossian to find her place in a world she thought gone forever.

As Lynch said in an interview about *Grace*, the novel is "an epic, Odyssean, five-year journey in which Grace becomes a bandit, a penitent, and finally a woman." Lynch has made it clear that his goal in the novel was to make the narrative eclectic—at once an adventure, a romance, and a coming-of-age story in the tradition of Cormac McCarthy's *All the Pretty Horses*. Lynch wanted to examine "what it means to be a person during enormous times of crisis." For Lynch the story is his attempt to write an Irish *Adventures of Huckleberry Finn* with a fourteen-year-old girl at the center. "The act of writing," Lynch has said, "is an act of divination." *Grace* chose him, not the other way around. The fundamental issue he wanted to explore in *Grace* was "the silence that came out of the Famine. There is a silence of which the Irish never really spoke about. They never spoke about what they did to survive.... The people who survived it just didn't speak about it." Grace has seen and done unspeakable things in her attempt to survive the Great Famine and to return home, and, unlike her father, a failed Ulysses, she finds her path back to Blackmountain, and she finds a way to bring new life into the world, a way to open her heart to living. When she returns to her home ground, Grace breaks the usual Irish silence, finding a means of forgiving herself and arriving at a profound understanding of what her past means. After more than a year of total silence, she finds her voice—"Her hands go to her belly and the words rise up and she says to Jim, 'This life is light.'" That is the power of *Grace*, filling the awful silence with words and the heartbreaking past with light.

The Writers' Landscape

"The modern novel should be largely a work of reference."
—Flann O'Brien, *At Swim Two Birds*

Ireland in October 2022, perhaps post-pandemic but still reeling from rumors of additional virus strains and recent global threats, facing a housing scarcity, oil shortages, and the potentially new world of Brexit, might have benefited from a tongue-in-cheek barrage of silliness from Brian O'Nolan or a savage satire from Jonathan Swift. The whole world might have profited from their perspective at that moment. As I wandered around the country in the fall of 2022, I carried inside me a vision of present-day Ireland from contemporary writers like Tana French, Kevin Barry, Paul Lynch, Rob Doyle, Roisin Kiberd, and Sally Rooney that amounted to a portrait of a country in flux, a country that I'm not sure I understood any more than my grandfather, Alfred Hunter, would have if I could have resurrected him.

It was a miserable, rainy day, the remnants of Hurricane Ian draped over Washington, D.C., when I flew out of Dulles Airport on Aer Lingus the evening of October 1. The weather, it seemed, was preparing me for the Irish variety that would most likely greet me when I landed. I flew into Dublin before sunrise the next morning, on October 2, and from a few thousand feet up the country was shrouded in darkness, the lights of the city shimmering like diamonds tossed carelessly on a dark carpet. My good luck was that it was not raining, but my bad luck was that I couldn't get into my hotel room for at least 7 hours, so I decided to take the DART north and hike Howth Head. I had been there before, but I figured why not try by a commodious vicus of recirculation to get back to Howth Castle and its environs, given that I was once again in Joyce country. If nothing else, it might clear up my clogged ears and help me shake off the jet lag. As I climbed up Howth Head, along with hundreds of tourists who had ridden out on the DART with me to celebrate a sunny Sunday in Ireland, I walked to the top and gazed down at what was once a sleepy fishing village and what is now one of the prettiest small towns in the country. It was nearly eight miles up and back, and when I got back to my hotel at 3:30 p.m., my room still wasn't ready. I had arrived at 5:30 a.m.—so jet lag nearly brought out the ugly American in me. But I slumped into the lobby sofa and played back mental images of Howth lighthouse and castle, the glistening bay and islands floating in it, and the delicious prawns I had eaten only a few hours before at Beshoffs Market and Sea Grill near the train station. Those images kept me from committing any act of jet lag violence against the hotel staff, and eventually I got my key and crawled into bed, dreaming of the new Ireland I had seen that day in Dublin and on the DART, a country that might have surprised even a writer with a wildly wide-ranging sensibility like Joyce. Thirty years ago, on my first visit to Ireland, pale skin and pug-nosed Irish features had been the norm, but the country now, surely Dublin and Galway, had gotten far more ethnically diverse. The cab driver who drove me from the airport to the Castle Hotel had emigrated from Nigeria, the clerk in the hotel was from India, the waitress in the restaurant was from Bulgaria, and on my way up North Great George's Street to visit the Joyce Centre there was a crowd of maybe one thousand Brazilians lining up to vote in their home country's elections. One of the men in the crowd told me that there were nearly seventy thousand of his countrymen and women in Ireland, living, working, and studying. Ireland was no longer a country dominated by red-headed, freckle-faced Gaels but of people of African, Asian, and Eastern European descent. Walking along any main avenue or side street is like taking a stroll through *Ulysses* and *Finnegans Wake* at the same time, various languages—Russian, Croatian, Portuguese, Spanish, German, Nigerian, Hindi, and a Babel-like variety—stream together in a way that makes them seem like one new language. Dublin, in particular, had become a melting pot that Joyce might have appreciated, even though the crowds were so large the Joyce Centre was forced to shut down for the day.

The next afternoon, in the vegan restaurant Cornucopia, a funky place on Wicklow Street off of Grafton, John Lawrence and I had lunch with the writer Rob Doyle and a former student of mine from the United States, Caroline Kelly, who was in the third year of her undergraduate degree at UC Dublin. Paul Lynch was supposed to join us for lunch but couldn't because he had recently undergone an unexpected surgery for an illness similar to one his grandfather had suffered from. I felt concerned and sorrowful when I heard the news about Paul but, irrationally surely, I felt envious that he had known his grandfather and his family history. I had no idea where my grandfather died or what his life amounted to after he deserted my mother and grandmother. Paul and I talked a week before his surgery, and he offered some insights into Irish literary culture and what it means to be an Irish writer today. Even though, for obvious reasons, he declined to speak too much about the current Irish writers he admires most (a literary landscape that some think overpopulated by commercially successful writers grinding socio-political axes), he did express his admiration for Irish writers like Mike McCormack, Mary Costello, Rob Doyle, Mia Gallagher, Billy O'Callaghan, and others whose books were filled with mystery and strangeness and genuine metaphysical enquiry. "Most serious Irish writers find themselves working outside the mainstream conversation," Lynch said. "If you are an established name with major UK prize credentials, there is room for you within the general culture, but you are expected to talk about current affairs or your family. The truth of the matter is that serious literature remains a minority pursuit. Room for discussion within the media has diminished along with the readers who have the reading muscle. Attention spans have atrophied. Considerably fewer men read fiction. We are now at one with the machines." He knows, of course, that the problem is not exclusive to his country. "This is now a universal truth and is not unique to Ireland," he went on. "In the mid–60s, Saul Bellow's brilliantly cerebral *Herzog* spent 41 weeks on the NYT bestseller list. There is just no way now that a book like that would succeed as a mainstream proposition today." Even though Lynch is a unique writer, his concerns about contemporary culture might not be all that different from Sally Rooney's as expressed by her writer character Alice in *Beautiful World, Where Are You*, who wonders "whether celebrity culture has sort of metastasized to fill the emptiness left by religion."

Lynch elaborated in a way that made the problem of the Irish writer today seem to be similar to the one faced by James Joyce, Frank O'Connor, and Edna O'Brien. "While there are always exceptions, to be an Irish writer now means general indifference, lower sales and existential anxiety about whether your next book will be published based on prior sales. I'm told by older writer friends that it was not always like this and that a lot has changed in twenty-five years. I read John McGahern's letters recently and the patronage and encouragement he received by editors when he had low sales is largely absent today." Perhaps, times are tougher for a literary writer in Ireland today, but the likelihood of having their books banned by the Catholic Church and government authorities is negligible.

Lynch went on to quote John Cage who once mused that "we live in a time not of mainstream but of many streams." He feels that this could be said now for Irish writing. "There was a time when most serious Irish writers seemed to belong to the tradition in one way or another," Lynch said, "but now there are only a handful who remain committed to the 'knitting factory,' as a writer friend of mine once put it. The tradition has exploded into myriad styles and approaches and the post, post-modern space is unpredictable and ever-changing. We are now at 'delta.' Today, Irish artists have a global imagination and if you look at Irish writing now, many are setting their books outside the country. Geographically, Ireland is a small place and its traditional themes have been thoroughly explored. We are no longer a cultural backwater. Irish writers are now citizens of the world."

Speaking then about his own work specifically, he said, "I realize that my first three novels took on distinctly Irish themes, but I write against the tradition. (And yet when I travel to Europe, I am seen as a distinctly Irish writer.) Many of my primary influences come from Europe,

Chapter 9. Writers of the New Ireland 173

the US and South America and I seek to push the form in a manner that follows my preoccupations. Ireland now is distinctly post–Catholic and my generation of irreligious heathens have taken charge. Politically, the next decade or two will be shaped by how the establishment meets the needs of our lost generation. People in their twenties and thirties are being crushed by the same economic forces that are squeezing most first-world countries. They are going to vote Sinn Féin into power—politically unthinkable until recently. And it is possible they might encounter a resurgent conservatism later on. I once met former UK prime minister Gordon Brown in a green room at a Scottish book festival and we spoke about Ireland. He suggested that secular liberalism comes with a price and that we are about twenty years behind the disruption and decline of political and cultural values that has recently beset the UK. I hope he was wrong about that."

Although Paul wasn't able to meet us for lunch, he graciously invited us to his house for tea in the Drimnagh suburbs right outside of the center of Dublin. "I need an excuse," he said "to get dressed and put on shoes. And I need some literary conversation." In the late morning, on another surprisingly sunny day in Dublin, Caroline, John Lawrence, and I had stopped by Paul Lynch's house in Drimnagh, a short bus ride from the center of the city. Paul was in the beginning of his recovery but seemed strong and surely was eager for conversation after weeks of rest and recuperation.

So, the three of us knocked on his door, carrying scones, notebooks, and cameras. Paul brought out tea and his mother-in-law's homemade jam and we chatted amiably for two hours about books and politics, the state of the publishing world, his previous life as a journalist and film critic, and how he transitioned from a film critic to a novelist. After tea, he took us to his modest office on the second floor of the house, where a copy of Roberto Bolano's *Between Parentheses*, a collection of the writer's essays, articles, and speeches sat cater corned a few feet from a coaster bearing the image of Groucho Marx. Paul is slim and handsome, as dark-haired as a Spaniard, but the photos he showed me of his tow-headed four-year-old son and nine-year-old daughter didn't match up until he showed a photo of his stunningly beautiful blonde-haired wife that balanced on one of the bookshelves. On the wall hung a typed reading list—he is in the habit of creating such lists for himself, and this one was both eclectic and serious—Sophocles, John Donne, and William Golding, among the group.

"I dropped out of UCD," he said, casting a quick glance in Caroline's direction, perhaps trying to acknowledge her accomplishment becoming the editor of the college magazine. "I couldn't bear with all the isms spouted by the professors I had. I was studying literature, but it seemed as if I were in a sociology course." Paul went right from UCD to one of the major Irish newspapers and stayed there, rising among the ranks, until when he was thirty years old he told his wife that he was in the wrong profession and was meant to write fiction. She told him he was right and said do it. Around that time, the idea for *Red Sky in Morning* rose up in him and when he began to write it, he knew he was on the right path and said to himself, "Holy fuck where is this coming from." And for more than a decade, he has stayed on that path. We talked a bit about the news that Cormac McCarthy was publishing two novels sixteen years after his last one, *The Road*. "He had to wait until he was nearly sixty to garner a wide readership and financial success. I guess that might be the serious writer's lot in Ireland."

Paul Lynch's thoughts about being a writer in Ireland ricocheted around in my mind as I sat in Cornucopia with Rob Doyle, Caroline Kelly, and John Lawrence. And when I looked at Caroline, tall, athletic, with Irish good looks, all I could think about was her father, John Kelly, who had been my good friend for nearly three decades. John Kelly and I had met on the basketball court. I was an avid player, and he was a great one. He had played college ball at Rutgers, in one game guarded Larry Bird, and had an illustrious career after as a professional in Ireland. When John and I met in Virginia, he was an assistant basketball coach at Old Dominion University and a part time instructor in the English Department. Besides bonding over our passion for basketball, John and I shared a deep interest first in the work of William Faulkner and then in Irish literature. After a coup in the basketball program, John became a high school English teacher and in the summers a lieutenant on the lifeguard force at the Virginia Beach oceanfront. Multi-talented, handsome, and born with the Irish gift of gab, John seemed indestructible. In the spring of 2020, he asked me if his daughter, Caroline, could take my Irish literature course, even though she was on a gap year after high school and had not yet been officially accepted into any university. I said yes, and she turned out to be a sweet-natured and brilliant student. After the course, she asked me to write a letter of recommendation for University College Dublin, which I did, of course. She was accepted and started studying there in the fall of 2020. With his ex-wife and younger daughter, John visited Caroline and Ireland in the summer of 2021. He left his younger daughter in Dublin to visit with her sister, planning to pick her up a week later in the Washington, D.C. airport. As he entered the airport the next week, right after his younger daughter just sent him a text to say that she had landed, he died of a massive heart attack near the baggage claim area. When I looked at Caroline across the table from me, sitting next to Rob Doyle, my thoughts

Chapter 9. Writers of the New Ireland 175

cut through the pleasant chatter of our conversation and traveled in the direction of mystery and mortality, taking me back to John Kelly's death and Alfred Hunter's disappearance a lifetime ago.

After our tea at Paul Lynch's house and our lunch at Cornucopia, for some reason AE's description of literary Dublin had popped into my mind—"a city of gossips, cliques, and eccentrics, a writerly town where artists hate each other cordially." It was still a city that had more literary talent per square foot than most other cities in the world, quite a bit of cordiality, and quite a few eccentrics as well. A quick visit to Sweny's before we headed out to Dalkey and Sandycove to visit Rob Doyle in one Martello tower and the ghost of Joyce in another, we decided to make a brief stop at Sweny's, which sits on the edge of Trinity College, the James Joyce Heritage Visitor Centre on the edge of Trinity campus. Sweny's underscored the eccentric character of Dublin literary life for me. About twenty years ago, P.J. Murphy, in his own words, "rescued the pharmacy mentioned in *Ulysses*, keeping it from becoming another coffee shop." P.J. is red-cheeked and white-haired, and ready, it seems, at a moment's notice to bring out his guitar and sing a tune in the Irish language. He greeted customers in their language, be it Spanish, French, or Italian. He readily mentioned his familial relationship to Samuel Beckett as he sold bars of lemon soap to anyone who wants to follow in Leopold Bloom's footsteps. Each week, P.J. hosted readings of *Ulysses* and *Finnegans Wake* at Sweny's, and they were hallucinogenic affairs, tourists from all over Europe, reading Joyce's work in an array of accents that nearly matched Joyce's variety of neologisms.

* * *

P.J. Murphy's wonderfully eccentric project, one it would be hard to imagine outside of Ireland, seemed to have something in common with Rob Doyle's current home in a Joyce-like Martello tower in the village of Dalkey outside of Dublin. As I listened to Rob Doyle talk about the film the studio had made of his first novel, *Here Are the Young Men*, I couldn't help feeling like I was a character in the opening chapter of *Ulysses*. John and I had gone to dinner the night before at Davy Byrnes's Pub in Bloom's honor, and a middle-aged man sitting near us said to his friend, "She's a nice woman, sure, but she has a face like a boiled owl. I can't see myself dating her. Does that make me a bad person?" And Dr. Johnson's line about the Irish squeezed itself into my mind—"a fair people: they never spoke well of anyone." Even themselves, it seemed. So, I ate a bleu cheese salad, the closest I could come to gorgonzola on the menu, and looked forward to my visits to two writers and two towers, linking the past to the present.

Doyle had been offered the residence rent free by an American artist and Joyce scholar and very wealthy woman, Susie Lopez, a Harriet Shaw Weaver of his very own. From the roof of the Bartry Tower, where he lives with the writer Roisin Kiberd, he can see Joyce's famous tower in Sandycove, a short walk away. Rob had just turned forty and carried his slim six-foot six-inch frame with a boyish ease. His thick grey hair, a bit tousled by the wind off the Irish Sea, made him look like a boy who had disguised himself as a middle-aged man, but his mod pea coat with the Dostoyevsky pin on the lapel and his good-natured smile made it impossible not to feel as if you were in the right company, a man who was smart and serious but not too taken with his own importance.

After a tour of the Bartry Tower and the modernist glass house that Susie Lopez had built and attached to the stone fortress by a steel walkway, John Lawrence and I had tea with Rob and Roisin. They might have thought we were monosyllabic American morons because we uttered the word *wow* about two dozen times as we toured the buildings—infrared saunas, ultra-contemporary kitchens and bathrooms, bedrooms with original prints of Sally Mann's 1994 photograph "The Three Graces," and graceful stone walls thick enough to withstand a nuclear attack—but they never rolled their eyes at any *wow* that slipped out of our mouths. Surprisingly, neither Rob nor Roisin had ever met Susie Lopez, their patron, or even spoken to her on the phone. Their relationship existed exclusively in texts and emails. Impressed by his writing, Susie had contacted Rob, and both Rob and Roisin were as amazed as we were by her patronage and their good fortune. Roisin, the niece of the renowned Irish history and literature scholar Declan Kiberd, is

P. J. Murphy in Sweny's.

Chapter 9. Writers of the New Ireland   177

waif-like enough to be taken for someone about to turn eighteen years old instead of a young woman in her early thirties. She is slim and pale-skinned, and when she stands next to Rob, looks even more diminutive than she is. She has the shy and pretty smile of a teenager, like the protagonist of a Sally Rooney novel, thinking worriedly about taking her Leaving Certificate exams, but there is nothing adolescent about her writing.

On the DART to the Bartry Tower to visit Rob and Roisin, a few days after seeing Edna O'Brien's play *Joyce's Women* at the Abbey Theater, I found myself reading Roisin's review of the play in *The New York Times* and her take on Edna O'Brien's life and career. It was a sympathetic, smart, and lucid look at Joyce and O'Brien, and I couldn't help but think as I was reading it—*These two Irish women, one of the mid-twentieth century and the other in the twenty-first, have a lot in common. They're both tough-minded women who wrote in exile, of sorts, from their homeland. O'Brien in London and Kiberd on the internet, physically in Ireland but farther away, perhaps, than O'Brien's London had been from Tuamgraney. And both have a propensity to shock their readers.* Kiberd's review in the *Times* also made me think about her and Rob's own Joycean situation with their patron, Susie Lopez. In her *Times* article, Kiberd described Harriet Weaver, a Quaker who joined the Communist party, bankrolling Joyce over the years with an estimated 1.7 million dollars in today's money. Kiberd quotes the actor who plays Weaver in the play—"It became almost like her [Weaver's] religion to support these people." Kiberd goes on to write in the article that O'Brien's play "dismisses the present-day debate about separating art from the artist, arguing that to draw a line between Joyce's life and his works would be impossible." That made me see Rob Doyle and Roisin Kiberd following in the tracks of Joyce as he described the writer in *Portrait of an Artist*—"a priest of the eternal imagination, transmuting the daily bread of experience into the radiant body of everliving life." Despite, or because of, their early religious upbringing, both Rob and Roisin might find the sacred images absurd in the world they inhabit, but it could be argued that this is exactly what both of them do in their writing, making experience and the imagination intersect, making it hard to distinguish one from the other.

Kiberd's essays in her recently published collection—*The Disconnect: A Personal Journey Through the Internet*—are incisive and unflinching, by turns a wickedly funny and deeply disturbing account of living online. As she says in the book, she is the new flesh, born in 1989, at the inception of the internet, and she speaks with a blistering authority to a whole generation of young people who know nothing else but life seen through cell phones, iPads, and computers. Like many young women of her generation, she struggled with both anorexia and bulimia, and she sought solace and a new self on the computer screen. "Technology rewrote time," she says, "and told us not only what we wanted to hear, and in the process, I believe, it helped to destabilize the truth. It seems little coincidence to me that this was also the year of 'fake news,' a period in which troll farms and data mining interfered with democracy."

Kiberd's Ireland is not James Joyce's or Alfred Hunter's. It's not the mythic land of William Butler Yeats or Lady Gregory, not the grounded peasant folk of John Millington Synge, the rugged farm life of Seamus Heaney, or even the iconoclastic country girls of Edna O'Brien. Kiberd's imagined land is an Ireland connected to the world through the worldwide web. It is surely not an Ireland my grandfather could ever have fathomed or even imagined, but what he might have understood perfectly are the alienation and the loneliness that Kiberd sees at the heart of the new world that the internet has fashioned for Ireland and the planet at large. It is unquestionably a brave new world that exists on computer screens, for as she explains—"As I write this, at least 4.5 billion people use the internet every day, sending an estimated 23 billion text messages and 293 million emails, making 154,200 Skype calls and 1.6 billion Tinder swipes per day."

For Kiberd, the new world she was born into in 1989 was founded on a reverse Prometheus scenario "where human fire has been stolen by the machine." And the machine, the internet, is a new god, as paternalistic an entity as any described in the Koran or the Old Testament of the Bible—"Technology is among the most powerful, sophisticated and profitable industries the world has ever known—an economic force on par, in history, with the Catholic Church, and almost as unlikely to listen to women." She suggests that the internet is a new sort of god but maybe not all that different from the Catholic Church in its historical influence in Ireland and around the globe. It consumes its users and monetizes their every thought and gesture. As Kiberd convincingly argues, a company like Facebook is "the biggest surveillance-based enterprise in the history of mankind ... a cybernetic black hole that swallows up human behaviour and regurgitates it as ad revenue." And, if Kiberd's figures are even near accurate, it is a plutocrat's dream for Mark Zuckerberg who "earns an average of $6 million per day." The internet, the thing that ostensibly entertains us, is constantly watching us and profiting from its surveillance.

The Disconnect traces Kiberd's struggle to come to terms with her life on the internet, with her parallel, and apparently connected, history of insomnia and failed relationships accrued on dating apps (like food apps except "you're ordering a person"), and, ultimately, the debilitating loneliness that is a consequence of a mediated existence online. "The internet," she writes, "is full of solitary insomniacs ... data objects," caught in capitalist algorithms. The internet cycle, she explains, is symbiotic, "the more lonely we feel, the more we look to technology, and the lonelier it leaves us in turn."

In person, Roisin Kiberd emits a sense of sweet wariness and vulnerability, but on the pages of her essays and book, her candor is unblinking. And, for the reader, it feels impossible to look away from the scene of devastation she depicts. Reading her essays is like watching an alien creature strip her skin off to show us what is beneath, and warning us that we might actually be cyborgs without having realized. However, the trajectory of Kiberd's narrative brings her to an Ireland of the past, one closer to Yeats and Synge, it seems to me. She is on the Dingle Peninsula with her partner, watching him walk the hillside, as she stands by the window of a tiny stone hut—"a clochan ... it's been here for centuries, one of the many scattered across the surrounding county. Some historians date them to the twelfth century, others as far back as AD 800. Some stand in clusters, in networks of cells, while others are alone, like this one. The origins are steeped in mystery: historians speculate that they were once used by hermits, or by pilgrims on the way to Mount Brandon." She has made that leap of faith, as a writer and a pilgrim, as a human being, stepping away from the computer screen into Ireland's past and into the lonely but exhilarating freedom the lived world has to offer.

After tea, Roisin said, with more than the hint of an ironic smile, that she had a podcast to do online and exited, leaving Rob, John, and me in the kitchen talking about writing novels. His new novel, Rob told us, is tentatively titled *Cameo*, and he seemed to enjoy explaining its postmodern twists and turns. "It's a critical bibliography," he said, "of an author who is me in a parallel timeline, and the conceit is that next year, 2023, the author, Rob Doyle, me, has a major creative turnabout and writes a novel called *Old Rob Has Seen a Few Things*. I was going to call the novel that instead of *Cameo*, but in the end, I didn't have the courage for that. I lost my nerve for that one. *Cameo* is a better title overall, anyway."

Roisin came out of the back room and Rob asked if we were being too loud. We weren't, she said, picked up a pen and notebook, as if to ground her in the physical world, and headed back for a momentary excursion into cyberspace.

"The novel is a massive global success," Rob continued, returning to *Cameo*, "sells in the millions and his career is transformed. He goes from being a cult author to being a celebrity. Having written in this down home, ambling, style, he begins turning out books using the *Old Rob* persona, rapidly writing one after another. This novel, *Cameo*, becomes the parallel story of the author, his travails, his fluctuations, the oscillations of his career, telling the story of each of the novels he writes over the next ten years. The narrative strands intertwine."

I could see why he chose the title *Cameo* over *Old Rob Has Seen a Few Things*, perhaps allowing him a bit more space to hide behind the screen of fiction in a novel that might be initially read as a Joycean leg-pull. Like many contemporary Irish writers and their view of Joyce, Rob Doyle has a good dose of ambivalence. Even the idea of being an Irish writer sets his head spinning a bit. "I have a thorny attitude to this whole notion of being an Irish writer," he said, "in that while a probably inaccurate and definitely jaundiced conception of Irish writing is something I've noisily kicked against ever since they started publishing me, by now it's clear to me that that instinct to define myself *against* Irish literature has helped me to invent myself ... as an Irish writer! The fun and the challenge is to remake this globally marketable archetype in one's own twisted image, bending and subverting the image of the Irish writer till it looks less like it used to look ... and more like me! For the past decade I've been cynical about the direction Irish culture has been developing in, while never quite having the political-economic facts on hand to back up my suspicions. On the one hand, a priggish liberal-progressivist doctrinairism favors cultural production that is meek, inoffensive and anodyne, while on the other hand, neoliberal homogeneity reinforces this boring cultural situation. Dublin is now a rich person's city and it's looking ever more like a cultural boneyard. To do anything deep or weird or vital, it's often necessary to move abroad—to Berlin or Athens or Lisbon or somewhere like that, which is what many out-priced young artists are doing. Irish culture will continue to be renewed from the outside, by the jaundiced malcontents who have always been its saving grace."

Like Joyce, I thought, or Edna O'Brien. And I wondered aloud what Irish writers had nurtured him as an artist. "I'm wary of delivering one of those long lists by which a writer invariably betrays which cliques he belongs to, which palms he hopes to grease and the nature of his political ambitions," he said prudently. "Besides which, my perception of my closer contemporaries is distorted by a fanatical competitiveness—so I'll content myself to mentioning a mere handful. Philip O'Ceallaigh, who has published three superb collections of short stories including *Notes from a Turkish Whorehouse*, is an inspiration, not only for his writing but the restlessly internationalist life he's lived. At more than a risk of seeming biased, I must mention my girlfriend Roisin Kiberd, author of *The Disconnect*: if it seems suspect that I would mention her as an Irish writer I admire, I would point out that my attraction to her and the fact that we got into a relationship at all is inseparable from my interest in her writing, beginning with her Motherboard column on technology which I used to follow before we lived together. There's been a massive wave of new young female novelists in recent years, and of those I've read the one who seemed to me most strikingly talented is Naoise Dolan, author of *Exciting Times*. Of the Irish novels I've read in recent years, the other one that struck me as formidably good—and perhaps scandalously overlooked—was Paul Lynch's *Beyond the Sea*."

It seemed to me a good place to end the conversation, a full circle, connecting Edna O'Brien and Roisin Kiberd, Rob Doyle and Paul Lynch—so we reluctantly left Rob and Roisin and the Bartra Tower, and John and I walked the mile along the sea to the Joyce Tower and The Forty Foot swimming place.

I had swum there many times over the years but never with a dozen men and women dressed in Santa hats. Because that's what I saw when I got there—men and women of various ages and shapes in Santa hats, dipping their toes in the sea and making exaggerated gestures to indicate how cold the water was. It was actually around fifty-six degrees Fahrenheit, a bit warmer than I was used to from my previous plunges in the winter. There was a sign up that said that Pull the Trigger Production Company was filming a commercial that day for a supermarket chain. I asked one young production assistant what food chain they were

Roisin Kiberd and Rob Doyle in the Bartry Tower, Dalkey.

Forty Foot, Sandycove.

creating the ad for, and she touched my forearm gently as if I had just uttered *wow* a dozen times and said, "If I told you, I'd have to kill you."

So, like a character in *Old Mike Has Seen a Few Things*, I jumped in the frigid waters of the Irish Sea, my absurdist baptism in view of both James Joyce's ghost and Rob Doyle's binoculars, if he had any available to him that afternoon. The water was cold but I'd dived in when it was colder. I felt reborn, even though I was uncertain what that might mean amidst the cameras and Santas and the crowd of onlookers.

On my last night in Dublin before I headed to the airport and back to the United States, I ambled down O'Connell Street past Cuchulainn's shadowed statue in the window of the GPO. There was a crowd gathered around on the sidewalk in front of the building, cell phones in hands, like a circle of paparazzi filming a celebrity event. From a distance, I imagined a busking scene similar to the ones in the movie *Once*, but when I got closer I saw that I was wrong. It was more like a scene from Kevin Barry's *City of Bohane*. A teenaged black man and an early-middle-aged white man were pounding away at one another in the middle of the street, side-stepping and punching each other in the face, while two young women, apparently their girlfriends or wives, rocked baby carriages, shared a cigarette, and laughed like two drugged

Swimmers in Santa hats, Forty Foot.

groupies at a rock concert. After a few bloody minutes, the young black man stepped aside, and another young man stepped up to fight.

I took out my phone to film it, thought for an instant of putting a video on Facebook, but then I thought about Roisin Kiberd's *The Disconnect* and walked back along the crowded streets to my hotel on the edge of the dark, mysterious waters of the Liffey.

Epilogue: Hunter and the Hunted—Ireland Today

> "Were we not born to wander?"
> —William Butler Yeats, *Deidre*

    My guess is that Alfred Hunter cherished the silence and mystery of his story. He could have been the poster boy for Heaney's line, "whatever you say, say nothing." His desire may have been to leave no trace of himself, to remain a blank page that allowed (or forced) those he left behind to make up a story that would fit their own dreams about him and themselves. Like my mother when she spoke of him, Alfred, finally, didn't have much to tell me. He didn't leave any evidence to sift through, no letters or photos, no books, diaries, maps, or holy medals. He left nothing when he exited, that is, except for my sweet and big-hearted mother, and for that alone he won a place in my heart. He may have had an Irish wake with friends and family drinking and singing and wishing him *bothar maith* when he left County Armagh, or he might just have slipped away in the same ghostly fashion that he did when he left my mother and grandmother behind in their apartment in the south Bronx.

    Given that there were no family anecdotes passed down and no paper trail other than marriage and birth certificates, I looked for my grandfather in fiction and history, in the Irish landscape, in the talk of the people. He would have grown up with his parents and grandparents telling him about An Gorta Mor, and maybe the great hunger in him and his surname were the kind of inheritance from which he could never escape. Even though I never met him and knew little about him when I was a child, I may have inherited my wanderlust from him. That much we surely had in common. That hunger connected us.

    As I stood on the O'Connell Street Bridge overlooking the Liffey, scanning the grey waters for Joyce's Anna Livia Plurabelle, I realized that I was a Hunter and always would be. Even my mother, who was loyal

Epilogue: Hunter and the Hunted—Ireland Today

to a fault, had something of him in her, perhaps, a desire to see what was beyond the horizon, an incurable curiosity. But my mother was and is the known world for me, and Alfred is, and always will be, the unknown. When he abandoned my mother, and grandmother, he forsook his future grandson and great-grandsons and great-great grandchildren, too. Alfred Hunter is lost to me, except in books, in the literature of Ireland, in the stories I can imagine about him. He will never speak to me about his life or about the Ireland that he abandoned—or that abandoned him. All I have left of him are his surrogates, the writers he led me to, the country he left behind, the rain-bedazzled island that feels to me both like home and a forever foreign landscape.

Man walking near the Giant's Causeway.

Alfred Hunter is a collage of faces and voices for me. I see and hear him in the work and lives of James Joyce and William Butler Yeats and Frank O'Connor, in the art of John Millington Synge and Edna O'Brien and Seamus Heaney. Alfred Hunter is there, and I see and hear him also in the stories of contemporary Irish writers—Kevin Barry and Tana French, Paul Lynch and Roisin Kiberd, Rob Doyle and Sally Rooney—he lurks for me in the shadows of their narratives, in the silences and lost hopes, in the haze of alcohol and anger, in the loneliness and doubt and guilt, in the hopes for a new life, in the kind of laughter that stands in for tears. I even find him in the laconic and understated stories and novellas of Claire Keegan, in the silences and resentments, in the quite heroisms and ordinary decencies, of her characters. As I write these words, those of Holden Caulfield begin to hum in my ear—"Don't tell anybody anything. If you do, you start to miss everybody." Holden's warning is a fair one, for I miss the wild talk and wind-swept streets of Dublin and Galway already. I miss the bright chatter of the pubs, the conversations of Irish writers now at work, the way their discussion of books felt as important as life and death. I miss that island at the very edge of Europe but at the heart of so much that will always be necessary for me.

In a way, both Alfred Hunter and I are made of books, for literature has shaped my view of the world and my sense of who I am, and that has been the case since I was a child. Most of us dream ourselves into being, imagining ourselves into an identity. We make ourselves, as much as we are made by the people and the world around us. And what more profound dream machine than literature? Alfred Hunter and the stories of Ireland pointed me towards home, a place far away but part of me. Like my grandfather, Ireland is, ultimately, unfathomable, a silence that I will fill with my own stories, a beginning place.

At a certain point in my imaginative journey through Irish literature and my physical wanderings around Ireland, I began to hope that I had come to terms with the island in the manner that critic and novelist Thomas Flanagan had—"It is not the romantic, rather sentimental Ireland of many Irish Americans that I love, but the actual Ireland, a complex, profound, historical society, woven of many strands, some bright and some dark." However, Shakespeare was right too when he said we are such stuff as dreams are made on. I've trailed the ghost of Alfred Hunter through the counties of Clare and Longford, across Sligo and Mayo, up and down the hills of Wicklow and through Donegal, Tyrone, and Armagh. I've heard his voice in the pubs of Youghal and Clifden. I've seen his eyes in the faces of old men on the streets of Belfast and Kerry. I've tracked

Bloom plaque on the O'Connell Street Bridge, Dublin.

his ambitions and apprehensions, the limits and prospects that his time and culture might have offered him, in the poems of Yeats and Heaney, in the stories of Joyce and O'Connor and O'Brien, in the plays of Synge and McDonagh. Alfred Hunter is present for me—in those pubs, on those streets, between the lines of those poems and in the characters and conflicts of those stories. Alfred Hunter abandoned my mother and her family. For that, she never forgave him. But he left me a legacy of love—for Ireland, its people, and its literature.

In my dreams, my grandfather can be the darkness or the light, and sometimes both at the same time. He is at the bottom of Yeats's ladder in "The Circus Animal's Desertion," stopping for me among the old bones and rags, waiting for me to step down from my imaginative perch. He can be a history to cherish or a memory to shun. When I close my eyes to conjure him, his frown turns into a generous and compassionate smile. His angry monosyllables become a steady, heartfelt stream of consonants and vowels that drift toward me in the fierce and compelling accent of his Northern Ireland countryman Seamus Heaney. In that grandfatherly voice that sounds like Heaney's, Alfred whispers to me in his native language—*Sealgaire, sealgaire. Hunter, hunter.* That is who you are, he whispers. That is what you are.

Window in the Yeats Tower.

Acknowledgments

The Road to Dungannon, like all books, started with questions, not answers. I have many people to thank for helping me answer some of those questions and for making this journey one of the most fulfilling of my life. My mother, Dorothy Hunter, with her love and sense of wonder, put me on the right road many years ago. My wife, Jo-Ellen Kiernan, has kept me on the same path for a lifetime. My editor at McFarland, Gary Mitchem—sharp-eyed, understanding, and supportive—has been all that a writer could hope for as his book is ushered into print. For John Lawrence, who traveled for a time with me in Ireland, I'm deeply grateful for his companionship and artful photographs. To the contemporary Irish writers who invited me into their homes and lives and spent time talking with me—Paul Lynch, Kevin Barry, Roisin Kiberd, and Rob Doyle—it is your graceful voices I hear when I think of Ireland today. I owe a debt of gratitude to the friendly people of Ireland I met along the way, to the poetry of their everyday talk, to the breathtaking beauty of the land. I even owe a bit of thanks to my mysterious, ever-elusive maternal grandfather, Alfred Hunter, the question only my imagination could answer.

Appendix: A Starting Point—Books, Music, and Film

Fiction

Laurence Sterne—*Tristram Shandy*

Jonathan Swift—*Gulliver's Travels*
  —*"A Modest Proposal"*

Maria Edgeworth—*Castle Rackrent*

Bram Stoker—*Dracula*

Oscar Wilde—*The Picture of Dorian Gray*

James Joyce—*Dubliners*
  —*A Portrait of the Artist as a Young Man*
  —*Ulysses* (and for the art lover, the 2022 Eduardo Arroyo illustrated edition)
  —*Finnegans Wake* (if you dare)

Liam O'Flaherty—*Famine*
  —*Skerrett*
  —*The Complete Stories*

Flann O'Brien—*The Poor Mouth (An Beal Bocht)*
  —*At Swim-Two-Birds*

Joyce Cary—*The Horse's Mouth*
  —*The Best of Frank O'Connor*—edited by Julian Barnes
  —*The Collected Stories of Frank O'Connor*—introduction by Richard Ellmann

Frank O'Connor—*The Saint and Mary Kate*

James Plunkett—*Strumpet City*

John McGahern—*The Dark*
  —*Amongst Women*
  —*That They May Face the Rising Sun*

Appendix: A Starting Point—Books, Music, and Film

Mary Lavin—*In the Middle of the Field and Other Stories*

Benedict Kiely—*Collected Stories*

Edna O'Brien—*The Country Girls Trilogy*
—*Wild Decembers*
—*The Love Object: Selected Stories*
—*The Little Red Chairs*

Maeve Brennan—*The Springs of Affection: Stories of Dublin*

William Trevor—*The Collected Stories*
—*Last Stories*

Elizabeth Bowen—*The Heat of the Day*

J.P. Donleavy—*The Ginger Man*

Roddy Doyle—*The Commitments (and The Barrytown Trilogy)*
—*Paddy Clarke Ha Ha Ha*
—*A Star Called Henry*
—*The Dead Republic*
—*Love*

John Banville—*The Sea*
—*Mrs. Osmond*

Paul Murray—*Skippy Dies*
—*An Evening of Long Goodbyes*

Colum McCann—*Everything in This Country Must*
—*TransAtlantic*
—*Thirteen Ways of Looking*
—*Let the Great World Spin*
—*This Side of Brightness*

Lia Mills—*Fallen* (One Book One Dublin 2016)

Joseph O'Connor—*Ghost Light*
—*Star of the Sea*

Kevin Barry—*Dark Lies the Island*
—*There Are Little Kingdoms*
—*Beatlebone*
—*Night Boat to Tangier*
—*That Old Country Music*

Ciaran Collins—*The Gamal*

Ken Bruen—*The Guards* (or any of the Jack Taylor series)

Leon Uris—*Trinity*

Frederick Buechner—*Brendan*

Appendix: A Starting Point—Books, Music, and Film

Anne Enright—*The Green Road*
 —*Actress*
Alice McDermott—*Charming Billy* or *The Ninth Hour* (a take on the Irish American experience)
 —*Modern Irish Stories*—edited by Ben Forkner
Colin Barrett—*Young Skins*
Colm Toibin—*Brooklyn*
 —*Nora Webster*
 —*The Empty Family*
 —*The Blackwater Lightship*
Seamus Deane—*Reading in the Dark*
Thomas Flanagan—*The Year of the French*
 —*The Tenants of Time*
 —*The End of the Hunt*
Kevin Power—*Bad Day in Blackrock*
John Boyne—*The Heart's Invisible Furies*
Maeve Binchy—*A Week in Winter*
 —*Tara Road*
Frank Delaney—*Ireland*
Bernard MacLaverty—*Cal*
Sebastian Barry—*A Long Way*
 —*The Secret Scripture*
 —*The Whereabouts of Eneas McNulty*
Donal Ryan—*A Slanting of the Sun*
 —*The Thing About December*
Emma Donoghue—*Room*
 —*The Wonder*
Claire Keegan—*Antarctica*
 —*Foster*
 —*Small Things Like These*
 —*Walk the Blue Fields: Stories*
Tana French—*In the Woods*
 —*The Likeness*
 —*The Witch Elm*
 —*Faithful Place*
 —*Broken Harbor*
 —*The Secret Place*
 —*The Trespasser*
 —*The Searcher*

Appendix: A Starting Point—Books, Music, and Film

Brenda McKeon—*Solace*
 —*Tender*

Rob Doyle—*Here Are The Young Men*
 —*This Is the Ritual*
 —*Threshold*
 —*Autobibliography*

Benjamin Black (aka John Banville)—*The Entire Quirke Series*

Paul Lynch—*Grace*
 —*Red Sky in Morning*
 —*Black Snow*
 —*Beyond the Sea*

Anna Burns—*Milkman*

Sally Rooney—*Normal People*
 —*Conversations with Friends*
 —*Beautiful World, Where Are You*

Jess Kidd—*Himself*

Sara Baume—*Spill Simmer Falter Wither*

Christine Dwyer Hickey—*Tatty*

Lisa McInerney—*The Glorious Heresies*
 —*Blood Mercies*

Nonfiction

J.M. Synge—*The Aran Islands*

Frank O'Connor—*An Only Child*
 —*My Father's Son*
 —*The Big Fellow*
 —*Irish Miles*

Kevin O'Hara—*Travels with a Donkey*

Bill Barich—*A Pint of Plain*

Eric Newby—Round Ireland in Low Gear

John McGahern—*All Will Be Well*

Rosemary Mahoney—*Whoredom in Kimmage*

Flann O'Brien—*The Best of Myles*

Nell McCafferty—*Nell*

Edna O'Brien—*Country Girl*, a memoir

Appendix: A Starting Point—Books, Music, and Film

Tim Robinson—*Stones of Aran*
 —*Pilgrimage (Volume I)*
 —*Labyrinth (Volume II)*

Richard Ellmann—*James Joyce*
 —*Yeats: The Man and the Masks*
 —*Oscar Wilde*

Gordon Bowker—*James Joyce*

Maria Tymoczko—*The Irish Ulysses*

R.F. Foster—*W.B. Yeats*, a two-volume biography
 —*On Seamus Heaney*

W.J. McCormack—*Fool of the Family: A Life of J.M. Synge*

Dennis O'Driscoll—*Stepping Stones: Interviews with Seamus Heaney*

James Matthews—*Voices: A Life of Frank O'Connor*

F.S. Lyons—*Charles Stewart Parnell*

Timothy Egan—*The Immortal Irishman*

Pete McCarthy—*McCarthy's Bar*

Fintan O'Toole—*Ship of Fools: How Stupidity and Corruption Sank the Celtic Tiger*
 —*We Don't Know Ourselves: A Personal History of Modern Ireland*

Jack McCarthy—*Joyce's Dublin, a Walking Guide to Ulysses*

John Banville—*Time Pieces: A Dublin Memoir*

Edna O'Brien—*James Joyce: A Life*

William Trevor—*A Writer's Ireland*

C.S. Lewis—*Surprised by Joy*

Nuala O'Faolain—*Are You Somebody*

Frank McCourt—*Angela's Ashes*
 —*Tis*
 —*Teacher Man*

Kevin Birmingham—*The Most Dangerous Book: The Battle for James Joyce's Ulysses*

Patrick Radden Keefe—*Say Nothing: A True Story of Murder and Memory in Northern Ireland*

Hugh Mulrooney—*The Night of Other Days: The Life and Work of Seamus Heaney*

John Connell—*The Farmer's Son*

Colm Toibin—*Mad, Bad, Dangerous to Know—The Fathers of Wilde, Yeats and Joyce*

Roisin Kiberd—*The Disconnect—A Personal Journey Through the Internet*

Shirley Peterson, "Murder in the Ghost Estate: Crimes of the Celtic Tiger in Tana French's *Broken Harbor*," in *Clues: A Journal of Detection*, Volume 32, Number 1, Spring 2014, pp. 71–80.

Maureen T. Reddy, "Authority and Cultural Memory in *Faithful Place* and *Broken Harbor*," in *Clues: A Journal of Detection*, Volume 32, Number 1, Spring 2014, pp. 81–91.

Dan Sheehan, "Madness at the Edges: A Conversation with Kevin Barry, Author of *Beatlebone*," in *Electric Lit*, November 17, 2015.

Timothy Noonan, "Hibernians Present: An Interview with Author Kevin Barry," Ancient Order of Hibernians, January 30, 2021.

Sally Rooney, "Even if you beat me," *The Dublin Review*, Spring 2015.
—"An App to Cure My Fainting Spells," *The New Yorker*, November 20, 2017.

Lauren Collins, "Sally Rooney Gets in Your Head," *The New Yorker*, December 31, 2018.

Constance Grady, "The cult of Sally Rooney," *Vox*, September 3, 2019.

Christian Lorentzen, "I couldn't live normally," a review of *Beautiful World, Where Are You* in the *London Review of Books*, Vol. 42, No. 18, September 23, 2021.

Drama

John M. Synge—*The Playboy of the Western World*
Oscar Wilde—*The Importance of Being Earnest*
Samuel Beckett—*Waiting for Godot*
Martin McDonagh—*The Beauty Queen of Leenane*
 —*The Lonesome West*
 —*The Cripple of Inishmaan*
 —*The Lieutenant of Inishmore*
Frank McGuinness—*Carthaginians*
Oliver Goldsmith, George Bernard Shaw, Brian Friel, Tom Murphy, Brendan Behan, Lady Gregory

Poetry

W.B. Yeats
Patrick Kavanagh

Austin Clarke
Eavan Boland
Seamus Heaney
Paul Muldoon

Some General Histories

The Green Flag—A History of Irish Nationalism—Robert Kee
The Oxford History of Ireland—R.F. Foster
Ireland: A History—Thomas Bartlett
The Rising—Ireland 1916—Fearghal McGarry
The Graves Are Walking: The Great Famine and the Saga of the Irish People—John Kelly
The Great Hunger: Ireland 1845–1849—Cecil Woodham-Smith
How the Irish Saved Civilization—Thomas Cahill
Atlas of Irish History—Sean Duffy
The Irish Americans—Jay P. Dolan
Early Irish Myths and Sagas—Jeffrey Gantz
Inventing Ireland—Declan Kiberd
Irish Literature—A Backward Look—Frank O'Connor

Music (the island is filled with it)

Van Morrison, U2, The Dubliners, Glen Hansard, The Swell Season, The Frames, the Pogues, the Cranberries, Sinead O'Connor, Damien Rice, Mary Black, Wolfe Tones, The Clancy Brothers, Black 47, Damien Dempsey, the Tossers, John O'Neill and the Undertones, the High Kings, Fontaines DC....

Films/TV (a wide-ranging list)

Man of Aran, The Quiet Man, The Butcher Boy, My Left Foot, The Van, Once, Into the West, Kisses, In the Name of the Father, The Field, In America, The Commitments, The Wind That Shakes the Barley, Angela's Ashes, Michael Collins, The Country Girls, The Boxer, The Magdelene Sisters, The Snapper, Nora, Waking Ned Devine, Veronica Guerin, '71, Intermission, Educating Rita (it may be British but it's set in Trinity College), *The General, The Playboys, Bloody Sunday, The*

Crying Game, The Flight of Doves, Some Mother's Son, BBC version of *Strumpet City, War of the Buttons, Hunger, Noble, The Outsider, The Quare Fellow, Handsome Devil, The Secret Scripture, Shadow Dancer, Cal, The Boys and Girl from County Clare, P.S. I Love You, London Boulevard, Ryan's Daughter, Handsome Devil, Philomena, The Queen of Ireland, Jimmy's Hall, The Rocky Road to Dublin, South, The Siege of Jadotville, Divorcing Jack, Extra Ordinary, The Disappeared, Dancing at Lughnasa, Brooklyn, Sing Street, BBC Story of Ireland* (5-part documentary), *Normal People* (10-part series on Hulu) *Conversations with Friends* (12-part series on Hulu), *Peaky Blinders, Secret of Roan Inish, St. Saviours, Irish Drinking Culture Documentary, The Foreigner, What Richard Did, The Young Offenders, The General, Dublin Murders, The Irishman, Conor McGregor Notorious, The Secret Scripture, The Book of Kells, Calvary, Dating Amber, Good Vibrations, Rebellion* (two Seasons), *Kisses, Rosie, Sophie: A Murder in West Cork* (Netflix Series), *Calm with Horses, The Derry Girls, Here Are the Young Men, Belfast, The Banshees of Inisherin....*

Index

Allgood, Molly 94
Amado, Jorge 7
Armagh, County 8, 33, 37, 130, 142, 184
Auden, W. H. 27, 72–73; "In Memory of W. B. Yeats" 27
Austen, Jane 159

Banville, John 117; Black, Benjamin 144, 148
Barnacle, Nora 59, 66, 69, 125
Barnes, Julian 108–109
Barry, Kevin 20, 148–157, 182, 185; *City of Bohane* 149–150; *Dark Lies the Island* 20, 150–155
Beach, Sylvia 63
Beckett, Samuel 138
Birmingham, Kevin 63; *The Most Dangerous Book* 63
Black, Mary 139–140
Bloom, Leopold 18, 20, 54, 70, 92
Bloom, Molly 19
Bloomsday 19
Bolano, Roberto 173
Book of Kells 66
Bowker, Gordon 57
Brett, Sam 82, 84, 85, 125–126, 140–142
Bronte, Charlotte, Emily, and Anne 8
Bronx 1, 3, 4, 6, 17, 21, 49, 70, 123

Cahill, Thomas 12
Camus, Albert 8
Cather, Willa 7
Caulfield, Holden 185
Cervantes, Miguel de 3
Collins, Lauren 159
Coole Park 83, 85

Dedalus, Stephen 28, 49, 54
Dickens, Charles 8
Dillard, Annie 7
Dolan, Naoise 181

Donne, John 173
Doyle, Rob 146–148, 156, 171, 175, 179–182, 185; *Here Are the Young Men* 146–148
Dungannon 27, 29, 30, 31

Elie, Paul 4
Ellison, Ralph 4
Ellmann, Richard 51–52, 57, 61, 67, 71, 74–75, 78–79

Faulkner, William 55, 119, 165, 174
Fitzgerald, F Scott 7
Flaherty, Robert 26, 96; *Man of Aran* 26, 96
Ford, Richard 7
Foster, R. F. 71, 73, 77, 78, 127–129, 132, 134
Fowles, John 7; *The Magus* 7
French, Tana 144–146, 148, 185
Frost, Robert 128–129

Gebbler, Ernest 122
Gogarty, Oliver St. 60
Golding, William 173
Gonne, Maud 76–79
Great Hunger 35–36
Greene, Graham 7
Gregory, Lady Augusta 62, 78, 83, 85, 93
Guardini, Romano 5

Hannah, Barry 156
Hawthorne, Nathaniel 7
Heaney, Seamus 2, 84, 127–143, 185, 187; "Casualty" 135–136; *Death of a Naturalist* 130, 134; "Digging" 131; "Follower" 142–143; "Mid-Term Break" 129
Hemingway, Ernest 165; *The Sun Also Rises* 19
Hunter, Edwin Gray 34

197

Index

Hunter, Alfred 1–3, 9, 18, 21, 27–33, 35, 37, 50–51, 54–55, 92, 97, 130–131, 139–140, 143, 175, 184–187
Hunter, Dorothy 1–3, 28, 32, 184, 187
Hunter, Raymond 30–34
Hurston, Zora Neale 7
Huston, John 14, 15; *Moby Dick* (film) 14
Hyde-Lees, Georgiana 79–80

Imagined Places 8
Innocents Abroad Too 8
Irish history 37–42

Joyce, James 9, 11, 44–70, 82, 113, 144, 148, 164, 180, 182, 184–185, 187; "Araby" 20, 46–48, 51, 53–54; "The Dead" 52–54, 101, 118, 164; *Dubliners* 21, 44, 48, 50–51; "An Encounter" 20, 45–46, 51; "Eveline" 48–49; *Finnegans Wake* 52, 58, 63, 66, 68–69, 71, 114; *A Portrait of the Artist as a Young Man* 69; *Ulysses* 9, 12, 19, 20, 28, 70
Joyce, John 55–57, 60, 74
Joyce, Lucia 68–69
Joyce, May 56, 125
Jung, Carl 68

Keegan, Claire 185
Kelly, Caroline 171, 174
Kelly, John (friend) 174–175
Kelly, John (historian) 35; *The Graves Are Walking* 35
Kiberd, Declan 9, 72, 176; *Irish Classics* 9
Kiberd, Roisin 170, 176–181, 183, 185; *The Disconnect* 177–181

Lawrence, John 113, 139, 171
Leavis, F. R. 72
Lorenzten, Christian 160
Lynch, Paul 156, 164–175, 181, 185; *Beyond the Sea* 165; *Black Snow* 165; *Grace* 166–169; *Red Sky in Morning* 165

Mailer, Norman 161
Malamud, Bernard 58; *Dubin's Lives* 58
Mann, Sally 176
Marx, Groucho 173
Matthews, James 105–106
McBride, John 77–78
McCarthy, Cormac 7, 164, 169, 174
McCarthy, Jack 18; *A Walking Guide to Ulysses* 18
McCourt, Frank 31, 115; *Angela's Ashes* 31, 115
McDonagh, Martin 187

McGahern, John 117, 127, 156
McInerney, Lisa 144, 148
McKenna, Siobhan 122
McKeon 114–115
McPhee, John 8, 18
Melville, Herman 7
Millhauser, Steven 7; *Edwin Mullhouse* 7
Mitchell, Joseph 7
Muldoon, Paul 128
Mulligan, Buck 60
Murphy, P. J. 175; Sweny's 175
Murray, Paul 22; *Skippy Dies* 22

Nabokov, Vladimir 7; *Pale Fire* 7
Niamh 82

O'Brien, Edna 9, 55, 57, 117–126, 144, 177, 180; "The Connor Girls" 119; *Country Girl* 120–122; *The Country Girls* 117, 122–123; "The Creature" 119; *Girls in Their Married Bliss* 122; "Irish Revel" 117–119; *Joyce's Women* 125; *The Lonely Girl* 122; "The Love Object" 120; "Old Wounds" 119; "The Rug" 119
O'Brien, Flann 22, 148, 156, 169; *At Swim-Two-Birds* 22
O'Brien, Tim 7
O'Connell, Daniel 144
O'Connor, Flannery 7, 106, 156, 160
O'Connor, Frank 9, 67–68, 94, 98–116, 120, 148, 185–187; "The American Wife" 112; "Darcy in the Land of Youth" 112–113; "First Confession" 98–101; "In the Train" 111; "The Long Road to Unmera" 111–112; "The Mad Lomasneys" 110–111; *My Father's Son* 101; "My Oedipus Complex" 108–109; *An Only Child* 103
O'Driscoll, Dennis 129, 132
Oisin 82, 85, 167
O'Malley, Grace 168
O'Pray, Jenny Finlan 1, 28, 32, 37, 70
Orwell, George 110

Pamuk, Orhan 7
Parnell, Charles Stewart 75–76
Pearse, Patrick 93, 104
Percy, Walker 4–7; *The Last Gentleman* 4–7
Plunkett, James 22; *Strumpet City* 22
Pollexfen, Susan 73
Pound, Ezra 67
Pritchett, V. S. 67
Pynchon, Thomas 7

The Quiet Man (film) 24

Reading Life 8, 9
Regan, Carrie 70
Remarque, Erich Maria 110
Richards, Grant 49
Rooney, Sally 156–164, 185; *Beautiful World, Where Are You* 157–164; *Conversations with Friends* 157–164; *Normal People* 157–164
Rose, Charlie 129
Russell, George 49, 58, 101; *The Irish Homestead* 49; *The Irish Statesman* 101

Salinger, J.D. 159
Shaw, George Bernard 138
Sophocles 173
Steinbeck, John 7
Stevens, Cat 17, 138
Stoppard, Tom 138
Synge, John Millington 9, 26, 78, 86–94, 185, 187; *The Aran Islands* 92; *Deidre of the Sorrows* 90; *In the Shadow of the Glen* 91, 93; *The Playboy of the Western World* 9, 78, 86–89, 93, 167; *Riders to the Sea* 26, 90, 93; *The Tinker's Wedding* 90–91; *The Well of the Saints* 91

Thoor Ballylee 83
Toibin, Colm 60
Trevelyan, Charles Edward 35–36
Trevor, William 117
Twain, Mark 3, 102
Tyler, Anne 7; *The Accidental Tourist* 7

Vonnegut, Kurt 7

Warren, Robert Penn 7
Weaver, Harriet 68, 125, 177
Wells, H.G. 167
Woolf, Virginia 7
Wright, Richard 7

Yeats, John 73–75
Yeats, William Butler 62, 71–86, 91, 93, 105, 113, 138, 164, 185, 187; "In Memory of Major Robert Gregory" 86; "The Lake Isle of Innisfree" 82, 85; "The Stolen Child" 85; *A Vision* 79